ECONOMICS OF MARKETABLE SURPLUS SUPPLY

Economics of Marketable Surplus Supply

A theoretical and empirical analysis for China

PING ZONG
JOHN DAVIS
Department of Agricultural and Food Economics
The Queen's University of Belfast

Ashgate

Aldershot • Brookfield USA • Singapore • Sydney

338.1851
T88e

Published by
Ashgate Publishing Ltd
Gower House
Croft Road
Aldershot
Hants GU11 3HR
England

Ashgate Publishing Company
Old Post Road
Brookfield
Vermont 05036
USA

British Library Cataloguing in Publication Data
Zong, Ping
    Economics of marketable surplus supply : theoretical and
    empirical analysis for China
    1.Agricultural prices - Government policy - China
    I.Title II.Davis, John, 1951-
    338.1'8'51

Library of Congress Catalog Card Number: 98-70149

ISBN 1 84014 335 5

Printed in Great Britain by The Ipswich Book Company, Suffolk

Contents

v

List of figures

List of tables

Preface

The core of this book is based on work carried out for Ping Zong's doctoral thesis which was completed in The Queen's University of Belfast in 1997, under the guidance of John Davis. The authors are pleased to have this opportunity to disseminate the entire work more widely, especially in view of the current importance of the topics and issues which it covers. Grain production in China is a key focus of the country's political economy. It is also an area of growing global interest and concern, especially over the likely future effects of China's population growth, industrialisation and further socio-economic reforms on the levels of her grain self-sufficiency and trade. It is probably fair to say that the Chinese government will continue to be highly interventionist in the grain sector. The authors believe that it is important to understand better how these interventions may influence the further development of the grain sector. The work reported in this book is concerned primarily with the possible effects of grain price changes on Chinese farm households' grain marketable supply behaviour. Focusing on the reform period it adopts an economic modelling approach which attempts to take account explicitly of certain features of Chinese farm households and their environment; in particular their own grain consumption behaviour, and the dynamic interdependencies between these households and the rapidly evolving wider rural economy. Therefore, the book is ambitious in both its scope and remit and inevitably it leaves a number of issues which are inadequately covered and in need of further investigation. Nevertheless, the authors hope that it can contribute, in some small way, to the debate on these important issues. As always, with a book of this nature the material as presented frequently reflects a compromise in the styles and insights of the individual authors.

Ping Zong is a member of the Economics Faculty of Fudan University, Shanghai, China and at the time of writing was a graduate student in The Queen's University of Belfast, Northern Ireland. John Davis is Head of the Department of Agricultural and Food Economics and Director of the Centre for Rural Studies in Queen's University.

- / -

Dr Ping Zong, Dr John Davis
Department of Agricultural and Food Economics, The Queen's University of Belfast, Newforge Lane, Belfast, Northern Ireland, BT9 5PX.
e-mail: john.davis@qub.ac.uk

Acknowledgements

This book could not have been produced without the help, support and encouragement of a large number of individuals. We are particularly grateful to staff in the Department of Agricultural and Food Economics, The Queen's University of Belfast, especially Dr Seamus McErlean and Dr Christos Papadas for their detailed reading and valuable comments on earlier drafts. We are also deeply indebted to Mrs Hilary McErlean for her professionalism and painstaking preparation of the final camera-ready copy. Mrs Pat Coulter showed enormous patience and stamina in proof-reading earlier drafts. Library staff, especially Mrs Elaine Davis and Mrs Diana Greer, were extremely efficient and gracious in obtaining a large number of articles and books, often at very short notice! We are thankful to Professor Zhili Chen who helped us to solve a number of difficult mathematical problems.

1 Introduction

1.1 Background

Since 1978, China has been engaged in systematic reform of its traditional centralised planning system through greater use of price incentives and the market system. A series of grain price reforms were introduced as part of the reform package. The main effect of these reforms was to increase the state grain purchase price, with the aim of stimulating grain production. The fact that the state purchase prices were depressed to an artificial level was regarded as the main cause of the disincentives and the poor performance of the grain sector before 1978. After initiation of the rural reforms, the raising of grain prices became a major element of the reform process. Meanwhile, the government also made significant efforts to eliminate inappropriate administrative restrictions and to allow markets more freedom to guide economic activities.

These reforms resulted in rapid growth of grain production during the period 1978-84: the average annual growth in grain output was 4.2 per cent in this period (Rural Statistical Year Book of China, 1994, p169). The growth in agricultural production, and grain in particular, during this period was remarkable. However, production dropped significantly after 1985. Despite further adjustments in state purchase prices, grain production was stagnant until 1990. The average annual growth in grain output dropped to 1.96 per cent in the period 1985-92; while the output of rural non-agricultural industries and other sectors of the national economy continued to grow rapidly (Rural Statistical Year Book of China, 1994, p169). This raises a question about how China can achieve sustainable growth in grain supply through reliance on price incentives: more specifically what are the factors which influence supply response behaviour of farm households to grain price changes. There are many studies about grain price adjustment policies during this period, and debates are never ceasing (see Sicular, 1989, 1990, 1993; Claude, 1990; Ash; 1993; Cheng, et al. 1994; Gao, 1989). Grain price policy has become one of the most controversial issues in China over the last decade. Analysis of farm households' supply response to price policy changes has become an urgent task for agricultural economists.

A rigorous theoretical and empirical exploration of their production motivation and behaviour is needed. Improving our understanding of these factors should contribute to the development of a better framework for future grain price reforms and more informed policy choices.

1.2   Purpose of this book

The main purpose of this book is to examine the effects of grain price changes during the period 1978 to 1992 on the grain marketable surplus supply behaviour of Chinese farm households; taking account of the very significant changes in their institutional and economic environment. Specifically the book seeks:

(a) to examine the nature of the new economic environment after the initiation of reforms and how this has influenced employment and income structures in the rural economy;

(b) to investigate the nature of the upward grain price adjustments during the reform period and identify any price distortions;

(c) to set out a new modelling approach which integrates farm households' production, consumption and farm labour supply decisions into a unified theoretical and empirical framework; thus explicitly recognising the interdependence of these decisions;

(d) to utilise this framework to examine the quantitative effects of changes in the prices of household outputs and inputs, their own-consumption, and their non-farm activities on grain marketable surplus supply.

1.3   Modelling approach

According to conventional neoclassical theory, farm households' supply response depends on farm prices and profit. In this study, an alternative theoretical framework is used which emphasises three important features of Chinese reality. These are: (a) own-consumption behaviour; (b) farm labour input; and (c) non-farm activities. These features may alter the way in which households respond to grain price changes. This alternative framework is based on the assumption of farm household utility maximisation, rather than farm profit maximisation only.

Unlike conventional *ad hoc* approaches or the recursive model, the marketable surplus supply response model used in this study integrates production, consumption and labour supply decisions into a unified theoretical and empirical framework. This model satisfies the requirement that these decisions should be taken into account simultaneously. It facilitates identification of not only the direction but also the magnitude of the effects of key variables on grain marketable surplus supply.

1.4   Structure of the book

The book consists of two parts. The first, from Chapters 2 to 4, examines the policy factors which may influence grain price adjustment effects.

Chapter 2 discusses changes in the internal marketing system and institutional environment but also identifies certain relatively unchanged features which may influence the behaviour of farm households such as own-consumption of grain.

Chapter 3 examines grain prices and price adjustments in more detail and identifies areas of price distortion.

Chapter 4 explores the possible effects of non-farm policies on farm households' behaviour by looking at changes in the structure of rural production, employment and income.

In the second part, from Chapters 5 to 8, attention shifts to the theoretical and empirical analyses. Chapter 5 presents a wide-ranging literature survey covering the area of supply response analysis. Various theoretical and estimated models are reviewed; their theoretical development, application, and limitations are discussed.

Chapter 6 seeks an alternative theoretical and empirical approach in order to specify Chinese farm households' supply behaviour. Production behaviour for full income maximisation, rather than just farm income maximisation, is adopted as a theoretical footing. A non-recursive modelling approach is adopted, which estimates simultaneously the interdependencies among production, consumption and labour supply.

Chapters 7 and 8 explore policy issues in more detail. Grain marketable surplus supply models are estimated using aggregate panel data for the period 1978-92. Chapter 7 looks at the effects of own-consumption and farm labour supply on grain marketable surplus. Certain basic features of semi-commercial Chinese farm households and their implications for modelling are briefly discussed in order to highlight the importance of the integrated model. It is argued that marketable surplus supply response may become ambiguous due to two distinct effects of price changes. A pure price effect that renders own-consumption more expensive may lead to an increase in marketable surplus supply; but the income effect, arising from the increased value of farm output, may alternatively lead to an increase in consumption, this tending to reduce marketable surplus. Following the specification of the model, this ambiguous relationship is examined in two stages. In stage one, direct own-consumption responses to price are examined, firstly, ignoring the effect of full income; and then secondly taking the full income effect into account. Therefore, the dual effects of pure price and income on own-consumption are isolated. In stage two, the effects of price and own-consumption on marketable surplus are examined. Firstly, marketable surplus supply response to price is examined under the assumption that own-consumption is constant (conditional supply response). Secondly, the own-consumption effect is introduced and its impact estimated (unconditional supply response). Therefore, the effects of own-consumption on marketable surplus following changes in grain price and household income are disentangled.

Chapter 8 examines the possible impact of labour flows between the farm and non-farm sectors on grain marketable surplus. The assumption of full income (utility) maximisation is used to estimate simultaneously the effects of income from farm production and from non-farm activities on household supply behaviour. In stage one, the on-farm and non-farm labour supply responses, as measured by their respective income and cross income elasticities are derived from an indirect utility function. In stage two, marketable surplus supply response is examined firstly under the assumption that off-farm labour supply is constant (conditional supply responses). Then, it is estimated by simultaneously taking the effect of supply changes in off-farm labour into account (unconditional supply response). The net effects of off-farm income on on-farm labour supply and marketable surplus are estimated.

Finally, Chapter 9 draws together the main findings and conclusions of the work. It reviews the core theoretical arguments and the main changes in the rural economy which have affected farm households. It also briefly explores some possible policy implications and directions for future research.

4

PART ONE

GRAIN PRICE POLICY ANALYSIS

2 The rural economy and the institutional environment[1]

2.1 Introduction

Following 1978, comprehensive rural economic reforms were introduced in China. The major institutional reforms were the introduction of the Household Production Responsibility System (HPRS) and liberalisation of the rigid marketing system. The effects of price reforms depend, to a large extent, upon the institutional setting. Relevant aspects of the latter include the organisation of the system of production, the marketing system, the nature of the wider rural economy and other non-farm policies. These factors influence farmers' production behaviour. In order to increase understanding of China's grain price mechanism and correctly assess the outcomes of price reforms, it is essential to examine the institutional environment and the nature of the current rural economy in China.

The main objective of this chapter is to provide a background to the development of the institutions (organisation of the production and marketing system) and the nature of the rural economy before and after rural reforms; especially the functioning of prices in the reform period. In section 2.2, the People's Commune System and the 'Unified Purchase and Sale' marketing system are reviewed and the characteristics and problems of these systems are discussed. This is followed in section 2.3 by a discussion of institutional reforms including the establishment of the HPRS and changes in the marketing system since 1978. The dual characteristics

7

of the institutional environment after rural reforms are examined in section 2.4. The nature of the post-reform economy is discussed in section 2.5.

2.2   Planning and agricultural performance before reforms

The agricultural economic institutions established by the Chinese government in the 1950s, particularly after 1952, derived largely from the former Soviet Union. Two basic characteristics of the economic institutions at that time were the commune system (collective ownership) and 'unified production and sale' system (central planning). Economic institutions were designed to facilitate the heavy industry oriented development strategy. Individual production and marketing mechanisms were overridden by the centralised planned economic system.

To accomplish the overall strategy of economic development, grain price policy made by the Chinese government was designed to achieve the following three major objectives. The first objective was instituted to facilitate industrialisation. Heavy industry was regarded as a key factor to economic modernisation. Developing heavy industry, however, requires tremendous amounts of capital investment. The only source that could contribute to industrialisation in the early stages of development was agriculture (Timmer, 1988; Lin, 1991). The Chinese government, therefore, implemented low agricultural (including grain) prices to transfer resources from agriculture to industry (Lin, 1991).

The second government objective was to keep price stability. Although stability is a common reason for government intervention, it was particularly important to stabilise the market for China at that time. In order to receive popular support for the new Chinese government (Lardy, 1983a), price stability was an important component of the Communist Party's policies

The third objective was implemented because of China's limited foreign exchange reserves; this involved inhibiting the importation of grain from the world market. The policy was to aim at self-sufficiency. As industrial development and growth actually raised domestic demand, a price policy was required that ensured the state's acquisition and distribution of grain.

In order to achieve these objectives, three main policy measures were introduced: (a) abolishing the free markets for most agricultural products and introducing a unified procurement and sale system; (b) fixing product price and setting low prices for agricultural products by the state; and (c) introducing the commune system. In addition to these three measures, the free flow of all factors of production across regions and industries were prohibited.

There have been a large number of studies on China's 'unified purchase

8

and sale' system and commune system. The historical review here is focused only on the basic features, such as direct intervention in marketing and consumption through non-market mechanisms, the non-price measures and strict control of production through the commune system.[2] Many of the contemporary problems of grain supply in China stem from such a centrally administered system established in the early 1950s (Lin, 1991).

2.2.1   Direct intervention - the unified purchase and sale system

Prior to rural reforms, the state agencies monopolised most farm produce. One of the main institutional features was direct control of production and sales through a system called 'unified purchase and sale'. This system was set up in the early 1950's. It comprised two elements: compulsory purchase to control production, and rationing distribution to control consumption. Farmers had to sell specified amounts of grain to the state food agency which would then sell them through its local shops to enterprises and urban consumers, the latter purchasing it under a rationing system. Prices were set by the government and a low grain price was adopted. The unified purchase and sale system soon became a key element of China's agricultural economic system; in which a non-market mechanism and non-price measures were main features of the marketing system.

Non-market mechanisms   Agricultural production and marketing were strictly controlled through three practical measures under the unified purchase and sale system. Firstly, the government strictly controlled agricultural production and marketing. Before 1978, agricultural products were classified into three categories. The first category, including grain, cotton, oil-bearing crops and several kinds of medicinal herbs, was subjected to a system of 'unified planned purchase' by the state. The second category was also strictly controlled by the state under the system of 'assigned purchase'. This included certain sideline foods and major agricultural products for industrial inputs, such as swine, cows, sheep, eggs, vegetables, fruits, aquatic products and many other medicinal herbs. Unlike the first category, second category products could be sold in the free market after fulfillment of the state quota purchase. Mandatory procurement was imposed over these first two categories because prices were set at artificially low levels, particularly in comparison with industrial products. Almost 180 agricultural products were included in the first two categories. All remaining agricultural products fell into the third category, of which the state only purchased a portion at negotiated prices (Hu, 1989).

Secondly, private enterprises engaged in grain marketing were strictly limited, and were eventually eliminated. Before 1953, the main channel for grain marketing in urban areas was private enterprise. After the establishment

9

of the unified purchase and sale system, these private enterprises were strictly controlled. By 1955 most private enterprises were transferred into so called socialist state-private co-operative enterprises. Private grain marketing was abolished. Instead of private marketing, the state monopoly marketing system was established in which a number of state grain marketing agencies were involved in purchasing grain from farmers, collecting agricultural tax in kind and selling retail grain in urban areas.[3]

Thirdly, free market exchanges were strictly controlled and virtually abolished. The free market was closed between 1958 and 1962 and then reopened when the state tried to boost agricultural production. However, the free market was restricted and abolished again during the Cultural Revolution (1966-76). Even if exchanges of certain non-grain products in free markets were allowed in certain periods, the free market in grain was always prohibited. In theory, individual farmers could sell any surplus in markets after procurement quota was fulfilled. In practice, however, since the state procurement agencies purchased as much as they could extract, producers were left with little surplus (Perkins 1966, Ch.3). Overall, the government controlled almost all grain trade, not only from procurement to the retail stage, but also from production to the transport network. The free market and private trade essentially disappeared between 1953 and 1978, though black markets existed.

Non-price measures Under the unified purchase and sale system, the role of prices in resource allocation was dramatically reduced. Many non-price instruments, such as procurement quotas and planned sown areas, played important roles.

The procurement quota for grain was the principal measure used by government to directly control grain marketing. The quota was determined on the basis of average yield, deducting seed and the farmers' own-consumption requirements. The residual was then treated as marketable surplus. Since the large portion of output was considered as the quota to be sold to the state at the state procurement prices, the residual was rather small.

Production was also affected through the control of sown areas: mandatory sown area targets were enforced under the commune system. Before the sowing season the state decided the sowing areas for principal crops. Cropping quotas were designed to cover more than three-quarters of China's cultivated areas. Restricted by this kind of planning, farmers were unable to make their own production decisions freely in consideration of the principle of profit maximisation.

Demand for grain was also administered largely through a nation-wide rationing system at a fixed retail price. Local rationing of grain for urban residents began in 1953, it became nation-wide in 1955 and was maintained until 1993. Under the rationing system, food grain allocations varied

10

according to age and type of work. Each family received a ration book that listed its total quantity of rationed grain and purchased food grain at designated grain shops at a fixed retail price.

2.2.2 Production control - the people's commune system

The second feature of the control of production was through agricultural collectivisation. The basic organisational form was the collective farm, which owned almost all rural means of production including land and labour. The establishment of a collective team was based on the belief that socialist agriculture should eliminate private ownership and that public ownership was a key element of production efficiency. Under the anti-market philosophy of Stalinist economics, farm production activities were brought into line with the state administration.

The collectivisation of agriculture began in 1954 and went through four stages. The first was the 'Mutual Aid Team' (MAT) which emerged in the early 1950s and further developed in 1954. It was organised on the basis of four or five neighbouring households. Small groups of neighbouring farm households were obliged to work together, to exchange labour and to share their farm tools and draft animals. The harvest belonged to each household.

In 1955, the MATs were merged into larger 'Elementary Co-Operatives' (ECOs) in which about twenty to thirty neighbouring households pooled farm tools, animals and land under a unified management. The net income of such a cooperative was distributed in two categories: payment for renting farm animals and tools, and for the remuneration of work performed.

By 1956, the ECOs were further encouraged by the state to amalgamate into a new form of 'Advanced Co-Operatives' (ACOs) in which all means of production including land, farm animals and tools were collectively owned. The income of a family depended on the amount of work points earned by the family members and on the average income of a work point within the collective team.

In the autumn of 1958 the collectivisation of agriculture culminated in the formation of the 'People's Communes'. The commune owned all assets, and private plots were absorbed into collective fields. The traditional periodic markets were closed; much of the sharp drop in agricultural production between 1958 and 1961 was the result of a loss of producers' incentives. Grain output reduced by 15 per cent in 1959, and a further 16 per cent in 1960. Thirty million people are estimated to have died of starvation and malnutrition during this crisis (Lin, 1991).

However, communes were not abolished after the great crisis, only changed in their organisational scale. From 1962, agricultural operations and management groups were formed into much smaller units or

11

'production teams' which consisted of about twenty to thirty neighbouring households. In this system land was jointly owned by the commune, brigade and production teams. The production team was, however, treated as the basic operating and accounting unit. Income distribution, based on work points earned by each member, was undertaken within the production team. At the end of each year, the net income was distributed according to the work points accumulated by each team during the year. Generally, a farmer received fixed work points for a day's work regardless of the quality and quantity of his work. Egalitarian income distribution was the result of this system. Consequently, the incentive to work was low and productivity was stagnant.

2.2.3 Problems with centralised systems

During the period of these Stalinist institutions, output growth probably just kept up with population growth but at a high cost in terms of capital inputs. Total factor productivity before the reforms was only about three-quarters of that in 1952 (Wen, 1989; Wang, 1995). Farm labour productivity remained virtually unchanged for two decades. Moreover, the early changes in the Chinese rural institutions were followed by declines in output, and there was a huge loss of life in the accompanying famine, mainly in the period 1959-61. Urban grain consumption per capita declined by 15 per cent between 1954 and 1956, and the People's Commune movement worsened the shortage of grain during 1959-61. The efforts to boost grain production were at the cost of a precipitate decline in other agricultural sideline production such as vegetables, hogs and poultry production (Sicular, 1988, p254).

2.3 Rural reforms since 1978

Economic reforms in rural China, involving 80 per cent of the population, began in 1978. These reforms included three interrelated aspects: institutional change (including production organisation and marketing system), price reform and liberalisation of other economic policies. The purpose of reforms in these areas was to enhance production and farmers' income through a reduction of direct control and improvement to the incentive mechanism.

It is commonly recognised that the reforms can be divided into two stages: the first stage (1978-84) involved gradual changes in the rigid centrally planned system; the second stage (1985-92) was marked by a decisive step towards the complete elimination of the state planned system (Ash, 1993). The central policy issues in the two stages are summarised in Table 2.1.

Table 2.1

Strategic and policy issues in China's rural reforms

	Central strategy	Main policy issues
First stage of rural reform: 1979-84	Restructuring of rural economy through institutional change involving organisation of the production and marketing system based on the liberation of rural economy	* The establishment of the household responsibility system * Increasing agricultural product prices * Quota adjustment * Diversification of the agricultural and rural economies
Second stage of rural reform: 1985-1992	Restructuring of rural economy through an extension of the market, price adjustments and development of non-farm activities	* Further adjusting state purchase prices * Introduction of free market competitive mechanism * Diversification of production * Liberalisation of product and factor markets

2.3.1   The first stage of reform 1978-84: the incentive mechanisms

The immediate goal of the rural economic policy in 1979 was to ensure stable growth of agricultural production. Clearly, China could not adopt land-extensive measures to increase grain production due to the acutely limited cultivated area. Accordingly, policy reforms were to concentrate on institutional and economic measures, designed to raise land productivity through improvements of Chinese farmers' production incentives. Institutional changes became the focus of agricultural policy reforms during the first stage of rural reforms.

During the first stage of reforms, three aspects were involved: (a) decollectivisation of farm land and introduction of the Household Production Responsibility System (HPRS); (b) upward adjustment of the state quota prices and above-quota prices (discussed in the next chapter) and reduction of the mandatory procurement quota, which in turn increased the proportion of grain purchased at above-quota prices; and (c) encouragement of the rural non-farm economy (discussed in Chapter 4).

The household production responsibility system (HPRS)   The first and most important reform in 1978 was the introduction of the Household Production Responsibility System (HPRS). The HPRS was introduced in preference to the production team of the people's commune. It was first tried in Anhui province at the end of the 1970s and after several years of experimentation, spread nation-wide in 1982-83; 80 per cent of production teams adopted the HPRS in 1982 and 98 per cent by 1983.[4] The farm

13

household became the fundamental unit of production in the agricultural sector. The HPRS was based on a system of contractual relationships which defined the rights and responsibilities of state, collective and individual. In HPRS, the land was owned by the collective, and contracted to individual households usually based on household size or labour force (Kojima, 1988). Other collective assets were divided, sold or contracted to individuals or groups who were willing to manage them. The household was obligated to pay taxes, to make contributions to collective welfare funds, to provide its share of state procurement requirements, and to contribute labour to maintain the rural public infrastructure. After that, all residual products could be retained by the household. This system allowed farmers to sell surplus at a higher above-quota or market price once state obligations were fulfilled.

The introduction of the HPRS significantly improved incentives and the management of grain production. It provided substantial rewards to those farmers who were able to increase production: once quota procurement obligations were fixed in absolute terms rather than on a percentage of production basis, increases in production would bring direct profit to farmers.

Marketing reforms   The marketing system has also experienced a significant change since 1978 in order to facilitate market development in China's agricultural sector.

Firstly, market controls were relaxed. As early as 1978, the government began to encourage the revival of rural free markets. By 1980 all products except cotton were allowed to be sold on the market after the fulfillment of the state quota. Accompanying adjustment of the state purchase prices during 1979-84, the free market was reintroduced, reforming the Chinese rural economy. Markets rapidly developed in both urban and rural areas. The expansion of the free market provided an alternative channel for the sale of farm products, often at prices exceeding those offered by the state. As a result, the state monopolised purchase in grain markets was reduced. In 1982, grain sold through market channels accounted for 8 per cent of the purchased grain in the whole country (Zong, 1994, p137, Table 7.2). Although radical development of free markets did not occur until the second half of the 1980s, permitting market exchange of agricultural products was very important for rural development during this period.

Secondly, the compulsory quota was reduced and above-quota purchases were increased between 1978 and 1984. In 1978, the quota purchase of grain accounted for 69 per cent of farmers' total sales, but in 1981 it was reduced to 42 per cent. At the same time, above-quota sales rose from 25 per cent to 38 per cent, the remaining 17 per cent being sold on the free markets (Sicular, 1988). This proportion continued to grow, rising from 38 per cent of sales in 1981 to 67 per cent in 1984 (World Bank 1991).[5]

Thirdly, private trade was revived so that any produce which was not compulsorily purchased by the state could be sold through private trade channels. Starting from 1979, farm households were allowed to trade some agricultural surplus and sideline products on the free market. By 1982, restrictions on private long-distance trade had been abandoned. Farmers. as traders, were encouraged to engage in long-distance trading. Except for certain listed items including poisons, precious metals, grain coupons and similar items, all other commodities could be sold on the free market. In 1983, the further liberalisation of the free market was legally confirmed and was formally regarded as 'a component part of the unified socialist market'. All farm products other than grain were allowed to be sold in markets.

Finally, the role of the economic plan in production was weakened. The number of planning production categories was 21 before 1978, was reduced to 16 in 1981 and to 13 in 1982. The number of planning targets was 31 before 1978, and was reduced to 20 in 1981 (Sicular, 1989b).

2.3.2   The second stage of reforms: 1985-92

The major measures during the second stage of reforms included the following: introduction of the contract system; further relaxing of control of marketing activities; an increase in negotiated purchase; and expansion of the market system.

The contract system   In order to accelerate the pace of price reform towards the market system, the unified purchase system was replaced in early 1985 by voluntary contract purchase. The unified procurement of grain which had lasted for more than 30 years was abolished. The state no longer set the compulsory quota for farmers. Grain would be purchased on the basis of contracts negotiated with farmers before the sowing season. If the amount of voluntary contract purchase did not reach the state planned targets, the state would buy additional grain on the free market. Farmers could choose freely whether or not to contract with the state or dispose of their products on the market. However, the reform encountered a series of problems in the first year. The most difficult one was that the state was unable to fulfill its planned purchase through voluntary contracts. Chinese farmers became reluctant to contract with the government and in order to guarantee grain supply, the government began to emphasise that the grain contracts were not just contracts but also a responsibility (Wang 1995). In practice, the implementation of the contract system at the local level was far from voluntary (Oi, 1989).

Relaxing control of marketing activities   By 1985, the government had

15

reduced the number of commodities under state quota procurement from 180 to 21 (An, 1989). Furthermore, for the range of commodities still under contract procurement, the state procurement share of total social purchases had also declined. The proportion of state procurement of grain in total social purchase dropped from 98 per cent in 1978 to 74 per cent in 1985 (Table 2.2) but rose again in the late 1980s. By 1990, except for grain, oilseed crops and cotton which remained subject to the state quota procurement, other commodities were no longer strictly purchased by state quota procurement.

Increase in negotiated purchase   The liberalisation of the grain marketing system was also reflected in the steps adopted by the state to reduce contract quotas and increase negotiated purchase. The government gradually increased the proportion of negotiated purchase and decreased the proportion of quota at fixed prices for grains and oilseeds. The dual aim was to reduce state intervention and to allow the free market to develop: the result was the development of the dual procurement system.

Expansion of the market system   As early as in 1984, the attention of reforms was turning to the question of market expansion and a new market system was gradually established.   Firstly, free product markets were expanded; then markets for labour, and land gradually emerged.

Free markets for agricultural produce   The market for agricultural produce was expanded. The number of these markets doubled, and more importantly, the transaction's value soared from 18.3 billion Yuan in 1979 to 353 billion Yuan in 1992 (Table 2.3). The share of agricultural output sold through the market rose from less than 10 per cent of total agricultural output in 1978 to 40 per cent in 1992 (Chinese Statistical Abstract, 1993).

The number of rural free markets increased from 36,800 in 1979 to 64,678 in 1992. The number of urban free markets for agricultural produce also increased from 2,200 in 1979 to 14,500 in 1992. Rural fairs accounted for a large proportion of the total fairs but urban fairs also developed rapidly. Many agricultural products could now be exchanged in the free markets after fulfillment of the state procurement, whereas before the rural reform, only state commercial enterprises and marketing cooperative organisations were permitted to purchase grain.

Table 2.2 Marketing and state procurement of grain, 1977-91

Unit: million tonnes

Year	Total marketed grain[a]	State procurement[b] (1)=(2)+(3)+(4) As % of TMG		Of which: Quota Purchase (2) As % of State Proc		Above-quota purchase (3) As % of State proc		Negotiated Purchase (4) As % of State Proc	
1977	47.67	47.67	100.0	37.75	79.19	Na	Na	Na	Na
1978	50.73	49.47	97.52	34.04	68.81	12.16	24.58	3.27	6.61
1979	60.24	57.49	95.43	33.11	57.59	19.13	33.28	5.25	9.13
1980	61.29	57.16	93.26	28.29	49.49	20.28	35.48	8.56	14.98
1981	68.46	63.29	92.45	26.89	42.49	23.82	37.65	10.58	17.26
1982	78.06	72.63	93.04	28.21	38.84	26.94	37.09	17.48	24.07
1983	102.49	97.62	95.25	30.32	31.06	59.73	61.20	7.57	7.75
1984	117.25	110.08	93.88	27.86	25.31	73.62	66.88	9.30	8.39
1985	107.63	79.25	73.63	59.61	75.22	(-)	(-)	19.64	24.78
1986	115.16	94.53	82.06	53.34	56.43	(8.87)[c]	9.38	32.33	34.20
1987	120.92	99.20	82.04	56.92	57.38	(-)	(-)	42.28	42.62
1988	119.95	92.97	77.51	49.15	52.87	(-)	(-)	43.82	47.13
1989	121.38	99.57	82.03	48.02	48.23	(-)	(-)	51.55	51.77
1990	139.95	123.65	88.35	50.55	40.88	(29.36)[c]	23.74	43.74	35.37
1991	136.35	116.42	85.38	47.01	40.38	(15.81)[c]	13.58	53.60	46.04

Notes: (a) Total marketed grain is social purchase including state purchase and individual purchase in free markets. Quota prior to 1985 are for the state procurement quota and after 1985 are for the contract procurement.

(b) The state procurement included quota, above-quota purchase and negotiated purchase. The above-quota purchase has beem excluded in this Table due to the lack of data.

(c) The figure in 1986 is the amount of 'entrusted procurement', i.e., the central government entrusted the local government purchase, the figures in 1990 1nd 1991 were the amount of procurement for 'special grain reserve'.

Sources: Sicular, 1993 Table 6.4. China Commerce ED. Commercial Yearbook, 1990, p566, 571; Cheng, et al. 1994, The changing grain marketing system in China, China Quarterly, No. 4, Table 2; Statistical Yearbook of China, 1993, p607.

Table 2.3
The number and transaction value of rural and urban fairs

Year	Total	Rural	Urban	Total	Rural	Urban
	Number (Thousand)			Value (Billion Yuan)		
1979	39.0	36.8	2.2	18.3	17.1	1.2
1980	40.8	37.9	2.9	23.5	21.1	2.4
1981	43.0	39.7	3.3	28.7	25.3	3.4
1982	44.8	41.2	3.6	33.3	28.8	4.5
1983	48.0	43.5	4.5	38.6	33.0	5.6
1984	56.5	50.4	6.1	47.0	39.0	8.0
1985	61.3	53.3	8.0	70.5	52.4	18.1
1986	67.6	57.9	9.7	90.6	66.2	24.4
1987	69.7	58.8	10.9	115.8	81.1	34.7
1988	71.4	59.2	12.2	162.1	107.6	54.5
1989	72.1	59.0	13.1	197.4	125.0	72.4
1990	72.6	59.5	13.1	216.8	133.0	83.8
1991	74.7	60.8	13.9	262.2	154.3	107.9
1992	79.2	64.7	14.5	353.0	194.7	158.3

Sources: *Rural Economic Statistics of China (1949-86) 1989, p428;*
Statistical Yearbook of China, 1991, p605; 1993, p625.

Markets for labour   Substantial progress has also been made in expanding the role of the market in the allocation of labour. China has a dual labour market: official and non-official. Most non-official employment is in rural areas and smaller cities. The earliest rural labour markets emerged in areas where the small-scale industrial sector developed rapidly and farmers were able to shift into manufacturing employment and other non-farm industries. Labour exchanges in rural areas can be seen in the busy times i.e. the sowing and harvest seasons. Although in its infancy, the market seemed to be almost fully functioning. Wages were determined by an active market rather than being set according to the official standard. By 1993 the non-official market employed more than 110 million workers and produced a significant share of China's manufactured goods output. In 1990 it produced about $12.5 billion in export goods, a little over 10 per cent of China's total exports (Lardy, 1992a). In the state-owned sector, employment is still strictly regulated due to an array of social benefits. Wages are paid according to national standards.

Markets for land   Compared with the development of commodity markets, markets for land have developed slowly, though land transfers can be observed in some regions. Land in the rural areas is legally owned by the collective (previously by production teams) and leased to each of the households. Although land was leased to each farm household, this was not a transfer of land ownership. In 1984, land was also allowed to be subleased when a household engaged in non-farm activities. Usually the

18

sublessor received some compensation. This policy may eventually revive land markets in rural China. However, so far transactions in land exist only at the margin. There are probably two main reasons for this. Firstly, land transfer must be authorised by the collective. If a farmer wished land to be released during the contracted period, he would be required immediately to return the land to the village, after which it could be contracted to another farmer. Secondly, most farmers are reluctant to abandon their small plots of land even in the absence of long-term profit expectations: farm land in China plays a role not only as a factor of production, but also as a source of food security for farmers and their families (Zhu, 1991). Thus, most farmers have viewed farmland as a form of social insurance following the dismemberment of the people's communes (Kojima, 1988). Although little research has been done on this topic, it appears that formal transfers of subleased land are relatively few, though informal transfers can be frequently observed.[6]

2.4   The dual characteristics of the new institutional environment

Although grain production and marketing have undergone substantial changes since 1978, particularly after 1985, it is still hard to say that the perfect market system has been established in China. The broad rural reform has brought about new dual institutional characteristics, i.e. the imperfect planning and the imperfect market system. The role of grain price is still constrained by institutional factors in two respects: (a) government intervention; and (b) the imperfect market system.

2.4.1   Government intervention

The general approach to grain marketing liberalisation has been outlined in section 2.3.[7] However, even after opening up the grain markets, grain production and marketing remained under relatively heavy intervention by the government during the period 1978-92. Important elements of farm produce, including grain and cotton, remained under compulsory procurement throughout the 1980s, and until 1992 a large share of grain was sold through state commercial channels or the quasi-state channel of the supply and marketing co-operatives (Table 2.4).

Table 2.4

Grain marketing through the state commercial channels, selected years

Unit: million tonnes

Year	Total Social Purchase	Of Which: Through The State Commercial Channel	
			% of Total Purchase
1985	107.63	90.62	84.2
1990	139.95	122.56	87.6
1991	136.35	116.28	85.3
1992	132.46	111.46	84.1

Note: *Total social purchase is total national purchase by all sources including purchase by the state grain bureau, rural supply and marketing co-operatives, state commercial department, firms, foreign trade and individuals. The state commercial channel refers to the state grain bureau only before 1987, but after 1987, it includes the state grain bureau, the state commercial department and rural supply and marketing co-operatives.*

Sources: *Rural Statistical Yearbook of China, 1993, p166; Statistical Yearbook of China, 1993.*

It can be seen that during the later 1980s and early 1990s, more than 80 per cent of total social purchase was through the state commercial channels. This was mainly due to the continuance of compulsory purchase for a proportion of output, although in certain counties farmers were allowed to deliver only half of the quantity specified in their purchase contracts. To ensure market supply, the central government still instructed the provinces to purchase a certain amount of grain; this equaled the original quantity of state procurement, roughly a total of 50 million tonnes a year (World Bank, 1993). Indeed the State Grain Bureau still often forced farmers to deliver the full amount in a deficient year. Furthermore, government owned grain stations competed with other private dealers to purchase farmers' above-quota grain. Another reason was the backward nature of private purchasing channels which could not expand within a short period of time. A large private purchase required a huge investment in stock capacity: this was usually unable to be undertaken by private business as the bulk of farm output continued to be marketed through state marketing channels.

China still relied to a considerable degree on administrative measures to purchase outputs and distribute inputs for major elements of grain production during the period 1978 to 1992. Although there had been considerable loosening of the system and enlarging of the role of prices through recent reforms, the government continued to circumscribe the decision-making freedom of farmers. Thus, the quota and the assigned sown area for some crops was retained in order to ensure the state's acquisition and distribution of food grain. Under these circumstances, price was not the only signal influencing producers production and marketing decisions.

2.4.2   The imperfect market system

China has had considerable success in expanding the role of the market for agricultural products during the reform period. However, markets for factors of production, i.e., land, labour and capital, have developed slowly.

Free markets for agricultural commodities emerged in the early reform stage. With the development of rural reforms, the market became more complex and more efficient. The free market was initially along coastal towns, through itinerant traders and periodic markets. Later, as exchanges between regions grew, this forced the markets to expand beyond small scale trade for local consumption. It required specialised wholesale market sites with proper facilities. Some wholesale markets were established as early as 1980 and were administered by the local commercial department (Watson, 1988). There were no restrictions on the participants. Everyone who wanted to buy or sell was allowed to participate in the wholesale markets, including both private traders and government commercial agencies. However, there was little participation directly by producers (farmers) and final (urban) consumers. After 1983, the wholesale sector entered a period of rapid development. The number of wholesale markets in operation was over 1,000 in 1984 and reached 2,000 by the end of 1985 (People's Daily, 1986; Wang, 1995). These wholesale markets were mainly to handle trade in the agricultural produce such as vegetables, meat, fruit, eggs and other foodstuffs and might develop as a free network, parallel to the state marketing structure. After 1986, the wholesale grain market was also beginning to emerge, even though urban rations were still supplied through the state system at subsidised prices. For example, the Wuxi Rice market handled some 185,000 tonnes of grain and oils. This trade had established links with over 250 locations in 25 provinces. In 1987, a grain market was opened in Zhenjian dealing with merchants throughout Jiangsu province (Watson, 1988). By the end of 1992, a national wholesale market for grain trading (in Zhengzhou of Henan province) and seven regional markets had been established.[8]   The main participants in these wholesale markets included both private traders and state agencies such as private long-distance traders, peasant co-operatives, government and state commercial agencies. However, in contrast to wholesale markets in other agricultural produce, the wholesale grain markets were directly run and administered by the state or the local government commercial department. These markets began to play some role in the grain trade between regions. Although the amount handled through private traders was far smaller than through the state channels, the fact that the wholesale market trade in grain began to emerge, was a clear indication of the growing role of the market.

Despite the development in grain markets, the Chinese marketing system was still far from being mature even with all these reform attempts. Firstly, some of wholesale markets themselves were part of the Ministry of Commerce system. In these markets, the state agency both runs the market and participates in the trade. Secondly, even after the establishment of wholesale markets, the inter-regional flow of grain was mainly handled by the state food agency and the local government food agency. The central government still instructed the provinces to purchase certain amounts of grain. Farmers were required to fulfill the contract, then they were allowed to enter these markets. Thirdly, prices were still administered by the state through various means such as stipulating ceiling prices. Furthermore, markets were disarticulated and regionally isolated. The operation of the market was severely constrained by poor communications and difficult access to relevant market information. Apart from these fundamental market imperfections, there were other decisive factors which impaired the development of the market: (a) the imbalance of aggregate grain supply and demand; (b) the inadequacy of physical infrastructure, such as roads and means of transport; and (c) the absence of necessary legal regulations for a market economy.

Labour markets began to emerge, but the rural farm labour markets cannot be considered comparable with the urban labour markets in either opportunities for employment or level of income. Many factors made the labour market far from perfect: lack of skills and limited wages available from firms, caused constraints on the labour flow..[9] Land markets in rural areas were slow to develop although the reform of land and property markets in urban areas made dramatic progress.[10] The growth of grain production also depended upon the development of a capital market. After the establishment of HPRS, agricultural investment by the individual producers was constrained by their ability to save. The mobilisation of investments also depended upon the development of financial markets in rural China.

2.5   Unchanged aspects of the rural economy

In spite of improvement in the institutional environment following the reform, there remained unchanged features of the rural economy that affected the functioning of the price mechanism.

22

2.5.1 Own-consumption

During the period 1978 to 1982 the ratio of grain own consumption by households remained high, in response to rising household incomes. Indeed during that period, grain was by far the least commercialised of the major agricultural commodities, as may be seen in Table 2.5: by 1992 less than 35 per cent of grain entered commercial channels.

Table 2.5
Commercial ratios for major agricultural commodities, China, 1978-92

Year	Grain	Oil	Cotton	Pork	Aquatic
1978	20.3	55.8	94.3	53.5	67.7
1979	21.7	62.1	97.8	66.1	68.6
1980	22.8	71.1	99.0	65.0	62.3
1981	24.2	76.4	98.0	66.4	62.0
1982	25.9	71.9	97.2	66.7	65.3
1983	30.9	65.4	96.6	69.2	58.0
1984	34.8	67.4	95.9	71.9	58.2
1985	30.5	68.4	86.9	72.0	55.4
1986	33.8	74.9	107.2	76.3	44.9
1987	34.4	74.6	95.9	79.9	44.7
1988	34.9	74.1	91.1	80.6	41.2
1989	34.4	73.0	87.3	82.3	47.5
1990	36.6	72.4	90.7	85.5	46.5
1991	36.6	72.3	93.2	89.0	51.9
1992	34.6	69.1	96.7	91.5	50.1

Notes: (1) The commercial ratio equals the total amount of a product marketed as a percentage of total production.
(2) The cotton ratio in 1986 exceeded 100 per cent because some of the 1985 output was sold in that year.

Sources: Statistical Yearbook of China, 1993, p379, 608; Rural Statistical Yearbook of China, 1993, p146.

2.5.2 Labour-intensive production

Although agriculture had developed rapidly, production was still labour intensive. Three reasons can be identified.

Firstly, the limited land resources per person, which is one of the most important constraints on the development of China's agriculture. From the 1950s to the 1970s China's population grew rapidly, the total arable area declined substantially from its peak 111.8 million Ha in 1956 to 99.4 million Ha in 1978 and 95.4 million Ha in 1992 due to various development pressures (Statistics of Agricultural Economy 1949-83, 1983, p120).[11]   Thus, the arable land per person declined from 0.19 Ha in 1952 to just 0.11 Ha in 1975 (Rural

Economic Statistics of China 1982, p9). By 1992, the amount of farmland per person was among the lowest in the world at 0.10 Ha per person and at 0.22 Ha per agricultural labourer (Rural Statistical Yearbook of China, 1994, p41, 393).

Secondly, much of China's cultivated land was in semi-arid areas so that the growth of agricultural production was heavily dependent upon irrigation work. There were vast regional differences across China. Agricultural production in eastern areas enjoyed relatively large water resources for cultivated land. However, in the west and centre of China, where a large part of cultivated land was located in inhospitable areas, there were relatively limited water resources. This severely constrained the growth of agricultural production in these areas. Thus, the growth of grain production depended, to a large extent, on the development of irrigation network. This work was started from the late 1950s and around one quarter of China's cultivated land was drained and irrigated (Statistical Yearbook of China, 1993, p349). Through huge efforts by the communes to mobilise labour for the construction of irrigation network, China's drained and irrigated area rose from 27 million hectares in 1957 to 45 million hectares in 1978 (Statistical Yearbook of China, 1993, p349).

Thirdly, given the limited availability of farm land, the growth of agriculture in China depended to a large extent upon multiple-cropping of farmland. Approximately half of China's farm land mainly in middle and southern areas was cropped more than once in a year. Thus, China's Multiple Cropping Index (MCI), which is a ratio of sown area to arable area, is rather high. In 1992 it was estimated as 1.56 (Statistical Yearbook of China, 1993, 358, Rural Statistical Yearbook of China, 1993, p229); it reached 2.46 in Jiang Xi province in 1993 (Rural Statistical Yearbook of China, 1994, p389). China's annual grain yields per hectare of 'harvested' land was at 4.0 tonnes in 1992 (Statistical Yearbook of China, 1993, p371).

The increase in the irrigated area in the commune period can be directly attributed to state investment and other forms of state help, but there is little doubt that most of it was only possible due to farm labour inputs. It is well known that under the commune system China's rural farmers increased their efforts and spent most of their time changing their local production conditions including digging ditches and building reservoirs in wide irrigation systems. In addition, they also made great efforts at land reclamation and soil improvement. This intensive labour input contributed to the high irrigation ratio of the arable farmland areas after 1950 and it enabled China to attain higher yields per unit of land through the 1960s and 1970s. On the other hand, the adoption of new agricultural technology developed slowly, due to a decline in investment in agriculture after rural reforms.

24

Firstly, individual investment in agriculture declined in relative terms. Private rural savings increased to about 20 per cent of annual income in 1985 (World Bank's estimation, 1986). However, total private investment in fixed farm assets declined markedly as a percentage of total investment (Table 2.6). Most farmers' savings had been funnelled into housing construction or stock accumulation, reflecting a reluctance to make long term investments in agriculture.

Secondly, government investment also declined due to the increased budgetary burden. Capital construction expenditure on agriculture declined from 4.9 per cent of total state expenditure in 1979 to 2.0 per cent in 1992 (Table 2.7).

Thirdly, the use of agricultural machinery also showed a slightly downward trend, particularly in the mid-1980s after decollectivisation. There was also stagnation in the irrigated and power-irrigated areas. This underlines the labour intensive nature of much of agriculture in China.

Table 2.6

Farm household investment in fixed assets and household building, 1982-92

Year	Total investment (TI)	Investment in fixed farm assets		Investment in household building	
	Billion Yuan	Billion Yuan	As % of TI	Billion Yuan	As % of TI
1982	19.853	3.000	15.1	16.260	81.9
1983	30.505	6.100	20.0	21.454	70.3
1984	37.911	11.328	29.8	23.938	63.1
1985	47.843	12.830	26.8	31.315	65.4
1986	57.482	7.182	12.5	38.856	67.5
1987	69.535	9.218	13.3	48.721	70.0
1988	86.523	12.401	14.3	58.097	67.1
1989	89.203	9.788	10.9	64.168	71.9
1990	87.647	9.933	11.3	64.978	74.1
1991	104.256	13.008	12.48	75.925	72.8
1992	100.552	6.880	6.84	67.852	67.5

Source: Statistical Yearbook of China, 1993, p206.
Note: This table excluded certain other forms of investment.

Table 2.7
State budget expenditures on agriculture in selected years

Year	Total state agricultural expenditure		Of which: Capital construction expenditure		
	Billion Yuan	% total expenditure	Billion Yuan	% total state expenditure	% agricultural expenditure
1965	5.5	11.8	2.4	5.2	43.6
1975	9.9	12.1	3.6	4.4	36.4
1978	15.1	13.6	5.1	4.6	33.8
1979	17.4	13.7	6.2	4.9	35.6
1980	15.0	12.4	4.9	4.0	32.6
1981	11.0	9.9	2.4	2.2	21.8
1982	12.0	10.4	2.9	2.5	24.2
1983	13.3	10.3	3.4	2.6	25.6
1984	14.1	9.1	3.4	2.2	24.1
1985	15.4	8.3	3.8	2.1	24.7
1986	18.4	7.9	4.4	1.9	23.9
1987	19.5	8.0	4.7	1.9	24.1
1988	21.4	7.9	4.0	1.5	18.7
1989	26.4	8.8	5.1	1.7	19.3
1990	30.8	8.9	6.7	1.9	21.8
1991	34.8	9.1	7.6	1.9	21.8
1992	37.3	8.5	8.3	2.0	22.3

Sources: Statistical Yearbook of China, 1991, p209, 218; 1993, p215; Rural Statistical Yearbook of China, 1994, p95.

Table 2.8
Tractor-ploughed and irrigated areas

Year	Tractor-ploughed area (10000 Ha)	Irrigated area (10000 Ha)	Of which power-irrigated	Proportion of power-irrigated to the total irrigated area (%)
1952	13.6	1995.9	31.7	1.6
1957	263.6	2733.9	120.2	4.4
1962	828.4	3054.4	606.5	19.9
1965	1557.9	3305.5	809.3	24.5
1978	4067.0	4496.5	2489.5	55.4
1979	4221.9	4500.3	2532.1	56.3
1980	4099.0	4488.8	2531.5	56.4
1981	3647.7	4457.1	2523.1	56.6
1982	3511.5	4417.7	2514.5	56.9
1983	3357.2	4464.4	2526.5	56.6
1984	3492.2	4445.3	2506.2	56.4
1985	3444.2	4403.6	2462.9	55.9
1986	3642.8	4422.6	2503.2	56.6
1987	3839.3	4440.3	2482.5	55.9
1988	4091.4	4437.6	2608.3	58.8
1989	4259.3	4491.7	2610.7	58.1
1990	4825.5	4740.3	2714.8	57.3
1991	5019.0	4782.2	2762.9	57.8
1992	5146.9	4859.0	2828.3	58.2

Source: Statistical Yearbook of China, 1993, p349.

China's grain trade rose substantially in volume terms between 1978 and 1982. Exports increased by a factor of over seven, whereas, after 1979, imports remained relatively constant. China remained a net importer in all but three years of this period, although imports remained a relatively low percentage of total output.

In spite of the increase in grain trade, self-sufficiency may remain as the main policy objective for a rather long period in the future. China is unwilling to depend upon the world markets for food. There are two reasons for this. Firstly, China has a large population with rather low income levels and a huge demand for grain. China does not wish to depend on grain imports from the world market to feed around 24 per cent of the world's population. It perceives potentially catastrophic consequences if world market grain supplies were to reduce suddenly, for whatever reason. The fluctuations in world grain prices from the mid 1960s to the end of the 1980s reinforces the perceived risk. China's principal grain import is wheat, around 90 per cent of the total in most years.   The average unit price of China's wheat imports increased 21 per cent during the first large wave of imports (1978-82) and 66 per cent during the second wave (1987-89).

Table 2.9
China's grain imports and exports, 1978-92

Year	Imports		Exports		Net imports	
	Million tonne	% of total output	Million tonne	% of total output	Million tonne	% of total output
1978	8.8	2.7	1.9	0.6	6.9	2.3
1979	12.3	3.7	1.7	0.5	10.7	3.2
1980	13.4	4.2	1.6	.0.5	12.2	3.8
1981	14.8	4.6	1.3	0.4	13.5	4.2
1982	16.1	4.5	1.3	0.4	14.9	4.2
1983	13.4	3.5	1.9	0.5	11.5	3.0
1984	10.7	2.6	3.3	0.8	7.3	1.8
1985	6.2	1.6	8.9	2.3	-2.7	-0.7
1986	7.3	1.9	9.1	2.3	-1.8	-0.5
1987	16.3	4.0	7.1	1.8	9.1	2.3
1988	14.8	3.8	6.5	1.6	8.2	2.1
1989	16.4	4.0	6.2	1.5	10.2	2.5
1990	13.7	3.1	5.9	1.3	7.9	1.8
1991	13.5	3.1	10.9	2.5	2.6	0.6
1992	11.8	2.7	13.6	3.1	-1.9	-0.4

Sources: Statistical Yearbook of China, 1991, p623, 626; 1993, p364, 641, 644; Rural Statistical Yearbook of China, 1994, p169.

2.6   Summary

China's rural reforms can certainly be viewed as economic liberalisation with wide-ranging effects on production, consumption, investment and incentive structures. Decollectivisation of agricultural production was the most important part of China's economic liberalisation. The introduction of the HPRS in replace of the Commune system significantly improved producers' incentives in and enthusiasm for grain production. Marketing system reform also got underway alongside the institutional reform. An increase in agricultural (including grain) prices and relaxation of the monopoly marketing system, regarded as the most essential parts of economic liberalisation made agricultural production more profitable and attractive.

Institutional reforms created greater incentives for farm households to respond to changes in the economic environment. The key was in the creation of more direct linkages between farmers' efforts and their incomes. Farmers regained their responsibility for decision-making in agricultural production, and benefited from relaxations in marketing and upward price adjustments.

However, China has neither a typical planned system nor a free market system: she still relies, to a considerable degree, on administered measures for the output production of major crops, particularly grain, for input distribution and output marketing. A dual market system has emerged and free markets co-exist. Markets for labour, land and capital are still in the infant stage.

The current rural economy in China is still only semi-commercialised. Although the rural policy environment has dramatically changed since 1978, a high proportion of output for household's own-consumption and the pattern of labour intensive production remains largely unchanged.

The continuing high level of government intervention, the dual market system and the high level of household consumption of grain all serve to complicate any attempts to determine the effects of price changes on marketed grain supply. In the next chapter we look at some of the debate and issues surrounding actual grain price adjustments in China.

Notes

1. The institutional environment here includes the organisation of the production and marketing systems.

2. For the detailed evolution of the old marketing and commune systems, see Lin, 1991; Chen and Buckwell, 1991; Perkins, 1966; Chen and Galeson, 1969; Cheng, 1982; and Donnithorne, 1967.

3. For detailed information about marketing organisation, see Wang and Davis, 1992, 'The development of reform and the rural marketing system in China', in Vermeer, E B (ed) From Peasant to Entrepreneur: Growth and Change in Rural China, Netherlands, Pudoc Wageningen, pp 69-82.

4. For the development of HPRS, see Lin's paper (1991). 'Reforming the agricultural sector in China', China Working Paper, No 91/1, National Centre for Development Studies, Research School of Pacific Studies, The Australian National University.

5. According to the World Bank's estimation of 1991, above-quota purchases were 33 million tonnes in 1981 and 77 million tonnes in 1984, out of 63 million tonnes and 107 million tonnes of total state purchases, while quota purchases stagnated at 30 million tonnes.

6. Formal transfer means that land subleasing is made through the production team or via village government permission.

7. On April 1, 1993, the authorities implemented a national grain price deregulation policy. Firstly, the planned supply system instituted in the mid-1950's, which guaranteed urban residents grain and edible oil rations, was abandoned in most places. After April, sales volumes in government owned grain stores dropped dramatically. Competition from open markets forced many of these stores to radically change their business methods and services offered. Secondly, the planned purchase system was changed in 1993. The document in 1 April 1993 stated that the state purchases were not uniformly implemented throughout the country. In some counties farmers who had signed grain purchase contracts with grain stations still had to deliver the specified grain to the storage bins and were paid market prices. For surplus grain above the obligated quota, some individual grain dealers drove their wagons and trucks directly to farmers' fields to purchase the grain (State Council, China's Agricultural Development Programme for the 1990s, Renmin Rebao, January 19, 1994 p2).

8. Recently thirteen regional wholesale markets have developed. These markets are mainly concerned with inter-regional trade in grain and are administered by the regional commercial department. The Zhengzhou national wholesale market is directly administered by the central government for grain trade between regions.

9. A detailed discussion of labour flow will be presented in Chapter 4.

10. In the last few years, China has introduced land and building rights registration, land leasing, and profit-driven real estate companies. Market forces are emerging in the urban real estate market. Land increasingly has a value revealed by prices in the urban land transaction market. Land leasing has expanded especially quickly since 1992 in about 30 cities where the reform process is most advanced. However, in rural areas, land transfers and land markets are rare.

11. According to the most recent data published by the People's Daily, real total arable farmland is 133 million hectares which is nearly 40 per cent higher than the 95 million hectares published by the State Statistical Bureau (People's Daily, overseas version, 25 June, 1996, p1). In spite of this, the average arable farmland per capita in China is still low compared with the world average.

3 Grain price adjustments: the debates and issues

3.1 Introduction

The main aim of grain price changes in the reform period was to improve incentive mechanisms and farm households' income. Price reforms played a key role in economic liberalisation: the adjustment of grain prices provided higher incomes and greater incentives for production. This chapter examines the debates and issues about grain price adjustments since 1978. Special attention is given to the relationship between price and output changes in the periods 1978-84 and 1985-92. The chapter identifies price distortions remaining after price adjustments and their possible impacts on grain supply.

3.2 Adjustments to state purchase prices

3.2.1 Agricultural price distortion in the pre-reform period

It is commonly recognised that the grain price was seriously distorted against agricultural producers in the pre-reform period.

Agricultural price distortion before rural reforms had several aspects. Firstly, the price did not fully reflect the cost of production. Based on a survey of cereal production of 1,296 teams conducted by Yao (1981), production costs plus taxes per fifty kilograms averaged 11.6 Yuan, while the procurement price for the same amount of output was only 10.74 Yuan. Secondly, agricultural prices were relatively low compared to industrial prices. This is the well known 'price scissors'. As the major raw materials of industry came from agriculture and around two-thirds of light industrial product was sold in the countryside (Su, 1979), the price differences between industrial and agricultural products generated a considerable profit for industry. Although the industrial profit was high due to the low price of raw material from agriculture,[1] the state also imposed a high tax on the industrial firms. Thus, a large proportion of accumulated funding was transferred to the government. Thirdly, the state quota purchase price was lower than the market price. Prior to 1978, grain prices for quota delivery were initially fixed by the central government and set at a rather low level under the unified purchase and sale system: usually 20 per cent to 30 per cent lower than prevailing market prices (Perkins, 1966, p49-50). Fourthly, there were fewer price adjustments during the pre-reform period, particularly between 1966 and 1978 (Liang, 1982).

3.2.2   Adjustments in the state purchase price

The rural reform started in 1978 aimed at improving farmers' living standards and introducing the market mechanism to grain production. Price adjustment was the most important component of the rural reform. The purpose of price changes in the early stage of reform was to correct price distortions. It aimed at giving a correct price signal to farmers; gradually getting pricing right in order to improve their incomes and stimulate grain production.

Increases in quota and above-quota prices   To encourage grain production, the quota prices of selected products were raised substantially at the end of 1978 and in early 1979. The quota price rose 18 per cent for indica paddy, 21 per cent for wheat, 22 per cent for corn and 15 per cent for soybean respectively. The average increase for these four grain prices was 20 per cent.

The overall average increase in the quota price of grain, oil crops, cotton, sugar crops and pork was 17.1 per cent in 1979 (Lin, 1992). Quota price revisions were accompanied by higher above-quota price bonuses for grain, cotton, tobacco and certain other cash crops. Prior to 1978, grain and oil-crops had received a price bonus of 30 per cent for deliveries beyond the quota level. In 1979 this bonus was increased to 50 per cent. Between 1977 and 1983 above-quota prices rose by 36 per cent for grains, and 47 per cent for oils (Sicular, 1988).

Increase in the average price of grain   The upward adjustment in the state purchase price was also reflected in an increase in the average price of grain. As the proportion of quota purchase in the total state purchase declined while the proportion of above-quota purchase increased, this led to an increase in the average state purchase price for grain. Not only were both the quota and above-quota prices increased, the new above-quota bonus was calculated on the new increased quota prices. These resulted in a significant increase in the average price of cereals.

In addition to the adjustment of the state purchase price, the state also expanded a variety of material incentive programmes under which farmers were awarded certain scarce commodities at the low state price for delivering farm products to the state. For example, in 1978 the government raised the nationwide award of chemical fertilisers from 35 to 40 kg per 100 kg of cotton delivered to the state. Starting in 1979 it also gave farmers an award of grain at the low urban retail price for additional delivery of cotton.

The distorted price ratio between agricultural and industrial prices was partially adjusted as the state quota and above-quota prices increased significantly while the rural industrial price was kept relatively stable (increased only 0.1 per cent in 1979). The state above-quota price increased even faster than that of the free market price (Lin, 1992).

Table 3.1 shows that the state purchase price was adjusted much faster than the industrial price and free market prices in the early 1980s.

Table 3.1
Price indices in selected years (1978=100)

Year	State purchase price index	Rural free-market price index	Rural industrial product price index	State price as % industrial price index (4)=(1)/(3)×100	Free market as % industrial price index (5)=(2)/(3)×100
	(1)	(2)	(3)		
1979	130.5	100.0	100.1	130.4	99.9
1980	140.8	100.9	100.9	139.5	100.0
1981	154.5	99.5	101.9	151.6	97.6
1982	160.3	102.0	103.6	154.7	98.5
1983	176.9	98.0	104.6	169.1	93.7
1984	198.1	88.5	107.8	183.8	82.1

Note: *The state purchase price index used here is an average price index of quota and above-quota price published by the SSB recently.*

Sources: *The State Statistical Bureau, 1984, 1988; Lin, (1992). Rural Reforms and Agricultural Growth in China, Table 2. Price Yearbook of China, 1995, p295, 1994, p373; The Ministry of Commerce of China; Rural Statistical Yearbook of China; 1992, p185; 1993, p185.*

Price adjustments during 1978-84 encountered some difficulties. Firstly, the government found itself confronted with a severe budgetary burden. The state purchase price was increased significantly while the retail price remained unchanged at the levels of the 1960s, leading to state and retail price inversion.[2] Thus, the grain price subsidy leapt to 0.2 Yuan per kilogram in 1979. For edible oil, the subsidy was 1.6 Yuan per kilogram. Price subsidies amounted to 11.5 billion Yuan in 1979, and peaked at 28.3 billion Yuan in 1984. Subsidies accounted for more than one-fifth of government expenditure during the early 1980s (Table 3.2), and continued to be a severe burden until 1992.

Table 3.2
State revenue, expenditure and food subsidies, 1978-84

Unit: Billion Yuan

Year	Total state revenue	Total state expenditure (TSE)	Government deficit	Food subsidies	Subsidies as % of TSE
1978	112.1	111.1	1	Na	Na
1979	110.3	127.4	-17.1	11.5	9.0
1980	108.5	121.3	-12.8	17.2	14.2
1981	109.0	111.5	-2.5	25.0	22.4
1982	112.4	115.3	-2.9	24.3	21.1
1983	124.9	129.3	-4.4	26.3	20.3
1984	150.2	154.6	-4.5	28.3	18.3

Sources: *Statistical Yearbook of China, 1991, p209; World Bank for Reconstruction and Development, 1991, p146.*

The retail price of grain was increased to the level of the market price in 1992 when the government took further steps to reform the retail price system. It aimed at par with the state purchase price. Even so, the equalisation of the state purchase price and retail price of grain did not imply the elimination of subsidies. The state still had to subsidise the state-owned grain shops and urban consumers. Then the central government began to allow provincial governments to decide whether grain prices were to be further liberalised. In 1992, certain regions chose to liberalise immediately both the procurement and retail prices of grain, while others announced that similar measures would take effect in late 1992 or early 1993.[3]

Secondly, grain price signals were still being distorted by government intervention. For example, in order to encourage farmers to produce more grain, the government increased above-quota prices and purchased as much as farmers wished to sell in years of shortage and surplus. Thus, even though free market prices sometimes dropped below above-quota prices, eg. in 1982 and 1984, the government still had to buy the surplus grain at the higher above-quota prices, thus giving producers wrong signals.

Overall, the changes in pricing policy between 1978 and 1984, although important, did not reflect a radical break from the past, but rather an evolution of the previous price system. This was reflected in two aspects. First, the operation of the agrarian economy remained firmly under state supervision. Although prices were adjusted dramatically, they were still fixed by the state, rather than in the market place. Secondly, government still intervened in grain production through non-price measures. Although price administration was largely relaxed, the state procurement and rationing system remained unchanged. On the whole, pricing reforms during this period were mainly adjustments to state purchase prices, including bonuses and quotas rather than major changes in the state pricing system itself. Nevertheless, the flaws in the old system had been recognised and a new incentive system for grain producers was gradually being established.

3.2.3   Contract prices

Establishment of the contract price   In response to the budgetary problems and to accelerate the price reform towards the market system, the contract system was established in early 1985. The contract price was set equal to 30 per cent of the quota price plus 70 per cent of the above-quota price (Gao, 1989). It actually was a proportional price, i.e. 30 per cent of grain sales by farmers to the state was paid at the lower (quota) price and the remaining 70 per cent was paid at the above quota price. In this way, the two former kinds of state prices (quota and above-quota) were merged into a single price. This was intended to realise gradually a transition from planned prices to a market price system. At the end of 1985, to assure contract fulfillment, the state issued strict commands to deliver the contract purchase at the contract price set by the state. Aside from the contract purchase, the state also needed to purchase grain in the free market in order to meet the shortfall in grain purchases relative to government demand. This led to a dual purchase and price system, i.e., the state contract price and the free market price co-existed.

Further price adjustments   Further adjustments of contract prices were introduced in 1986 to deal with distortions in grain prices (Table 3.3). Price adjustments in 1986 raised grain contract prices by between 4 and 20 per cent over their 1985 levels. In 1989, the average contract price of grain was significantly increased by 26.9 per cent. The grain price declined slightly in 1990 and 1991, but increased in 1992. In late 1993, the state purchase prices for grain and oilseed were substantially increased again; as the state was worried about insufficient incentives for farmers to increase grain output and the low growth of rural income relative to urban income.

35

Taking Liaoning province as an example, in 1993, the government corn purchase price for fixed quota rose from 440 Yuan to 700 Yuan per tonne, an increase of 59 per cent or 40 per cent in real terms. The purchase price for paddy rice rose from 600 to 900 Yuan per tonne, a real increase of 32 per cent (Rozelle, 1994; Crook, 1994).

Figure 3.1 shows the trend in the real state purchase price index since 1978. It increased rapidly up to 1984 then declined slightly and stayed relatively constant up to 1989. It further declined in the next two years but the very large increase in 1994 pushed real price to its highest level in the reform era.

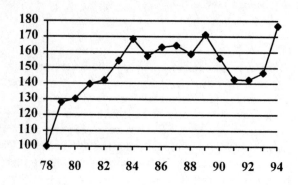

Figure 3.1   The real state purchase price index (1978=100)

Note: *State purchase prices were deflated by the national consumer price index.*

Sources: *Price Yearbook of China, 1995, 295; 1994, 373; Rural Statistical Yearbook of China, 1992, p185; 1993; p185; Statistical Yearbook of China, 1995, p233.*

Table 3.3
Adjustments in state prices, 1978-94

Unit: Yuan/Tonne

Year	State purchase price Yuan	Increase %	Rice Yuan	Increase %	Wheat Yuan	Increase %	Corn Yuan	Increase %	Soybean Yuan	Increase %
1978	231.9	0	220.0	0	272.5	0	168.1	0	264.1	0
1979	302.6	30.5	286.4	30.2	357.2	31.1	218.5	30.0	327.5	24.0
1980	326.5	7.9	308.9	7.8	385.0	7.8	235.5	7.8	361.8	10.5
1981	358.2	9.7	324.9	5.2	405.2	5.2	247.8	5.2	571.0	57.8
1982	371.7	3.8	327.4	0.8	420.4	3.8	257.2	3.8	593.5	3.9
1983	410.2	10.3	360.8	10.2	463.5	10.2	283.4	10.2	653.9	10.2
1984	459.3	12.0	360.8	0	466.2	0.6	283.4	0	653.9	0
Average increase:		12.4		9.0		9.8		9.5		17.7
1985	467.4	1.8	368.1	2.0	466.7	0.1	288.8	1.9	672.2	2.8
1986	513.8	9.9	391.2	6.3	486.6	4.3	333.7	15.5	807.9	20.2
1987	554.8	8.0	442.9	13.2	503.3	3.4	347.3	4.1	835.4	3.4
1988	636.0	14.6	530.6	19.8	579.8	15.2	363.6	4.7	911.4	9.1
1989	807.1	26.9	693.4	30.7	706.8	21.9	479.2	31.8	1119.3	22.8
1990	752.1	-6.8	642.2	-7.4	650.1	-8.0	467.8	-2.4	1101.3	-1.6
1991	705.5	-6.2	615.8	-4.1	612.5	-5.8	412.5	-11.8	1099.2	-0.2
1992	742.9	5.3	599.7	-2.6	674.4	10.1	446.5	8.2	1313.4	19.5
1993	866.9	16.7	747.3	24.6	710.6	5.4	532.2	19.2	1611.6	22.7
1994	1270.8	46.6	1150.8	54.0	1081.4	52.2	805.2	51.3	1846.9	14.6
Average increase:		11.7		13.7		9.9		12.3		11.3

Notes: (1) The state price before 1985 was the quota price and after 1985 the contract price.
(2) The state price is the average grain price, but this Table includes only four kinds of major crops and excludes other crops such as maize and potato.

Sources: The Ministry of Commerce Institute of Commercial Economic Research, 1990. Price Yearbook of China, 1995, p295; 1994, p373.

37

In the late 1970s, the state made a large adjustment in relative prices. The 'price scissors' (index of farm purchase prices as a proportion of retail prices of industrial products in rural areas) was reduced and moved in favour of farm produce by 13-14 per cent per annum between 1978 and 1980 (Statistical Yearbook of China, 1990). However, it encountered political constraints on further changes due to consumer grain price rises in urban areas. Thus it slowed down or reversed the process of improvement in the 'price scissors' in the 1980s. Furthermore, the state allowed the retail price of agricultural production inputs to rise faster than the overall price index of industrial products sold in the rural areas. Thus, from 1980 to 1989 the 'price scissors' for output prices (state purchase prices) relative to industrial product (mainly for agricultural inputs) prices for rice improved by just 6 per cent and for wheat actually fell by over 16 per cent (Statistical Yearbook of China, 1990; World Bank, 1993).

During the 1980s, the government allowed the overall retail price of subsidiary foodstuffs to drift upwards. Under the growing impact of market forces, retail prices of subsidiary foodstuffs increased more rapidly than for grain. For example, the average retail price of meat and eggs rose 157 per cent from 1983 to 1989, aquatic products by 197 per cent, compared to 78 per cent for grain (Statistical Yearbook of China, 1990, p251, World Bank, 1993). The disparity in retail prices between the state and free market had been reduced and gradually closed for most subsidiary foodstuffs. For example, for aquatic products the average gap between the state market and the free market fell from 59 per cent in 1980 to 22 per cent in 1988, for meat and eggs from 22 per cent to 14 per cent and for vegetables from 65 to 11 per cent (Rural Statistical Yearbook of China, 1989, p179). However, for grain and edible oil, the disparity hardly narrowed at all. In 1988, the difference was still 70 per cent for edible oil and 98 per cent for grain (Rural Statistical Yearbook of China, 1989, p175, World Bank, 1993). This situation did not change until the early 1990s. By 1991, the state retail price of grain was raised by about 50 per cent and edible oil by more than 100 per cent. At the same time, the government increased real incomes of urban workers: this enabled a large step to be taken towards free market prices for farm produce without major protest. Grain price adjustments in 1991 and 1992 were accompanied by substantial adjustment to urban ration prices. By mid-1992, urban ration prices and the state quota procurement prices were essentially equalised for the major food grains (wheat, maize, indica and japonica rice). Thus, the previous subsidy, at least within the government grain marketing system, was reduced. The remaining consumer subsidies cover the costs of the portion of the storage, handling, and distribution system devoted to official rations. These were estimated at 25 billion Yuan (World Bank, 1993). The massive reduction in explicit subsidies was not achieved at the expense of farmers. On the contrary, farmers benefited from substantial increases in quota prices over the decade.

In 1992, in many urban areas, a further increase in ration prices to near market levels and the coupon rationing system for grain and edible was abolished. By the end of 1992, over 400 counties (about 20 per cent of counties in China) had liberalised grain prices.[4] Reforms in this regard were further extended in early 1993. By the end of 1993, all regions in China had liberalised grain prices and abolished the delivery of grain coupons to urban residents (The only exception was 13 counties in Yuannan Province and 12 counties in Qinghai province).[5] However, large subsidies are still granted to urban consumers in the form of additional payments to urban workers' wages, but to a large extent these are no longer provided by implicit price subsidies.

3.3   Issues: the upward price adjustment and price distortions

In spite of the significant upward adjustments, the grain price remained distorted by government measures. Firstly, asymmetrical price control was operated. While most other agricultural price controls had been gradually eliminated, the grain price was still controlled by the government. Secondly, grain prices were substantially influenced by state market intervention, rather than determined by the market. Thirdly, grain markets remained insulated from the international market.

3.3.1   Price distortions quantified

Lutz and Scandizzo (1980) used the so called nominal protection coefficient (NPC), a ratio of domestic prices to international prices, i.e., $NPC = \dfrac{P_d}{P_w}$, as an indicator to measure the impact of market distortion on the incentives to producers. The price distortion in China can be measured at two levels: firstly, the state grain purchase price to the free market price; secondly, domestic producers' price to world market prices. There are three reasons for using the free market price and the international border price as the references to measure price distortion. First, there are no other more appropriate observables. Second, the free market and border prices represent true opportunity costs for farmers' exchanges. Third, because government intervention has become complex over the years, the only feasible way to measure price distortion is in terms of the ratio between

39

existing prices and opportunity costs, as measured by the free market or international prices. It should be borne in mind that this approach also has some limitations. Identifying world prices is difficult as there is no unique international market. Also, the domestic free market price itself may also be distorted due to government intervention such as imposing a ceiling price. Furthermore, the domestic to international price ratio may be affected by the use of an official foreign exchange rate: the shadow exchange rate may be more appropriate but it is usually unavailable from the official statistics. Despite these limitations, the domestic free market price and international prices give some indication of price distortions. Thus, the ratio of the state purchase price to the domestic free market price (SNPC) and the ratios of the domestic free market prices to the international price (NPC) are used to measure price distortion. The SNPC is given by $\frac{P_s}{P_f}$, where P_s is the state purchase price and P_f the free market price. NPC is given by $\frac{P}{rP^*}$ where, P is a composite of the state (P_s) and free market (P_f) prices; P^* is the border price; and r is the shadow exchange rate.

It can be seen from Table 3.4 that the difference between the state purchase and free market prices gradually narrowed. In 1979, the state purchase price was only about half of the free market price. By 1992 the overall state grain price was actually higher than the free market price. Wheat, corn and soybean prices in the late 1980s and early 1990s were quite close to the free market price. Rice was the most under-priced of the main grains, its price still much below the free market price.[6]

It can be seen from Table 3.5 that the state purchase price was significantly lower than the world market price up to 1986 and then moved much closer to parity. Rice and soybean prices remained at less than 50 per cent of parity whereas wheat moved much closer to the world price level. The domestic free market prices were typically at or above the world market price after 1986, although soybean remained stubbornly low. Thus although the situation generally improved during the 1980s, it is evident that considerable distortions remained. Moreover, as the free markets tended to operate only at the margins, many farmers were unable to access them successfully. It is clear that the prevailing prices during this period severely distorted the incentive mechanism and resource allocation in rural China.

Table 3.4

The ratio of state procurement price to free market price, 1979-92

Year	Ratio of the state procurement price to free market price (SNPC)				
	Total grain	Rice	Wheat	Corn	Soybean
1979	55.1	40.2	64.7	55.5	33.3
1980	58.9	42.5	69.1	61.7	36.1
1981	65.6	43.8	73.9	68.4	57.7
1982	66.4	43.2	77.3	67.0	60.6
1983	76.2	49.3	89.1	74.2	73.5
1984	94.5	56.2	96.7	83.9	83.2
1985	97.6	59.2	100.2	84.0	84.4
1986	92.1	54.7	94.1	79.1	86.5
1987	88.3	52.7	87.4	75.0	80.4
1988	85.8	49.0	82.2	70.7	75.3
1989	78.7	44.1	72.2	66.6	67.7
1990	90.5	50.3	81.6	80.1	82.2
1991	98.2	55.9	89.4	81.8	94.9
1992	103.7	54.6	98.2	90.6	113.7

Note: The state procurement price is quota price (before 1984) and contract price (after 1985). It is also a mix of various standards, grades and qualities.

Sources: Statistical Yearbook of China, (various issues); USDA, Agricultural Statistics of the People's Republic of China, 1949-90, p268-278; The Ministry of Commerce of China; Price Yearbook of China, 1995, p295; 1994, p373; Rural Statistical Yearbook of China, 1992, p185; 1993, p185.

Table 3.5

The ratio of domestic price to international price, 1978-92

Year	Ratio of domestic state price to international price[a]				Ratio of domestic free market price to international price[c]			
	Grain	Rice[b]	Wheat	Soybean	Grain	Rice[b]	Wheat	Soybean
1978	49.8	18.4	52.7	28.8	(-)	(-)	(-)	(-)
1979	58.5	33.1	60.3	34.1	106.2	82.3	93.3	65.7
1980	53.0	26.4	57.9	34.0	89.9	61.9	83.8	61.3
1981	53.8	25.0	58.8	32.9	81.9	57.0	79.6	55.4
1982	64.3	36.2	67.3	37.0	96.8	83.8	87.1	61.5
1983	79.6	51.7	82.9	45.9	104.4	104.8	93.0	66.2
1984	85.3	52.2	83.1	36.8	90.3	92.9	85.9	49.1
1985	60.2	33.0	56.2	27.6	61.8	55.8	56.1	35.0
1986	80.9	41.4	71.2	34.5	87.9	75.7	75.7	45.6
1987	106.4	48.2	95.1	40.1	120.4	91.5	108.9	52.2
1988	102.6	41.7	94.9	40.5	119.6	85.2	115.4	53.8
1989	93.5	47.7	80.7	45.7	118.8	108.1	111.8	64.6
1990	83.7	48.3	68.2	45.5	92.5	95.9	83.6	56.5
1991	100.9	50.4	92.1	44.4	102.7	90.1	103.0	49.4
1992	86.0	44.4	77.5	43.8	82.8	81.3	78.9	50.1

Notes: (a) The domestic state procurement price used is the quota (before 1984) and contract price (after 1985). The border price is based on China's import price from the world market at the shadow exchange rates. (b) As China is a rice exporter, the rice price in NPC calculation was based on export parity price. Others were based on import parity prices. (c) Export (import) parity prices were calculated based on the total value in US dollars of export (import) divided by the quantity of export (import). These calculations were based on FAO data.

Sources: Statistical Yearbook of China, (various issues); USDA, Agricultural Statistics of the People's Republic of China, 1949-90, p268-278, 315; The Ministry of Commerce of China. Statistical Yearbook of China, 1995, p295; 1994, p373; Rural Statistical Yearbook of China, 1992, p185; 1993, p185; FAO Trade Yearbook, (various issues).

42

3.4   The debates

3.4.1   Supply response

Rapid Growth, 1978 to 1984   The achievements in grain production during
the period 1978-84 were impressive. Grain production increased by 34 per
cent between 1978-84, with bumper harvests in 1982-84. Grain output grew
at an average annual rate of 4.3 per cent between 1978 and 1984, and 7.7 per
cent between 1982 and 1984 when it reached a historical high (since 1949) of
407.3 million tonnes. Deliveries of grain products to the state increased from
51 million tonne in 1978 to 142 million tonnes in 1984 (Statistical Yearbook
of China 1993, p609). The upward grain price movement was regarded as a
major contributor to the growth in production and marketing during this
period (Sicular, 1988; Lin 1991).

Slowdown in growth, 1985 to 1990   The second round of rural reforms
was marked by less impressive growth. After reaching a peak in 1984,
grain production fell substantially in 1985: marketed supply also dropped
significantly (Statistical Yearbook of China, 1993, p609). Production and
marketing of grain was stagnant in the following years until 1990 when it
began to recover. The average annual rates of growth in production and
procurement were 1.96 per cent and 1.63 per cent respectively.

The production of other crops also dropped during this period. Cotton
production continued its decline through 1986, recovering substantially in
1987-85 but still remaining lower than its record in 1984. Oil-seed and
sugar-cane production levelled off, while hemp and tobacco output fell
back to their original levels in 1978 (Sicular, 1993; Statistical Yearbook of
China, 1993, p365, 366).

3.4.2   Views on stagnation in the second period of reforms

There is little controversy among economists about the first period of growth.
The HPRS reform and adjustments to the state purchase prices (including
input prices) are regarded as important contributors (McMillian et al 1989;
Lin 1992). However, there is debate about what caused the stagnation in grain
production and marketing in the second period.

The completion of HPRS   Wen (1989) argued that the completion of the
HPRS may have been a major cause of the stagnation of grain production and
marketing in the second stage of reform. Although studies by Lin (1988) and
McMillian et al. (1989) revealed that the HPRS reform made significant
contributions to increased grain output and productivity during 1979-84, the
direct institutional effect of the HPRS may have been largely exhausted after
completion in 1983, in the absence of new incentive measures. He argued

Table 3.6

Grain production, gross procurement, state procurement 1978-92

Unit: Million Tonne

Year	Total production		Gross procurement			State procurement			
	mt	Growth % of previous year	mt	Growth % of previous year	As % of TP	Quota	As % of GP	Above-quota	As % of GP
1978	305		51		16.6	34	67.0	12	24.0
1979	332	8.85	60	17.6	18.1	33	55.0	19	32.0
1980	321	-3.4	61	1.7	19.0	28	46.0	20	33.0
1981	325	1.25	68	11.5	21.1	27	40.0	24	35.0
1982	355	9.23	78	14.7	22.0	28	36.0	27	35.0
1983	387	9.0	102	30.8	26.5	30	29.0	60	59.0
1984	407	5.17	142	39.2	35.0	28	19.7	74	52.1
Average annual rate:		4.2%		15.8%		-2.8%			
1985	379	-6.9	108	-24.0	30.6	60	51.7	(-)	(-)
1986	392	3.4	115	6.5	29.3	53	46.1	(8.86)a	7.7
1987	403	2.8	121	8.3	30.0	57	47.1	(-)	(-)
1988	394	-2.3	120	-0.8	30.7	49	40.8	(-)	(-)
1989	408	3.6	121	0.8	29.7	48	40.0	(-)	(-)
1990	446	9.3	140	15.7	31.4	51	36.4	(29.36)b	21.0
1991	435	-2.5	136	-2.9	31.3	47	34.6	(15.81)c	11.6
1992	443	1.8	132	-3.0	29.8	Na	Na	Na	Na
Average annual rate:		1.96%		1.63%		-3.5%			

Notes: (a) represents the amount of 'entrusted procurement'. (b) and (c) represent the amount of procurement for 'special grain reserve'.

Sources: Commercial Statistical Yearbook of China, 1985, p191, 547: 1988, p55; 1989, p613, 620, 714: Statistical Yearbook of China, 1985, p547; 1991, p346; 1993, p609. Cheng et al, (1994); Zong, P (1994) Table 7.2.

44

that, under the HPRS there was under-investment in rural infrastructure, especially farmland, which may have led directly to a decline in rural labour productivity. The small scale of operation under HPRS was probably a barrier to the introduction of new production technology. However, the extent to which completion of the HPRS slowed down growth is not clear.

Adverse weather and environment   Unfavourable weather has also been invoked as an important factor in the stagnation of grain production during this period (Kueh, 1993). In China, weather conditions were significantly correlated with agricultural performance (Kueh, 1993). Except for 1980, weather was reported to be good during the period 1979-84, and this was also a period of rapid growth in grain as well as overall agricultural production. During the period of agricultural stagnation, 1985-88, the weather was reported to be unfavourable for agricultural production. However, the statistical data shows that the deviation in arable land areas which was affected by natural disasters, such as drought, flood, low temperature injury and frost damage, in this period was the same as in 1989-90 (Statistical Yearbook of China, 1993, p391), so although weather conditions undoubtedly affected production in this period, other factors were also at work.

The deteriorating environment was also cited as a factor in the stagnation of grain growth during this period (Huang 1995). Environmental problems may explain the slowdown in grain output growth in 1985-88, but can hardly explain the recovery in production after 1990 as there was little, if any, improvement in the environment in this period.

Relatively low grain price   A number of studies hold the view that grain price was the underlying reason for stagnation in grain output in the second stage of the rural reform. Sicular (1993) argued that the decline in the marginal price worsened grain production and trade during that period; this argument has also been put forward by Wiens (1987), Claude (1990). Before 1985, the higher above-quota price was the marginal price for farmers. After 1985, the quota and above-quota prices were replaced by the single contract price. This single price increased the average quota price paid to farmers, but was lower than the old above-quota price. Thus it is possible that the loss of the higher marginal price adversely affected production and marketing in the second period.

In contrast to Sicular's view others raised doubts about the impact of price changes (Ash 1993; Crook 1994). Indeed other non-grain or non-farm activities may have offered better income prospects for farm households. As early as 1983 the policy shifted towards the encouragement of commercialised and diversified production in order to increase incomes. The most important change was that various forms of diversification of agricultural production were encouraged and non-farm employment opportunities emerged. Many farm households began to work part-time,

45

whilst continuing to cultivate their contracted land. As greater economic diversification occurred, more and more farmers would leave farming to engage full-time in non-farm activities. The dramatic change in income structure exerted a significant influence on farmers' supply response to price adjustments, which will be discussed in the next chapter.

3.5   Summary

This chapter has examined grain price adjustments and the impacts of upward movements on grain production and marketing during the period 1978-92. Although there have been clear efforts and movements towards greater reliance on the price mechanism, there still exists a high degree of state intervention in grain pricing. Substantial distortions to grain prices remained as a result of state involvement. The existence of dual prices and the move to a single contract price, alongside a free market price, complicated the picture and had unpredictable effects on producers' incentives. In one sense the changes to prices, at least until the early 1990s, arguably represented adjustment rather than reform. Economic diversification in rural society and the increased incidence of off-farm employment probably tended to weaken the effects of grain prices in creating incentives; this is examined in the next chapter.

Notes

1. In the 1950s, for example, a cigarette factory with a production capacity of 280,000 boxes per year could recoup its capital investment within two months, a sugar factory with a capacity of 30,000 tonnes would take ten months and a cotton textile factory with 100,000 spindles and 3500 looms would take fifteen months (Su xing, 1979, Social Science, No 2, p104). The major mechanism was the high profit made on light industrial products manufactured using agricultural raw materials. The amount of accumulated capital in this way was much greater than the one through taxation (Dong Fureng 'Relationship between accumulation and consumption' in Xu dixin et al China's search for economic growth, Beijing: New World Press, 1982, p71).

2. In the early 1950s state retail prices of grain and other food products were set higher than the planned purchase prices. The state commercial department made slight profit from its trade in grain (Wang, 1985 p51. Sicular, 1988, P269). In large and medium sized cities retail grain prices were 5 to 15 per cent higher than the state purchase price. (Wang 1985, p61. Sicular, 1988, p269). At the end of 1950s and early 1960s, but mainly

46

in 1958, 1960 and 1961, the state raised purchase prices without increasing retail prices, which first led to an inversion of the purchase and retail prices. It was estimated at roughly 0.04 Yuan per kilogram for grain (Xue, 1983 p45).

3. These regions included Guangdong, see Guangdong-Hong Kong Information Daily 5, April, 1992, p1; part of Sichuan, see Economic Information Daily, 25, November, 1992, p1; Zhengjiang, see Information Times, 15, September, 1992, p1; Hunan, see Rural Post, 30 November, 1992,p1.

4. See Economic Reference Daily (Jingji Cankaobao), 10 December, 1992, p1, the speech by Bai Meiqing, Vice-Minister of Commerce.

5. See China Commercial Daily, 10 March, 1994, p1; Cheng, et al, 1994.

6. It may be difficult to provide a precise comparison of the level of state quota prices to prices in non-state markets for three reasons. Firstly, market prices may be substantially above marginal cost because of excess demand in the markets. Secondly, urban market prices may include costs of transporting commodities from rural to urban areas whereas procurement price in the rural markets by the state may not. Thirdly, it may be difficult to judge the magnitude of the difference between average state procurement prices and the market price level empirically due to various market and price controls.

4 Emergence of the rural non-farm economy

4.1 Introduction

Major changes have occurred in Chinese rural policies, for example towards the development of township, village and private enterprises, labour mobility and non-farm economic activities. These have expanded income opportunities outside agriculture and lowered the relative attractiveness of farming. These sources of non-farm income may also have affected the farmers' supply behaviour. Although this has been recognised by certain researchers (Hinton, 1991; Sicular, 1993), there are still relatively few studies in the literature. The main purpose of this chapter is to examine the emergence of the rural non-farm economy and its implications for grain production and marketable surplus supply. Hopefully this will increase our understanding of Chinese farm households' grain supply behaviour and shed some light on the subsequent grain supply analysis.

In section 4.2, new rural policies, particularly towards the encouragement of diversified production and labour mobility, are reviewed. Structural changes in employment and production in rural China are analysed in section 4.3. The growing disparity between wages and the marginal productivities of labour in agriculture and rural industry are examined in section 4.4. The consequences of these developments for farm household incomes are considered in section 4.5.

4.2   New rural policies

Rural policies in China have changed significantly since 1978, particularly in the mid-1980s: farmer's production choices were expanded through further liberalisation of rural policies.   These included: (a) encouragement of diversified production; (b) relaxation of the private enterprise control and the development of township and village enterprises (TVEs); (c) encouragement of the development of rural industries through introduction of low taxes and subsidised bank loans; and (d) liberalisation of rural factor markets at the beginning of 1985.

4.2.1   Encouragement of diversified production

In order to further develop the rural economy, a series of new rural development policies were adopted in the mid-1980s.   The government enlarged the scope of private activities in procurement, transport and marketing of agricultural products.   In particular, it encouraged farmers to diversify production and allowed most agricultural products, including livestock, aquatic products, and processed foods to be marketed across county and provincial lines.

4.2.2   Relaxation of private enterprise control and the development of TVEs

One of the most important changes was the decision to relax restrictions on rural private businesses. In 1984, rural residents were permitted to move to small towns to set up in private business. Individuals from the countryside could now engage in urban-rural transport, set up stalls or stores in towns and hire employees to work in private enterprises.   Private or joint investment in capital goods, such as trucks and tractors, was encouraged and grew rapidly.   Moreover, the government implemented a range of measures to encourage the development of industry and services in the rural areas. Township and village enterprises as well as various types of private enterprise in rural areas were developed and became a major source of off-farm work.

4.2.3   The development of rural industries through the introduction of low taxes and subsidised bank loans

The fiscal responsibility system was implemented in the mid-1980s. After its adaptation, local governments gave priority to expansion of local rural industry in order to enhance their finances. Because of the distorted price structure, industry enjoyed much higher profit margins than agriculture.

Many local governments adopted low taxes and subsidised bank loans to encourage the development of rural industries. Restrictions on industrial production were removed and the expansion of rural industry was also facilitated by banking system reform. One direct result of the banking reform was the explosion of bank loans in 1984 and at the beginning of 1985 (Kojima, 1989). In 1984/8 the government allowed rural credit cooperatives to provide credit for rural industrial and commercial enterprises. By 1986 the share of non-agricultural loans had risen to 47 per cent of the total, while the share going to agriculture had fallen to only 33 per cent (Statistical Yearbook of China, 1993, p667). The diversion of funds from agriculture was further facilitated by policies on fund raising outside bank channels. A large part of this extra credit went to rural industries.

4.2.4   Liberalisation of rural factor markets

Before the rural reform, labour mobility was not allowed. The government strictly controlled labour movement between rural areas through the household registration and urban grain rationing systems. The household registration system signified the status of the legal residence of an individual. People who had legal urban status held a city household registration book and could obtain grain coupons to purchase commercial grain at the state (low) retail price from the state food grain shops. However, people who had so called 'rural household registration' were not issued coupon tickets. They obtained their grain rations directly from their production teams, either monthly or, more commonly, semi-annually after each harvest, to ensure planned consumption. They had to participate in collective agricultural production in order to obtain their yearly food grain from the collective. Without this participation and without grain coupons, even if they had money, they would not be able to buy food grain in the market. Those who needed to travel outside their village had either to apply for special grain coupons from their brigade leaders or carry food-grain with them. This system severely limited farmers' movement.

After the rural reform, several new policies were introduced. Firstly, households were allowed to exchange labour with each other and a limited amount of labour could be employed for farm work (Kueh 1985). Secondly in 1983, the government eased barriers to urban entry by allowing farmers to work in small towns while retaining their rural household registrations (Hu, 1985). Then, a further loosening of constraints on rural-to-urban migration took place in 1984. The government allowed farmers to transfer their household registration to small towns but required them to obtain their own food and not rely on urban grain reserves. These policies meant that voluntary migration to urban areas was allowed and a rural labour market

51

began to emerge.

4.3 Structural changes

The liberalisation of factor markets and product markets facilitated the re-
allocation of resources between different sectors and between different
regions. Farm households had more choices in maximising income growth.

4.3.1 Farmers' choices and family strategy

The development of the non-grain economy in the mid-1980s gave farmers
tremendous opportunities to work outside agriculture. Chinese farmers
responded actively by adopting new family strategies. A large number of
farmers transferred from farm to non-farm production. The channels of
transfer of rural labour out of grain production were multiple. The first was
a transfer from growing grain to industrial crops; the second is a transfer
from growing crops to forestry, animal husbandry, fishery products and
agricultural sidelines; and the third was from agriculture to non-agriculture.
In developed areas, 80 per cent of those who left grain production
transferred to non-agricultural sectors while 20 per cent transferred within
agriculture. In semi-developed areas, almost half of the transfers were to
the non-agricultural sector, and 52 per cent within agriculture. Transfers
out of grain production in undeveloped areas were mainly within
agriculture, particularly to other crops (Deng, 1989).

These movements led to structural changes in rural employment and
economic integration between grain production and non-grain production.
Certain family members engaged in factory work and others, often women
and older members of the family, worked the family's fields. In
mechanised areas in particular, it is possible for one person to work the land
and the other three or four family members to work in factories. During the
busy farm season, family members who worked in factories would come
back to assist with the farm work.

4.3.2 Employment in the rural township and village enterprises

The most important development in the rural economy for farmers was the
rapid expansion of the rural industrial sector during the reform period.
Before, and in the early stage of economic reform, farmers had few
opportunities to work in non-farm activities. The rapid growth of the rural
industrial sector provided farmers with more employment and investment
opportunities. The rapid development of township and village enterprises
started in 1984 and continued during the period 1985-88 (Table 4.1). The

number of rural township and village enterprises increased by 351 per cent in 1984 over the previous year. The number of TVEs continued to grow until 1988. The real value of gross output of the rural industrial sector increased at an average annual rate of 21 per cent during the same period. In 1992, TVEs' total output value accounted for 32 per cent of total social output value and 48 per cent of total national industrial output value (Statistical Yearbook of China, 1993, p50, 57, 396). At the same time, private enterprises also grew rapidly.

Table 4.1
The development of rural TVEs

Unit: Ten Thousand

Year	Enterprises (number)	Increase % on previous year	Employees (number)	Increase % on previous year	% rural labour force
1978	152.4		2826.6		9.2
1979	148.0	-2.9	2909.3	2.9	9.4
1980	142.5	-3.8	2999.7	3.1	9.4
1981	133.8	-6.3	2969.6	-1.1	9.1
1982	136.2	1.8	3112.9	4.8	9.2
1983	134.6	-1.2	3234.6	3.9	9.3
1984	606.5	350.6	5208.1	61.0	14.5
1985	1222.5	101.6	6979.0	34.0	18.8
1986	1515.3	24.0	7937.4	13.7	20.9
1987	1750.2	15.5	8805.2	10.9	22.6
1988	1888.2	7.9	9545.5	8.4	23.8
1989	1868.6	-1.1	9366.8	-1.9	22.9
1990	1850.4	-1.0	9264.8	-1.1	22.1
1991	1907.9	3.1	9609.1	3.7	22.3
1992	2079.2	9.0	10581.1	10.1	24.2

Sources: Rural Statistical Yearbook of China (1994), p41, 333, 337.
Statistical Yearbook of China, 1993, p97, 395, 397.

As a result, many farmers found jobs in TVE enterprises. The number of people employed started from a small base of only 28.3 million in 1978 but increased to 52.1 million in 1984, and to 69.8 million in 1985 (Table 4.1). Employment growth was brisk during 1984-88 at an average rate of 10.3 per cent. Total employment in rural industries increased to 95 million in 1988 which was almost one-quarter of the rural labour force. It slowed in 1989 due to economic retrenchment. In 1990, rural industry and construction employment held steady, and rural job growth was primarily in agriculture, with small gains in transport and commerce. The average annual growth rate in TVE employment was 9.2 per cent during the period of 1978-92.

4.3.3   Employment in urban areas

Apart from labour mobility between rural areas, the growth of employment opportunities in urban areas also stimulated the rural labour force to enter the city to look for jobs. At the beginning of reform, the pursuit of regional self-sufficiency in grain was abandoned and producers were free to consider local conditions. Specialisation of production was encouraged. Therefore, regional trade and resource flows occurred. Though official segmentation between the urban and rural sector has not been abolished, labour migration into urban areas was common. During the period of economic reform the urban expansion led to an upswing of urban construction and house building which generated a huge demand for construction workers. At the same time, tertiary industries developed rapidly. As a result, a large number of rural workers shifted away from agriculture and looked for jobs in urban areas, particularly in coastal and major metropolitan areas. Most of the rural labour was recruited in the construction sector. Others were engaged in tertiary industries such as, child minders, shoe-repairers, private-retailers and causal workers in the cities and towns. Detailed data about the amount of rural labour working in urban areas are not available; but detailed information about changes in employment structure in rural China was provided by the Rural Survey Team of the State Statistical Bureau. According to a 1992 report, during the period 1985-90, the number of employees in the industry and construction sectors increased by 21 per cent in the eastern coastal area, 26 per cent in the central areas, and 23 per cent in the western areas respectively. The total growth of the tertiary (service) sector was 38 per cent in the eastern coastal area and over 30 per cent in the western area (Banister and Harbaugh, 1992).

More detailed information is presented in Figure 4.1. The agricultural labour force accounted for 90.7 per cent of the total rural labour force in 1978 but declined to 75.8 per cent by 1992. The liberalisation of labour markets during this period and the expansion of TVEs after 1984 jointly created a favourable environment for the transfer of rural labour out of agricultural production.

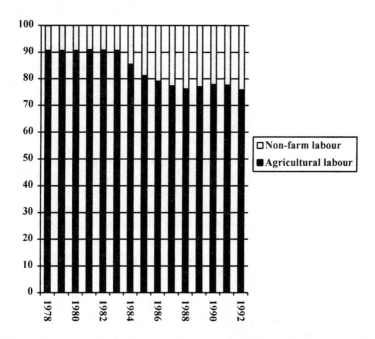

Figure 4.1   Structural changes in rural labour, 1978-92

*Note: The non-farm labour only includes employment in rural township
          and village enterprises; it excludes non-farm employment in urban
          areas due to the lack of data.*
Source: Statistical Yearbook of China, 1993, pp97, 395.

4.3.4   The speed of transfer of rural non-farm labour

The liberalisation of factor markets and changes in employment structure
had dramatic effects on the output structure of the rural economy. In 1978
agriculture accounted for 93 per cent of the total output value and rural
industry for a mere 7 per cent. By 1985 agriculture had declined to 57 per
cent, rural industry had grown to 28 per cent and other sectors had emerged
including construction (8 per cent) and transport (3 per cent). By 1992
agriculture had further contracted to 36 per cent and rural industry
expanded to 50 per cent.

4.4　The motivations for farm labour mobility

There may have been various reasons for the trend of rural labour migration out of agriculture. However, in this section we concentrate on two main factors: (a) the disparity in wage incomes between farm and non-farm activities; and (b) the relatively low agricultural labour to industrial labour productivity.

4.4.1　The disparity in wage incomes

The disparity in wage incomes between farm and non-farm industries is frequently observed in China. According to a report by the Beijing Review in 1986, in one village, those who worked in the fields earned 240 Yuan a year, but those who worked in a village paper factory earned 600 Yuan. In another area, a farmer earns less than 1,000 Yuan a year from work in the field, while one who works in the local factories earns 3,000 Yuan a year. A very rough comparison of wage income between farm and non-farm activities is presented in Figure 4.2.

The income derived from crop production in 1978 was higher than income from rural industries and the two were broadly comparable until 1981. This is due to the fact that the income derived from rural industries was still strictly administered by the commune. In spite of relatively high profits in rural industries, the workers still only received a level of income roughly equivalent to farm workers. However, this situation changed after the dismantlement of communes. Income from rural industries increased significantly relative to crop income: indeed by 1992 the latter was less than one half of the former. The relatively high non-farm income was undoubtedly one of the main reasons for rural labour migration out of agriculture.

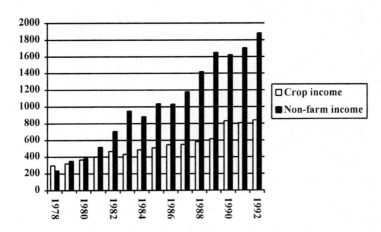

Figure 4.2   Average yearly income from crops and non-farm activities, 1978-92

Note: *These are average crop income per worker per year in the agricultural sector and non-farm income per worker per year in non-farm sector respectively. These were calculated from the data of crop income, non-farm income, on-farm labour and non-farm labour statistics and rural population.*

Sources: *Rural Economic Statistics of China 1949-86, pp 558-559; Statistics of Agricultural Economy (1949-83) pp 522-23; Statistical Yearbook of China, 1991, p 295; 1993, pp312.*

4.4.2   Agricultural versus industrial labour productivity

In this section we examine the evidence concerning agricultural and industrial labour productivity. Between 1985 and 1992 there was no real evidence of major technology advances in Chinese agriculture. However, there were rapid improvements in non-farm production technology. In order to evaluate productivity differences we carry out a simple regression analysis. The translog function is as follows.

$$Ln(Y_i) = \alpha_i + \sum_{j=1}^{3} \beta_{ij} \ln(X_{ij}) + \gamma_i T + +\varepsilon$$

57

i=1,2; j=1,..., 3.

Where Y_i is the total output value of agriculture and TVE; i=1 represents agriculture and i=2 represents TVE; X_j are the production factors including land, labour and capital for agriculture; labour and capital for TVE; T is the time trend; and ε is statistical error. National time series data for 1978 to 1987 were used.

The dependent variable for agriculture is the total value of crops (Y_1). The sown acreage of total crops was used as the land variable and the number of on-farm workers was used as the labour variable. These data were derived directly from the Statistical Yearbook of China, 1993, p335, 341, 358. Capital in the agricultural sector includes the sum of the values of draft animals, non-draft animals, poultry and machinery; it is therefore difficult to measure due to its the high degree of heterogeneity. The most accessible capital variable was the amount of agricultural machinery employed, measured in Watts of power used.

The dependent variable for rural industries is the gross output value of rural industries (Y_2). The number of employees in rural industries was used as the labour variable. The published capital value of TVEs was used as the capital variable (Statistical Yearbook of China, 1993, pp395, 396, 397). The regression results are presented in Table 4.2, with T-values shown in brackets.

Table 4.2
Estimated production functions for agriculture and TVEs

Variables	Agriculture		Rural TVEs	
Intercept	-66.485	(-11.693)	-2.947	(-2.738)
Labour	1.646	(6.647)	0.528	(4.648)
Capital	1.317	(29.998)	0.856	(4.330)
Land	3.715	(7.831)	(-)	
Time Trend	(-)		0.012	(0.285)
R^2	0.99		0.99	
Adjusted R^2	0.99		0.99	
DW	2.91		0.92	
F	1590.41		1369.67	

All estimated coefficients in Table 4.3 are statistically significant except for the time trend variable, and all sign of parameter estimated in the models are in line with expectations. The explanatory power of the equation is high for both agriculture and rural industry. This is further supported by the F-test which is highly significant for both agriculture and TVEs equation. (The low DW value for the TVE function may be due to the time trend being correlated with labour and capital.) The results from Table 4.3 indicate that, in the agricultural case, land was most important to agricultural growth. In the TVE sector, capital input was the most important factor for production growth. Whilst we recognise the limitations in this simple modelling approach, the contrasts between the two sectors are nevertheless interesting and informative.

We then estimated annual values for marginal labour productivity for each sector from the Cobb-Douglas function (Table 4.3).

Table 4.3
Marginal value product of labour, agriculture and rural TVEs

Unit: Yuan/Per Worker

Year	Agriculture (1)	TVEs (2)	(1) as % (2)
1978	63.44	92.03	68.9
1979	74.21	99.45	74.6
1980	78.68	115.54	68.1
1981	85.21	132.41	64.4
1982	93.70	144.58	64.8
1983	101.61	165.85	61.3
1984	117.49	173.21	67.8
1985	124.76	206.26	60.5
1986	136.86	235.36	58.1
1987	154.74	285.46	54.2
1988	176.76	359.02	49.2
1989	191.61	418.41	45.8
1990	225.33	481.85	46.8
1991	229.26	638.09	35.9
1992	249.79	896.29	27.9

In 1978, the agricultural MVP was 69 per cent of that in the TVEs. However, the MVPs in TVEs increased by almost ten-fold during the period compared with a four-fold rise in agriculture in the same period.

By 1992 the estimated MVP in agriculture was only 28 per cent of the TVE sector. This disparity in marginal productivities is the fundamental reason for the differences in wage ratio and the migration out of agriculture in the second half of the 1980s. This estimation is consistent with the income data analysed earlier. Income disparity between these two sectors is not as large as that in productivity; this is mainly due to the fact that a large proportion of TVEs' profit was reserved for firm's development funds and not distributed as income.

4.4.3   Constraints on labour flows

Although labour mobility began to occur after 1985, labour flow was still subject to many non-economic constraints. Firstly, rural industries aimed to absorb mainly local rural labour thus reducing regional flows. Secondly, there were relatively few employment opportunities for farmers in towns and cities. China suffered from an acute shortage of places where additional labour could be productively employed (Banister et al. 1992).   Urban industries could not absorb large   numbers of rural labourers due to an already high urban population density. During the latter half of the 1980s, fewer than 2 million urban jobs were assigned annually to rural workers. Urban employment of rural workers hit low points in 1989 and 1990. There was a slight rebound in 1991, when rural workers were given 1.4 million urban jobs, or 18 per cent of the 7.65 million urban jobs assigned that year (A Statistical Survey of China, May 1992, p16,17, 19; Banister et al. 1992). Thirdly, it was very difficult for rural labourers to obtain permanent registration as urban residents, due to the strict urban household registration system and the controlled growth of the urban population in the early 1980s. As a result the rural labour force was channelled into seasonal and temporary work in urban areas. In fact, relatively few rural people left agriculture to find permanent employment in urban areas.

In spite of these constraints Chinese farm households during this period did increasingly have greater flexibility and freedoms to adjust and allocate their labour in response to changes in incentive structures.

4.5   Farm household income changes

4.5.1   The period 1978 to 1984

Before 1978, personal income distribution in a production team was, in principle, based on an individual's ability and work effort. In practice, there was equal distribution to all members within the team for social reasons. Everyone received equal amounts of grain, vegetables, cooking oil and fuel within their own production team. During this period, the Chinese farmers' incomes were very low. The national annual average net income per capita of farmers was 72.92 Yuan in 1957 and only 133.57 Yuan in 1978 (Compilation of Historical Provincial Statistics in China, 1949-1989, p35). The real income increased only by 18.42 Yuan over this period. The income of Chinese farmers was amongst the lowest in the world. The national annual average consumption expenditure per capita of farmers was 70.68 Yuan in 1957 and 116.06 Yuan in 1978.

By 1978, the portion of cash income in total income was only 47.8 per cent (Jiang et al, 1989). Rural farmers' cash income was only one-sixth of the urban wage.

After introduction of the HPRS, the improvements in a household's income depended mainly on the prosperity of their farm, since the farm household, instead of the production team became the basic production unit. Thus, grain price adjustments gave farmers stronger incentives to increase their grain production.

Detailed data on the effects of grain price increase on farmers' income is not available. However, a rough estimation made by the State Council Rural Investigation Team in 1984 indicated that price adjustment in the early 1980s made a considerable contribution to the increase in farmers' income. According to their survey, increases in the price of grain and other agricultural sideline produce in the early 1980s alone contributed an additional 45 billion Yuan to the farmers' income in the three years 1979 to 1981 (Jiang, et al. 1989). As a result, the national annual average net income per rural resident, jumped from the 133.57 Yuan in 1978 to 355.33 Yuan in 1984. The average annual growth rate of net income per capita was over 15 per cent in the period 1978 to 1984 (Figure 4.3). The real average annual farm income per capita was increased by over 11 per cent in the period 1978-84 (Statistical yearbook of China, 1993, p312). Enhanced incomes resulted from increases in both yields and prices. Taking the index of state purchase prices for four crops, the average annual rate of grain price increase from 1978 to 1984 was 3.5 per cent. Farmers certainly benefited from grain price adjustment.

Further details are available from a survey of three counties (Yanshi, Yichun, Songxian) in Henan province by Zhu (1991). In late 1978 he highest income per capita was 280 Yuan, whilst the lowest was only 32 Yuan. Almost half of the sample households (47.1 per cent) had less than 100 Yuan in 1978. In 1985, the income level of all sample households showed a general rise compared to 1978. The range between the highest and lowest increased from 40 to 605 Yuan. Average per capita income in the sample amounted to 397.60 Yuan, almost double that of 1978.

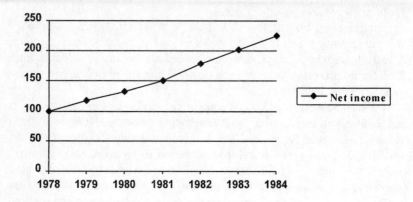

Figure 4.3   Rural real net income per capita 1978-84

Note: Net income is deflated by the rural retail price index.
Source: Statistical Yearbook of China, 1987, p698; 1991, p229, 295.

Prior to 1984, farm households' main income source was crop production. It can be seen from Table 4.4 that the income derived from crops accounted for 77.6 per cent of total net income in 1978 and 51.2 per cent in 1984. Non-farm income was relatively low at 7 per cent of the total net income in 1978, 10.7 per cent in 1981 and 18.2 per cent in 1984. As there was not much non-farm income available, farmers had to rely mainly on their farm income, especially from crops During this period the highly centralised administrative system still largely controlled households' production activities: it aimed at 'taking grain production as the key link'.

4.5.2   The period 1985-92

The liberalisation of labour mobility gave farm households more opportunities to increase family income. Associated with the structural changes in rural employment as analysed in the section 4.3, the income structure of farm households also changed significantly after 1984. Table 4.4 shows that the non-farm income element began to increase rapidly and by 1992 accounted for almost 30 per cent. Thus the second half of the 1980s was a period of fairly dramatic change in both the level and structure of farm households' incomes.

Table 4.4

Composition of farm households' net per capita income

Unit: Yuan

Year	Net income	Crop income	% of NI	Non-farm income	% of NI	Other income	% of NI
1978	133.57	103.68	77.6	9.39	7.0	20.50	15.3
1979	160.17	112.76	70.4	14.20	8.9	33.21	20.7
1980	191.33	130.30	68.1	16.77	8.8	44.26	23.1
1981	223.44	145.02	64.9	23.93	10.7	54.49	24.4
1982	270.11	175.31	64.9	33.50	12.4	61.30	22.7
1983	309.77	162.67	52.5	51.14	16.5	95.96	31.0
1984	355.33	181.86	51.2	64.70	18.2	108.77	30.6
1985	397.60	191.46	48.2	86.26	21.7	119.88	30.2
1986	423.76	205.03	48.4	95.70	22.6	123.03	29.0
1987	462.55	207.80	44.9	117.56	25.4	137.19	29.7
1988	544.94	222.16	40.8	148.38	27.2	174.40	32.0
1989	601.51	240.19	39.9	168.64	28.0	192.68	32.0
1990	686.31	330.11	48.1	167.10	24.3	189.10	27.6
1991	708.55	323.53	45.7	178.30	25.2	206.72	29.2
1992	783.99	337.91	43.1	216.60	27.6	229.52	29.3

Note: Other incomes represent non-crop income such as forestry, animal husbandry, sidelines, fishery non-productive income.

Sources: Rural Economic Statistics of China 1949-86, pp 558-559; Statistics of Agricultural Economy 1949-83, pp 522-23; Statistical Yearbook of China, 1991, pp295; 1993, pp312.

Another very interesting feature of farm household income changes during this period was the effect of non-farm incomes on household income distribution. A survey by Zhu (1991) in Henan province showed that the high income groups had a much greater involvement in non-farm activities than low income groups. Similar results were obtained by Jiang and Luo (1989) based on three regional studies. They found that agricultural income accounted for over 90 per cent of family income in households with annual per capita income below 200 Yuan, but only about 50 per cent in households where annual per capita income was over 1,000 Yuan.

4.6   Summary and conclusions

In this chapter we have examined the emergence of the rural non-farm economy during the reform period.   Several new characteristics were identified.

There was rapid and fairly dramatic economic diversification following emergence of the non-farm industries. Township and village enterprises became increasingly important in rural areas: their share of output value increased quickly while that of agriculture declined.

As a result, labour choices for farmers and their households expanded and non-farm employment and income became important, especially after 1985. Indeed it became the main source of household income growth.

These changes undoubtedly had implications for agriculture and for grain production in particular. The opportunity cost of household labour became increasingly important in household decision making, specifically the amount of labour to be allocated to grain production and the amount to be allocated to the non-farm economy. In these changed circumstances we believe that the effects of grain prices may be expected to have changed. Whereas in the relatively closed rural economy where grain prices and income were the main signals for producers, in the much more open situation in the 1980s their impact may have been weakened by the alternative income opportunities available to households.

The chapters so far have set the scene for the analytical chapters which follow. We would highlight again two particular features of the Chinese rural economy which we believe have important implications for any analysis of the marketable surplus supply of farm households. These are firstly, the levels of grain own-consumption of households and secondly, the growing importance of non-farm income opportunities. We believe that these features may have influenced the responsiveness of farm households to grain price changes. However, we recognise that there are likely to be complex linkages between grain price and off-farm wage changes, on-farm and off-farm labour allocation, household income, household consumption

64

and grain marketable surplus supply. In the remainder of this book we attempt to develop a modelling approach which allows us to take account of these complexities and to test our ideas empirically.

PART TWO

SUPPLY RESPONSE ANALYSIS

5 Review of supply response issues

5.1 Introduction

Of the present grain policies in China, price policy is one of the most important. The effect of price policy on grain production clearly depends upon the supply response of farm households in China. Therefore, it is essential in a study such as this to examine the nature and magnitude of their supply response behaviour.

The objective of research on supply response, according to Nerlove and Bachman (1960), is to improve understanding of the effects of the price mechanism on supply. For policy purposes, a knowledge of the direction and magnitude of supply response is of crucial importance. However, the measurement of this response in a semi-subsistence economy is complex. Farm households' supply response is influenced by their production, consumption and labour supply behaviour. Therefore, the critical point is how to value the effectiveness of the price mechanism within the prevailing complex socio economic and market conditions. Supply response analysis should, if possible, take account of these complex inter-relationships.

Over the years there have been many studies of supply response. Such work has been extensively reviewed elsewhere (see in particular Askari and Cummings, 1976; also Colman, 1983; Rao, 1989; Behrman, 1989; Henneberry and Tweeten, 1991). Previous research in the field of agricultural supply response has provided a wide range of estimates for price elasticities. In this chapter we review theoretical and empirical supply response studies connected with policy analysis. The chapter focuses on theoretical and methodological developments and their limitations.

Section 5.2 reviews general issues in the theoretical and empirical development of supply response. Sections 5.3 and 5.4 then concentrate respectively on theoretical analyses and empirical studies of supply response in China. The theoretical and empirical issues are briefly summarised in section 5.5.

5.2   Supply response analysis in general

Although supply response analysis has been pursued with much vigour for the last 70 years, it still remains an important and controversial area. The analyses conducted so far have raised many theoretical and empirical issues.

5.2.1   Total output and marketable surplus

It is important to distinguish between output or production and marketable surplus. Colman (1983) states that, 'supply is defined as the amount of a commodity offered for sale in a particular market during a specific time interval at the prevailing values of prices and any other relevant conditioning variables'. However, it should be emphasised that in a semi-commercial rural economy producers themselves may be the major holders of stocks. Therefore, it is not appropriate to equate production with supply onto the market, i.e. the amount of marketable surplus. The latter is the total grain output remaining after farm households' own consumption needs have been met. The marketable surplus is regarded as an important concept in development economics.

5.2.2   Normal and negative supply

In conventional economics, 'supply response' in underdeveloped agriculture generally means the variation of agricultural output and acreage mainly due to a variation in prices' (Ghatak, et al. 1984, p172). In simple terms output supply response is expressed as a function of an expected price.

$$Q_a = f(q_{t-1}, A_t, W_t, U_t) \dots\dots\dots\dots\dots\dots\dots\dots (5.1)$$

Where, Q^a is the amount of output; q_{t-1} is previous period price, a proxy for the expected price; A_t is acreage; W_t is weather condition and U_t is a statistical error term. Although yield variation is implicit in U_t, output is

70

expected to vary positively with past price (q_{t-1}) and land (A_t), and either rise or fall with changes in weather and other non-price factors, i.e.,

$$\frac{\partial f}{\partial q_{t-1}} > 0; \frac{\partial f}{\partial A_t} > 0; \frac{\partial f}{\partial W_t} \gtrless 0.$$ This means that the slope of the supply

curve is positive and the elasticity of supply with respect to price change is greater than zero. In any case, supply response has a consistent direction with changes in price. Such an analysis is within the neoclassical theoretical framework of profit maximising behaviour.

In contrast to the normal output response, the possibility of negative supply response in undeveloped agricultural countries has been raised by many researchers (Olson, 1960; Mathur and Ezekiel, 1961). There are two possible negative responses that can occur in underdeveloped agricultural countries. Scenario one is where farm production is for farm household consumption only and not for the market: positive price changes may not induce farm households to produce more. In this case, the supply elasticities will be equal to or less than zero. The second scenario is where an increase in output prices may actually lead to a decline in marketable surplus supply due to household income, consumption and other social effects. In such a case, the elasticity of supply with respect to price will be negative.

Much of the initial work on negative response concentrated on marketable surplus supply. This was related to the controversies surrounding the effects of the surplus food disposal programme of USA Public Law 480 in the 1960s upon agricultural development in the recipient countries. Schultz (1960) believed that supply response to price changes in the recipient countries was normal and positive. He argued that the USA P.L 480 programme was deleterious to agricultural development in these countries since it reduced food prices in recipient countries by increasing overall supply. As a result, farmers were unwilling to increase domestic production due to the depressed food prices.

In contrast Olson (1960) argued that the programme was irrelevant because supply response in these countries was perverse, as a large proportion of production was consumed by farm households and a small proportion was for the market. Thus, even if average price was lowered by the programme, farmers may still have had to increase production in order to meet their own food requirements. Conversely, if price increased, this could lead farmers to retain more of their output for consumption since a smaller volume of sales could meet their monetary requirements. Thus, the USA P. L. 480 could actually increase marketed supply in the recipient countries. However, it should be evident that Schultz and Olson were actually discussing two different types of supply response: the former referring to total production and the latter to the marketable surplus only (Livingstone, 1977). Marketable surplus response may differ from total output supply response. The price elasticity of total output may be generally positive, whilst the elasticity of marketable surplus supply may theoretically assume either sign (Bardhan, 1970).

5.2.3 Hypothesis of supply behaviour

A number of explanations or hypotheses have been put forward in order to capture the complexity of supply behaviour in subsistence or semi-commercial settings; i.e. situations where a significant proportion of output may be retained for family consumption or other issues.

'A fixed cash needs' First proposed by Mathur and Ezekiel (1961), who argued that subsistence farmers have an inelastic demand for cash. An increase in grain prices allows farmers to satisfy their monetary requirements by selling a smaller quantity of food grain than before. Therefore, prices and marketable surplus tend to move in opposite directions. However, there are certain weaknesses in this argument. It implies that there is zero income elasticity of demand for non-farm commodities and zero substitution effects at the subsistence level. Moreover, this assumption implies that, if prices were fixed, the marketable surplus would be fixed. If this were true, farmers' own-consumption would be residual and would absorb all the variation in total production. Farm output in fact would have no effect on prices.

'A fixed own-consumption' Rather than the farmer's own-consumption being residual, Krishnan (1965) argued it is more likely that the level of farmers' own-consumption is fixed and marketable surplus is residual.

$$M = Q(1-r) \dots \dots \dots (5.2)$$

Where M is marketable surplus; r is proportion of output consumed by the farmers themselves; Q is total output of food grain.

The quantity of own-consumption is a function of prices (q) and income (qQ). Using a Cobb-Douglas production function, this can be specified as:

$$rQ = Aq^{-\alpha}(qQ)^{\beta} \dots \dots \dots (5.3)$$

Where q is the price of food grain; α is price elasticity; β is income elasticity. So

$$r = Aq^{\beta-\alpha}Q^{\beta-1} \dots \dots \dots (5.3_a)$$

$$M = Q(1 - Aq^{\beta-\alpha}Q^{\beta-1}) = Q - Aq^{\beta-\alpha}Q^{\beta} \dots \dots \dots (5.4)$$

Differentiating (5.4) with respect to q, then we have:

$$\frac{dM}{dq} = -(\beta - \alpha)\,AQ^{\beta}\,q^{\beta-\alpha-1} \quad\dots\dots\dots\dots\dots\dots\dots\dots\dots (5.5)$$

This equation can be rewritten in elasticity form as,

$$\frac{dM}{dq}\cdot\frac{q}{M} = -AQ^{\beta}q^{\beta-\alpha-1}(\beta-\alpha)\cdot\frac{q}{Q-AQ^{\beta}\cdot q^{\beta-\alpha}}$$

$$= -(\beta-\alpha)\cdot\frac{AQ^{\beta}q^{\beta-\alpha}}{Q-AQ^{\beta}q^{\beta-\alpha}}$$

$$= -(\beta-\alpha)\cdot\frac{(AQ^{\beta}q^{\beta-\alpha})}{Q(1-r)}$$

$$= -(\beta-\alpha)\cdot\frac{r}{Q(1-r)} \quad\dots\dots\dots\dots\dots\dots\dots\dots\dots\dots\dots\dots\dots\dots\dots (5.6)$$

Where r will lie between 0 and 1, so r/(1-r) is always positive. Thus, the sign of the elasticity of the marketable surplus is determined by the magnitude of income and price elasticities. Using Indian rural credit survey data, Krishnan estimated an elasticity of marketable surplus of -0.30.

'An uncertain own-consumption' Rather than fixed own-consumption, Nowshirvani (1967) argued that we cannot rule out the possibility of negative supply response due to the fact that own-consumption is uncertain: a price rise may lead to an increase in income which leads to an increase in food consumption, and to households retaining more of their own production. Thus, if the income effect outweighed the substitution of alternative consumption goods, the negative response may occur. The negative supply response is, to a large extent, dependent upon the price and income elasticities of own-consumption.

'Consumption preference and monetary savings preferences' Krishna (1963) argued that increased income following an agricultural price rise will encourage farm households to consume more non-agricultural goods. In addition, a strong preference for monetary savings in many developing countries would encourage farm households to sell more to the market. Thus, supply response of farm households to price changes would be most likely positive.

Using such an assumption, he analysed the relationship among prices, income, consumption and marketable surplus in the following way.

$$M = Q - C \quad\dots\dots\dots\dots\dots\dots\dots\dots\dots\dots\dots\dots\dots\dots\dots\dots (5.7)$$

Where M is marketable surplus; Q is the total output; C is amount of output consumed by farmers themselves, and consumption (C) is a function of prices (q) and income (I).

Differentiating equation (5.7) partially with respect to price, we can derive the effect of price changes on marketable surplus as follows.

$$\frac{\partial M}{\partial q} = \frac{\partial Q}{\partial q} - \frac{\partial C}{\partial q} - \frac{\partial C}{\partial I} \cdot \frac{\partial I}{\partial q} \dots\dots\dots\dots\dots\dots\dots(5.7_a)$$

Krishna argued that if a peasant was only a producer of a crop, an increase in the price of the crop would lead to an increase in his income. On the other hand, should the peasant only consume the crop, an increase in the price of the crop would result in a decrease in his income. Krishna hypothesised that a peasant would be both a producer and a consumer. In this case, the peasant gains as a producer but loses as a consumer. The net effect of a change in price is the algebraic sum of the above two effects.

$$\frac{\partial I}{\partial q} = Q - C = M \dots\dots\dots\dots\dots\dots\dots\dots(5.8)^1$$

If equation (5.8) is substituted into equation (5.7$_a$), we have equations (5.9) and (5.10).

$$\frac{\partial M}{\partial q} = \frac{\partial Q}{\partial q} - \frac{\partial C}{\partial q} - M\frac{\partial C}{\partial I} \dots\dots\dots\dots\dots\dots\dots(5.9)$$

$$\frac{q}{M} \cdot \frac{\partial M}{\partial q} = \frac{Q}{M} \cdot \frac{q}{Q} \cdot \frac{\partial Q}{\partial q} - (\frac{Q}{M} - 1)[(\frac{q}{C} \cdot \frac{\partial C}{\partial q}) + \frac{M}{Q} \cdot \frac{qQ}{I} \cdot \frac{I}{C} \cdot \frac{\partial C}{\partial I}] \cdot$$
$$\dots\dots\dots\dots\dots\dots\dots\dots\dots\dots(5.10)$$

$$\text{or } E = rb_1 - (r-1)(g + mkh) \dots\dots\dots\dots\dots\dots(5.10_a)$$

Where E is the price elasticity of marketable surplus; b_1 is the output price elasticity; g is the consumption price elasticity; h is the consumption income elasticity; and r is Q/M, m is M/Q and k is Q/I.

Equation (5.10) is Krishna's final expression for the price elasticity of marketable surplus of a subsistence crop. Krishna concluded that farm households responded positively to price changes. This model has received considerable attention and has prompted several empirical investigations of marketable surplus.

The most novel aspect of this analysis was the decomposition of the consumption term into income and substitution effects. In addition, the output of food grain was allowed to vary. Krishna (1962, 1963) examined different ranges of price elasticities of marketable surplus in India and concluded that the price elasticity of marketable surplus of a single crop was likely to be positive.

Krishna's original model was further modified by many others, such as

74

Behrman (1966, 1968), Bardhan (1970). Behrman (1966) introduced the ratio of grain prices to other crop prices and also considered the retention of food-grain for purposes other than own-consumption. Bardhan and Bardhan, (1971) estimated the price elasticity of marketable surplus of total food grains for both the short- and long-run respectively.

Not only do the theoretical perspectives on supply behaviour differ, empirical studies also present conflicting results. For example, Krishna's (1965) positive price elasticity conflicted with Krishnan's (1963) negative price elasticity for marketable surplus in India. Bardhan (1970) estimated the marketed surplus elasticity using cross-sectional village-level data for India at between -0.33 and -0.60. Haessel (1975) subsequently employed the same data but allowed for the interaction between (simultaneous determination of) marketing and prices. The estimate of the short-run elasticity ranged between 2.7 and 3.3. Haessel's results from village level data were not consistent with the results derived from a macro-econometric model in which the marketed surplus and food prices were simultaneously determined by many other variables relating to the agricultural and manufacturing sectors (Ahluwalia, 1979). Behrman (1966) estimated elasticities of marketed surplus for rice in Thailand to be around 0.45 in the short run and about 1.04 in the long run. Results from a series of systematic and wide-ranging studies by the World Bank and others tend to suggest that both output and marketable surplus supply response are strongly positive with respect to price changes (Schiff et al. 1992). The variation in results derived from the empirical studies stems from the diversity of methodologies adopted and the different contexts of the studies.

5.2.4. *Methodologies for estimating supply response*

Estimating supply response is both a science and an art (Colman, 1983). The modelling of agricultural supply response traditionally falls into two categories: linear programming and econometrics. The choice of approach is governed by the objectives of the research, the nature of the system being analysed, and the data available.

Linear programming A mathematical programming model usually consists of two elements: an objective function and a set of conditions constraining the objective function. Programming models, typically the linear programme, have been widely applied to estimate supply elasticities. The procedure involves estimating a linear model which describes the production system (Colman, 1983). The system involves an objective function, eg. profit, and a set of endogenous and exogenous variables. The endogenous variables are the output and input levels for each farm, given the production technology. The exogenous variables include output and input prices. By solving this system of production for various sets of prices, one can trace the relationship between supply and the price of each commodity. The total supply response can be obtained by aggregating this supply-price function for individual farms in the reference groups (Henneberry et al. 1991). The main advantage of this approach, as mentioned by Colman (1983), is that the empirical process follows the steps prescribed by the profit maximising assumption for a given production technology. Another advantage is its capacity to handle the complexity of inter-relationships arising from the multi-product nature of the farm. Thus, the programming procedure provides a way to solve the optimum level of output and inputs. Meanwhile, it takes full account of the competition between products; given the limited resources available. The main disadvantages are concerned with the difficulties in summarising the relationship between prices and output in a formal functional statement; in selecting and classifying reference farms; in calculating price elasticities; and in collecting reliable data at the farm household level (Henneberry et al. 1991).

Econometrics   Econometric modelling has probably been the most frequently used approach in supply analysis. We discuss three aspects below: (i) direct estimation using ad hoc econometric models; (ii) indirect estimation using farm household firm theory; (iii) the duality approach.

Firstly, direct estimation using ad hoc econometric models. The *ad hoc* econometric model is the most popular method used in analysing supply response behaviour. This approach provides an understanding of the causal factors through estimation of a supply function (Henneberry and Tweeten, 1991). Based on a hypothesised causal relationship, explanatory variables are varied and a functional form changed until the 'best' result is obtained. Various elasticities can be derived directly from the estimated model. Many agricultural supply studies have employed a single equation approach. Supply may be directly estimated for the grain sector as a whole, and then for individual crops, such as rice, wheat, soybean and other grain.

Output supply models   Based on neo-classical economic theory, a single supply response function typically was used to explain the response of acreage or output to economic signals (Nerlove, 1956, 1958, 1979; Colman 1972; Askari and Cummings, 1976; Sanders and Ruttan 1978). The directly estimated model proposed by Nerlove (1958), in which the lag price variable was introduced, is worthy of special mention. In the Nerlove model, optimal output (Q_t^*) was specified as a function of expected price (q_t^e) and non-price shifters (Z_t). The expected price was based on past experiences. Thus, the change in expected price is proportional to the deviation between actual and expected prices in the last period. The price and other elasticities were estimated directly from the output function. The

Nerlove model consists of the following three equations:

$$Q_t = a_0 + a_1 q_t^e + a_2 Z_t + U_t. \dots\dots\dots\dots\dots\dots\dots\dots\dots\dots\dots\dots (5.11)$$

$$q_t^e - q_{t-1}^e = \beta(q_{t-1} - q_{t-1}^e)\dots\dots\dots 0 \le \beta \le 1\dots\dots\dots\dots\dots\dots\dots (5.12)$$

$$Q_t - Q_{t-1} = \delta(Q_t^e - Q_{t-1})\dots\dots\dots 0 \le \delta \le 1\dots\dots\dots\dots\dots\dots (5.13)$$

Where, q_t and Q_t are actual price and output at year t; U_t is an error term; α_i, β and δ are parameters that need to be estimated in the model. Thus, supply response was estimated directly in his model.

Over the years the basic Nerlovian model in a slightly modified form has been applied by a number of researchers in estimating supply response behaviour in many developing countries (Askari and Cumming, 1976). The main modification in subsequent works was on the lag variable expression. For example, Koyck (1964) used the price lag variable in his 'learning' process on the part of cultivators. The expected price in his model was expressed as the gap between the last period price and the current price.[2] Later, Almon (1965) further modified the basic distributed lag variables by using weights on the past prices.

In empirical studies, some researchers have emphasised the importance of yield responses to prices, where a substantial increase in yield has substituted for a limit on acreage (Nerlove, 1958). Others have emphasised the price elasticity of acreage and assumed that the price elasticity of yield is negligible (Falcon, 1964; Askari and Cummings, 1976). The idea of regressing acreage rather than output is not very difficult to understand. Acreage can be regarded as a proxy of farmers' real response to an expected price. Arguably, using output as a measure of farmers' supply response to expected prices is problematic as actual observed output probably differs from expected output. The actual output may be influenced by many other random factors (e.g., weather), rather than prices only. However, acreage cannot be influenced by factors such as weather and generally reflects farmers' real price expectations. Using an acreage response function, Nowshirvani (1968) examined the supply response for two states (UP and Bihar) in India, and Askari and Cummings (1976) estimated supply response of rice and wheat in most parts of India and Pakistan. The Askari and Cumming's (1976) basic model can be written in the following simple way:

$$A_t = f(q_{t-1}^h, W_t, A_{t-1}, T) \dots\dots\dots\dots\dots\dots\dots\dots\dots\dots\dots (5.14)$$

Where A_t is crop acreage in period t, q_{t-1}^h is previous period farm harvest price, W_t is an index for rainfall that shows deviation from normal rainfall, and T is the trend variable.

Mangahas et al (1966), analysed supply response in the Philippines and concluded that the price mechanism played a reasonably efficient role in resource allocation, but output response was not always confirmed due to a

77

weak yield response.

The *ad hoc* approach has been substantially developed over time: from a single equation to a system model; from complete to partial adjustment; and from a one product to a multi-product emphasis. Other factors have been incorporated in the basic model such as quantifiable social and technological variables. However, the basic approach still tends to involve predominantly single equation estimation using the ordinary least-squares technique.

The marketable surplus model   The *ad hoc* econometric approach has also been commonly employed in marketable surplus supply analysis. If the relationships among price, income, consumption and marketable surplus and are to be incorporated in supply analysis, the price elasticity of marketable surplus can be derived as follows.

$$M = Q - C. \dots \dots \dots \dots \dots \dots (5.15)$$

Where M is marketable surplus; Q is total output; and C is own-consumption. Output (Q) is specified as a function of price (q), farm household characteristics including fixed input (z) and production technology (k).

$$Q = Q(q, z, k). \dots \dots \dots \dots \dots \dots (5.16)$$

Own-consumption (C) is specified as a function of prices (q), household characteristics which affect tastes (η), full income (y). Full income is in turn a function of prices, fixed inputs, production technology and household characteristics affecting total time available.

$$C = C(p, y(q, z, k, \pi), \pi(q), \eta). \dots \dots \dots \dots \dots (5.16_a)$$

The consumption price and marketable surplus price elasticities can be derived from equations (5.15) and (5.16).

(1) The consumption price elasticity is

$$\frac{\partial C}{\partial q} \cdot \frac{q}{C} = \frac{\partial C}{\partial q} \cdot \frac{q}{C}\bigg|_{dy=0} + \frac{\partial C}{\partial Y} \cdot \frac{\partial Y}{\partial \pi} \cdot \frac{\partial \pi}{\partial q} \cdot \frac{q}{C}$$

$$= \frac{\partial C}{\partial q} \cdot \frac{q}{C}\bigg|_{dy=0} + \frac{\partial C}{\partial Y} \cdot \frac{Y}{C} \cdot \frac{C}{Y} \cdot \frac{\partial Y}{\partial \pi} \cdot Q \cdot \frac{q}{C}$$

$$= \frac{\partial C}{\partial q} \cdot \frac{q}{C}\bigg|_{dy=0} + \frac{\partial C}{\partial Y} \cdot \frac{Y}{C} \cdot \frac{qQ}{Y} \cdot \frac{\partial Y}{\partial \pi} \dots \dots \dots \dots (5.17)$$

The first term on the right hand side represents the uncompensated consumption price elasticity, and the second term, the effect of income on consumption.

(2) The elasticity of marketable surplus is

$$\frac{\partial M}{\partial q} \cdot \frac{q}{M} = \frac{\partial Q}{\partial q} \cdot \frac{q}{Q} \cdot \frac{Q}{M} - \frac{\partial C}{\partial q} \cdot \frac{q}{C} \cdot \frac{C}{M} \dots \dots \dots \dots (5.18)$$

78

This equation is a weighted difference of output price elasticity and consumption price elasticity. However, it is impossible to derive this price elasticity of marketable surplus supply by directly estimating a single equation. In order to estimate it, a number of assumptions must be imposed upon the estimated supply function. For example, Behrman (1966) assumed that $\dfrac{\partial C}{\partial q}$ and $\dfrac{\partial C}{\partial Y}$ were both equal to zero, thus, only price affected marketable surplus through its influence on production. Bardhan (1970) and Haessel (1975) assumed that production was fixed, hence, price affected marketable surplus only by changing consumption. Toquero et al. (1975) and Chinn (1976) estimated marketed surplus function assuming that production was fixed but then allowed production to vary when computing price elasticities.

Estimates of marketable surplus supply elasticities in these models, therefore, may be viewed as consisting of combinations of component elasticities, i.e. independent output, income and consumption elasticities. It is not possible to take account of the effects of interactions among the various causal factors in estimating a total marketable surplus elasticity as set out in equation 5.18.

Secondly, indirect estimation using household models. Farm household theory was initially drawn from Chayanov's subjective equilibrium analysis in the 1920s: the theory developed rapidly in the 1970s and 1980s (Nakajima, 1970, 1986, Singh et al. 1986). One of the major theoretical directions in farm household theory was to apply utility theory to supply decisions, taking the interdependent effects among prices, incomes, consumption and labour supply into account. Early applications were carried out by Lau et al. (1972) and Barnum and Squire (1979) and Strauss (1982, 1984).

The theoretical assumptions underlying marketable surplus analysis by Strauss are: (a) markets exist for all goods and labour; (b) family and hired labour are perfect substitutes in the production function; (c) the disutility of farm and off-farm work is identical, and farm and off-farm work are perfect substitutes in the utility function. The household utility function is

$$U = u(X_i^C, L). \dotfill (5.19)$$

Where X_i^C and L are vectors of goods and leisure consumed by households.

Households maximise the utility function subject to three constraints: (a) a production constraint; (b) a time constraint that equates with total household labour time available; (c) a full income budget constraint that is equal to the sum of farm income, and other income (A).

The total time and budget constraints can be written as

$$A + \sum_{i=1}^{N} q_i(Q_i - C_i) + P_N(T - L - L_T) = 0 \quad \ldots \ldots \ldots \ldots \ldots (5.20)$$

Rearranging terms, we have

$$A + (\sum_{i=1}^{N-1} q_i Q_i - p_N L_T) + p_N T = \sum_{i=1}^{N-1} q_i X_i^c + p_N L \quad \ldots \ldots (5.20_a)$$

Where A is other income; T is total time available to the household; L is household leisure; L_T is total labour demand (including hired labour); P_N is labour prices; Q_i is total output; X_i^c is consumption of goods; and q_i is prices of goods.

It can be seen that the farm profit element $\Pi = q_i(Q_i - C_i)$ is part of full income, and will be influenced by price changes. This so called profit effect should influence consumption positively: however, the response of marketable surplus to price may be influenced by two potentially opposing effects, a direct positive effect on production but a negative effect as a result of a profit induced increase in consumption. In contrast to earlier studies such as Behrman (1968) and Haessel (1975) the price elasticities of consumption and marketable surplus supply are no longer obtained by direct estimation, but from production and expenditure functions. Household behaviour effectively is represented by two separate maximisation problems: profit maximisation in production, subject to a production constraint, and utility maximisation in consumption subject to a full income constraint.

Thirdly, the duality approach. The duality approach to estimating supply response has become increasingly popular in the last fifteen years. Duality theory had its beginnings in the work of Hotelling (1932). A pioneering book by Shephard (1953) provided the first comprehensive treatment of the subject and proof of the basic duality of cost and production. Extensions of the formal theory of duality were later made by McFadden (1962), Uzawa (1964), Diewert (1971) and Lopez (1982, 1984). Many of the basic duality results were also obtained by Gorman (1953), working independently. Lopez (1982, 1984, 1986) used duality theory as a basic tool for analysing supply response behaviour, taking both production and consumption into account.

The foundations of the duality approach are the indirect profit and cost functions, obtained from the primal profit maximization and cost minimization problem. The indirect profit function is defined as the maximum profit associated with given output and input prices. Similarly, the indirect utility function is defined as the minimum expenditure required to meet a given level of utility at given factor and output prices. The

80

indirect utility function is specified as a function of certain variables including output and input prices and their quantities. Using the Hotelling Lemma, the output supply and input demand equations can be derived by taking partial derivatives of the indirect profit function with respect to the prices of output and inputs. The duality approach has been increasingly used in applied economic analysis, as it has the advantage of being able to take account of all the various influencing factors simultaneously. It is possible to use more complex functional forms with less restrictions on the estimating equations, thereby, permitting a closer relationship between economic theory and practice (Lopez, 1982). As with other methods used to estimate supply response, the duality approach is also not without its limitations. As Henneberry (1991) mentioned, duality theory implies an assumption of profit maximization which may be difficult to sustain in certain developing countries; and the elasticities obtained from the dual method may be difficult to categorise as short or long run values. However, this approach, in integrating various determining factors and in analysing interdependent effects, has considerable theoretical and applied value.

5. 3   Theoretical analysis of supply response in China

In contrast to the vast amount of theoretical and empirical work in supply response analysis, some of which is reviewed above, the amount of formal theoretical and empirical analyses of Chinese agriculture is very limited. The modelling literature on Chinese agriculture, by Chinese economists, has only really developed since 1978 (Chen and Buckwell, 1991). Apart from the fundamental institutional and managerial difference between the Chinese and western market system, a substantial impediment for theoretical and empirical analysis is the lack of an appropriate theoretical framework for producer and consumer behaviour under the Chinese economic system and environment.

5.3.1   Supply response under the planning system

Perkins (1966) was the first to analyse Chinese agricultural transformation from the market system to a planned economy in the period 1950s and 1960s. He argued, in his work, which was regarded as a classic on China's planned agricultural system, that the farm households will not respond to price changes under such a system.   As marketing and prices were strictly controlled and quotas imposed by the government, price no longer plays a role in guiding quota production, or even the above-quota production.

    In contrast to Perkin's view, Chou (1984) argued that farm households will respond positively to changes in the state purchase price. As the price paid by the state was lower than the market equilibrium price, the farmer would suffer a 'loss'. However, as long as total revenue was above total cost, or the state purchase price greater than average cost, farmers would still tend to respond positively to the state purchase price.

An (1992) held the same view as Chou. He argued that, even if the state quota purchase was viewed as an invisible tax imposed on farm households, Chinese farm households would still respond to changes in the state purchase price since a rise in this price would increase farm households' income. Using a simple mathematical equation, he specified that the Chinese farm household would respond to changes either in quota, or the state purchase price. In his equation, invisible tax A (P-P') was defined as the difference between the state purchase price (P') and free market price (P) times total quota (A). The tax rate was a ratio of total quota to total output in physical terms (A/T), or in value terms (A (p-p')/PT)., where T is total output. Thus, the rate of the extra tax depends on quota (A), the state purchase price (P') and total output (T) at a given level of market price (P). Hence, both total output and net cash income are sensitive to changes in the state purchase price (P').

5.3.2   Supply response under the two price system

Song (1987) argued that farm households would mainly respond to changes in market prices. According to his view, in the period before 1978, there was little room for a producer to choose how much he could sell on the market under the planning system. Hence the state purchase price lost its production regulating role: price was more a quota tax. More specifically, it was a product tax in kind since both the amounts of quota and the level of quota price were unilaterally decided by the government. The farmer's quota was compulsory without any room for bargaining. However, he argued that although peasant farm households did not respond positively to the state purchase price, they did respond to the market price. If producers did not produce grain, they had to purchase grain in the free market at the higher market price to fulfil the quota. On the other hand, if a producer delivered the state quota he could sell the remainder in the free market and benefit from the higher market price. Thus, farm households could be seen to respond positively to changes in the free market price.

However, in contrast to Perkin's view, Song argued that although the state purchase price has no direct influence, it did have an indirect influence on grain production. The reason was that although the grain sown area was controlled by the government, farm households still responded to state purchase prices in other ways. For example, farm households could allocate different qualities of land to different crops; they could interplant one crop with another on the same piece of land; or change the allocation of non-land

and land inputs for different cropping activities. Thus, if the state purchase price was lower than the market price, farmers would choose the poor land for the state quota. This would directly influence relative yield and output. If the state purchase price was favourable, the higher quality land would be used for grain production and output would increase. Thus, the state purchase price had more influence on yields than sown areas. In this sense, farm households could also be said to be responding positively to changes in the state purchase price. However, Song only provided observations, no real evidence to support his argument. This was investigated empirically by Wang and Davis (1991). Their results further confirmed that the state purchase price had a relatively strong influence on yield, rather than on sown areas.

Sicular (1988a) argued that farm households respond to the market price changes only: farm households' marginal production decisions depend on market prices. Even if the market price for certain products was lower than the state purchase price, farmers could buy the grain from the market and sell it to the state. This would bid up the market price until it was equal to or higher than the state price. Sicular's model implied that the state purchase price and quota did not really have any influence on farmers' supply behaviour: they influenced production and consumption through their effects on income and market equilibrium prices. However, the conclusions drawn from her analysis are questionable.

Subsequent studies, for example, Gao (1989 a & b), Ke (1991), Jin (1990), Wang and Davis (1992) and Cheng et al. (1993) concluded that farm households respond positively to *both* the state purchase and market prices. The salient feature of these studies was that they took account of household consumption, the level of state imposed quota and the relationship between the state and free market prices. The levels of own-consumption and state quota were both assumed to be fixed in the short-run as was the relativity between the state and free-market prices. The studies nevertheless provided valuable theoretical expositions of some of the interrelationships which can influence grain marketable surplus under the planned system.

Jin (1990) argued that farm households respond to changes in marginal prices, i.e. the higher prevailing price whether it be state or free-market. He put forward the idea of quantum jump adjustment in supply. This could occur if the free-market price were sufficiently above the state price to compensate producers for the implicit loss in state quota sales: when the free-market price reached a critical level a quantum jump in output could be predicted, from the quota level of output to some higher level, which would be sold in the free market. These ideas were also developed in subsequent work by Wang and Davis (1992) who showed that supply could be influenced by both the state quota and free-market prices. Cheng et al.

83

(1993) also provided a supplementary analysis to Jin's model in which he introduced the idea of a double-peak profit function. His model also incorporated the idea of a critical level of free-market price. If the market prices were below this level producers would attempt to avoid quota and maximise profit at some lower level of output. If it rises above the critical level producers would have an incentive to fulfill quota and maximise profit at some level of output above quota, i.e. the profit function would have two peaks.

5.4   Empirical analysis of Chinese grain supply response

The literature on empirical modelling of Chinese grain supply has only really developed since the early 1980s. There has been a growing number of studies in recent years, mainly using econometric models. The following discussion focuses on these studies.

5.4.1   Econometric models for forecasting and simulation

These were mainly to aid forecasting using relatively straightforward methods. The studies involved the simple linear production model (Tang, and Stone, 1980); the quadratic function model (Noh, 1983) and the input-output model (Rock, 1985).

The simple linear production model   One of the earliest efforts to model Chinese agriculture was that of Tang and Stone (1980) who constructed a simple linear model to project China's agricultural production for the years between 1977 and 2000. The output in his model was specified as a function of technique, and inputs (labour capital and land). He assigned weightings of 0.55, 0.25, 0.10 and 0.15 to labour, land, capital and current input respectively, which were derived from data in the period 1952-77, then estimated the output index and input indices for the period 1977-2000.

Quadratic function model   Analogously, Noh (1983) estimated China's grain production through a quadratic time trend using data over the period 1949-81. This model incorporated fluctuations in grain output, but it did not investigate the economic mechanism in rural China. The model was limited in the form used, and in the fact that Chinese grain production exhibited an erratic path linked to various institutional and policy changes.

Input-output model   Rock (1985) estimated Chinese grain production through an input-output method. This approach provides a method of examining the intersectoral relationships. He found, not surprisingly, that the Chinese grain production is not totally independent from other sectors to the economy.

5.4.2 Econometric models for policy analysis

In more recent works the emphasis has shifted away from forecasting towards policy analysis. These models have focused on identifying those factors which affect supply behaviour, including the formulation of the supply function and the selection of explanatory variables. The *ad hoc* approach has been widely used to specify Chinese farm households' supply response to economic signals. Most studies have been based on a single commodity supply function using direct estimation of output supply rather than marketable surplus. In these models, yield or acreage was chosen as the dependent variable: these were generally specified as a function of own price, other related product prices and non-price variables such as weather, technology and policy.

Price was employed as one of main explanatory variables in Carter and Zhong's (1988) econometric model. The sown acreage equation for grain was specified as a function of population, grain prices and the price ratio between grain and cash crops. The yield equation was specified as a function of technique (the time trend was chosen as a proxy of technique change), grain prices and the price ratio between grain and cash crops. The different variables chosen in their supply function reflected their attempt to take explicit account of a number of key variables.

Using the state purchase price, state retail price of farm inputs, and weather as explanatory variables, Kueh (1988) examined the effects of price and weather on farmers' income. He concluded that weather is a much more important factor than price in influencing farm households' supply behaviour. The slow-down in the income growth from 14.7 per cent to 6.58 per cent between 1984 to 1986 was due to the effect of weather. The effect of the increase in state purchase price was greatly offset by bad weather. However, the dependent variable in his model was income, rather than the quantity of agricultural output. The income variable did not distinguish between on-farm and non-farm income. This was problematic, particularly in view of the growth in non-farm income after 1985.

Using regional panel data (combination of time-series and cross-sectional data) from 1979-86, Carter and Zhong (1991) attempted to project China's grain trade. The yield and acreage responses to the state purchase prices were estimated separately.

A more detailed model for the Chinese grain sector was developed by Chen and Buckwell (1991). Total output supply was estimated through a single supply function: it was specified as a function of the state purchase price, the state input price, the acreage, the production technique (time trends) and the policy (dummy) variable. The authors used time series data from 1952 to 1984 to estimate output supply for a range of grain crops.

Using an agricultural production function, Lin (1992) explored the sources of agricultural growth in China since 1979. In his model, grain output was specified as a function of prices (both the free market and the state purchase prices), institutional change (i.e. the proportion of production teams under the HPRS), technical progress (time trend), and regional dummies.

The main development over the last few years was in the formulation of the supply function and selection of explanatory variables. Wang and Davis (1991) examined the main factors which determine peasants' supply response behaviour in China's grain sector. Prices (including output prices, input prices and cash crop prices), techniques (time trend), non-price policies and weather were employed as major explanatory variables in their models. Dummy variables were used to indicate institutional changes in the pre and post-reform eras. Thus they tried to capture the complexity of factors influencing supply. They found that government policy measures had a very significant effect on the share of sown acreage taken by grain production and that institutional changes had strong effects on grain yield.

Huang and Rozelle (1995) explored the influence of environmental factors on grain yield including, erosion, salination, soil exhaustion and degradation of the local environment. Yield was specified as a function of inputs, technology, institutional change and environmental stress. Using provincial production data from 1975 to 1990, they concluded that environmental pressures may have been partially responsible for the slowdown of grain yield in the late 1980s in China.

In recent years many studies have attempted to estimate the different effects of the state purchase price and free market price using *ad hoc* econometric models. As the marketing of grain in rural China after 1985 involved a dual price system, farmers had to sell a certain amount of grain (quota) to the government at the state purchase prices. After the fulfillment of the quota, grain was exchanged in the free market. Using national aggregate data and a very simple model, Jin (1990) estimated the supply response to both the state purchase price and market price. Output supply was specified as a function of the state purchase price and the market price.

$$Q_t = \alpha_1 + \alpha_2 q_f + \alpha_3 q_s + \alpha_4 q_f q_s + D + \varepsilon \ \ldots \ . \ (5.21)$$

Where q_f is the market price; q_s is the state purchase price; $q_f q_s$ is the interaction term of the state purchase price and the free market price; D is a dummy variable, ε is statistical error; and α_i are parameters to be estimated. He concluded that output supply responds positively to both the state purchase and the market price.

A similar approach was taken by Wu (1995). In his marketable surplus models, the state purchase price and the free market prices were introduced as two independent explanatory variables.

86

$$M_t = \gamma_1 Z + \gamma_2 q_m + \gamma_3 q_o + \gamma_4 I + \gamma_5 POP \ldots\ldots\ldots(5.22)$$

Where M is marketable surplus supply; Z is total output; q_m is free market price; q_o is state purchase price; I is income; POP is rural population; and γ_i are parameters.

He found that marketable surplus supply responded positively to the state purchase price but negatively to the free market price. However, this single supply function approach is not without its problems. For example, using the two prices in the single equation may lead to serious multicollinearity. Also, in using panel data it is difficult to distinguish the time series (price) effects from the cross-sectional (regional) effects.

Du (1995) estimated marketable surplus supply response using Toquero's (1975) method. Marketable surplus supply in his theoretical analysis was affected by two main factors: own-consumption and total output. However, as own-consumption in his model was assumed to be constant, there was no scope for estimating the effect of income on consumption: marketable surplus was dependent on the output effect.

Based on this assumption, marketable surplus (M) was specified as a function of grain prices (q) and output (Q). The output was specified as a function of grain price (q) and a non-price variable (Z).

$$M=f(q,Q) \ldots\ldots\ldots\ldots\ldots\ldots\ldots\ldots\ldots\ldots\ldots (5.23)$$
$$Q=g(q,Z) \ldots\ldots\ldots\ldots\ldots\ldots\ldots\ldots\ldots\ldots\ldots (5.24)$$

The effect of changes in price on marketable surplus can be written as

$$\frac{dM}{dq} = \frac{\partial f}{\partial P}|_{\partial Q=0} + \frac{\partial f}{\partial Q} \cdot \frac{\partial Q}{\partial q} \ldots\ldots\ldots\ldots\ldots\ldots\ldots (5.25)$$

Therefore, the elasticity of marketable surplus supply can be written as

$$\frac{dM}{dq} \cdot \frac{q}{M} = \frac{\partial f}{\partial q} \cdot \frac{q}{M}|_{\partial Q=0} + (\frac{\partial f}{\partial Q} \cdot \frac{Q}{M})(\frac{\partial Q}{\partial q} \cdot \frac{q}{Q}) \ldots\ldots (5.25_a)$$

From his theoretical analysis, the total price elasticity of marketable surplus consists of two partial price elasticities, i.e. (a) a partial price elasticity of marketable surplus at a given output ($\frac{\partial f}{\partial q} \cdot \frac{q}{M}|_{\partial Q=0}$); (b) an induced price elasticity assuming that the total output can vary ($\frac{\partial f}{\partial Q} \cdot \frac{Q}{M} \cdot \frac{\partial Q}{\partial q} \cdot \frac{q}{Q}$).

However, his empirical model was specified as follows.

$$M = a_0 + a_1 q_t + a_2 Q_t + a_3 FRET_t + a_4 RIL_{t-1} + a_5 RPOP_{t-1} + a_6 D + \mu$$
$$\ldots\ldots\ldots\ldots\ldots (5.26)$$

Where M is the amount of marketable surplus; q is price; Q is output; FRET is amount of chemical fertiliser applied; RIL is ratio of rural industrial labour to total rural labour; RPOP is size of rural population; and D is a dummy variable.

Although this model enabled him to estimate marketable surplus elasticities with respect to each of the component variables, it was impossible to derive the total marketable surplus elasticity as defined in equation 5.25a. The interdependent effects between marketable surplus, price and output were lost.

5.5   Summary and conclusions

In this chapter we have sought to review the main issues in supply response in a general sense and, in particular, the main theoretical and empirical developments concerning grain supply analysis in China. We have attempted to capture something of the flavour of the rich debates which have been going on. The distinction between total output and marketable surplus has been emphasised. The basic theoretical issue is to explain the complex interdependencies between price output, income, consumption and marketable surplus supply. Our view is that, despite the burgeoning theoretical and empirical literature on grain supply response in China, these interdependencies have not been adequately accounted for. The big questions about the complexity of factors influencing grain marketable surplus supply, especially in the context of the changing Chinese rural economy, remain largely unanswered. However, from a policy perspective they remain absolutely central. In the remainder of this book we attempt to establish an appropriate theoretical and empirical framework to address these issues.

Notes

1. Here the author used the Hotelling Lemma $\dfrac{\partial \pi}{\partial q_i} = Q_i * (q_i)$. π and Q are replaced by I and M respectively. We can derive (5.9) by substituting (5.8) into (5.7$_a$)

88

2. Output (Q) is dependent on the price in the following way:

$$Q_t = \alpha q_{t-1} + \alpha \lambda q_{t-2} + \alpha \lambda^2 q_{t-3} + \alpha \lambda^3 q_{t-4} \ldots\ldots$$

where 0<λ<1 then,

$$Q_t - \lambda Q_{t-1} = \alpha q_{t-1}$$
$$or\, Q_t = \alpha q_{t-1} + \lambda Q_{t-1}$$
$$or\, \Delta Q_t = Q_t - Q_{t-1} = \alpha q_{t-1} + (1-\lambda) Q_{t-1}$$

Here, α illustrates short-term response to price, and α/(1- λ) is the long-term equilibrium response; λ indicates the speed of cultivators' adjustments.

6 An analytical framework

6.1 Introduction

There is general agreement that own-consumption is a fundamental factor determining Chinese farm households' supply behaviour. Own-consumption and marketable surplus supply are intimately linked through price and income changes. Meanwhile, there is increasing recognition that agriculture has become more closely integrated with the rest of the economy as a result of economic liberalisation and development in China. Farm household decision-making has been influenced increasingly by off-farm opportunities. Thus, there are increasingly complex linkages between grain prices, income, consumption, labour supply and output. Taking account of these interdependencies offers a particular challenge to agricultural economists.

If this challenge is to be met, three questions which were raised in the previous chapter must be addressed: (a) what is the correct theoretical basis for modelling supply response behaviour in China? Is the farm profit or the utility maximisation framework applicable?; (b) on the empirical side, which method can be adopted to deal most adequately with the interdependencies discussed above?; (c) is the use of aggregate data for empirical work appropriate in the Chinese situation? We devote most of this chapter to an exploration of these points, especially the theoretical and empirical issues.

In what follows we explore the theoretical and empirical footing for analysis of Chinese farm households' supply behaviour. We focus on a price response mechanism in which farm production (including own-consumption) and the development of external linkages with the non-farm labour market are explored. The chapter is organised as follows. Alternative theoretical

91

frameworks are discussed in the section 6.2. Empirical approaches are discussed in section 6.3. Finally, other issues such as the appropriateness of aggregate analysis and data type etc. will be covered in section 6.4.

6.2   Alternative theoretical frameworks

Many econometric models are based on a coherent theory of profit maximising behaviour of producers or of utility maximising behaviour of consumers. The conventional theory of profit maximising behaviour treats the household as a farm firm, operating in fully competitive input and output markets. Profit is the sole goal of farm production.

6.2.1   Supply response and farm profit maximisation

In the standard neoclassical theory, producers are assumed to be profit maximisers (or income maximisers) and price-takers under a perfectly competitive market. Profit maximisation regarding the level of output and technique for a firm is described mathematically in terms of a constrained optimisation problem:

$$\underset{Max}{\pi} = \sum_{i=1}^{n} q_i Q_i - \sum_{j=1}^{m} q_j X_j \dots \dots \dots \dots (6.1)$$

subject to $f(Q,X)=0$

Where Q_i is an output vector; X_j is an input vector; q_i is an output price vector; q_j is an input price vector and π represents farm profit. $f(Q,X)$ is the transformation function which captures the technical constraints governing production. In a single output case, it may reduce to an explicit form $Q=f(x)$, known as the production function. Neither the transformation function nor the production function is entirely arbitrary; and they satisfy a set of certain 'regularity properties'. There is no universally accepted set of regularity properties, but they usually include: (a) non-regularity; (b) monotonicity; (c) twice continuous differentiability; and (d) concavity or quasi-concavity.[1]

Using the Lagrangian method, the first order conditions for the profit maximisation problem given in (6.1) are as follows.

$$F = \sum_{i=1}^{n} q_i Q_i - \sum_{j=1}^{n} q_j X_j - \lambda f(Q,X) \dots \dots \dots \dots (6.2)$$

92

$$q_i + \lambda \frac{\partial f}{\partial Q_i} = 0,$$

$$-q_j + \lambda \frac{\partial f}{\partial X_j} = 0,$$

$$f(Q, X) = 0$$

i=1,.., n; j=1,..., m;

where λ is the Lagrangian multiplier. Rearrangement of the first order condition yields the well-know result:

$$-\frac{\partial f \big/ \partial X_j}{\partial f \big/ \partial Q_i} = \frac{\partial Q_i}{\partial X_j} = \frac{q_j}{q_i} \quad \ldots\ldots\ldots\ldots\ldots\ldots\ldots\ldots\ldots\ldots .(6.3)$$

(i=1,..., n; j=1,.., m)

Thus, at the optimum, the marginal product for output i with respect to input j is equated to the reversed ratio of those input and output prices.

Solution of the set of simultaneous equations given in (6.2) yields the optimal output supply and input demand function:[2]

$$Q_i^* = Q_i^*(q_i, q_J), \ldots\ldots\ldots i = 1, \ldots n. \quad \ldots\ldots\ldots\ldots\ldots .6.4)$$

$$X_j^* = X_j^*(q_i, q_j), \ldots\ldots\ldots j = 1, \ldots m \quad \ldots\ldots\ldots\ldots\ldots .(6.5)$$

Equations (6.4) and (6.5) represent the uncompensated or Marshallian output supplies and input demands. Substituting these optimal levels into expression (6.1) yields the profit function:

$$\pi^* = \pi^*(q_i, q_j) = \sum_{i=1}^{n} q_i Q_i^*(q_i, q_j) - \sum_{j=1}^{m} q_j X_j^*(q_i, q_j)$$

$$\ldots\ldots\ldots\ldots\ldots\ldots .(6.6)$$

Equation (6.6) sometimes is called the 'indirect' profit function in order to distinguish it from the expression in equation (6.1) for the original problem. Note that it corresponds to the maximum, long-run profit obtainable by the firm since all inputs are being treated as variable. The above analysis can be adapted to take account of fixed output levels, fixed factors (the short-run), or other exogenous influencing factors such as the weather and technology.

The expressions given in (6.4), (6.5) and (6.6) represent the solution to the individual firm profit maximisation problem given the technological and market environment. They provide information on optimal choice of output, technique and profit level. They also can provide information concerning the distribution of income, substitution possibilities between factors of production, the existence of decreasing, increasing or constant returns to scale, technological change and the effect of changes in the market environment. These results will be dependent on the choice of functional form used to specify the production or transformation function and the availability of data for parametric estimation.

Using duality theory, output supply and input demand can be derived from the profit function. Through partial differentiation with respect to the price of k's output, thus,

$$\frac{\partial \pi^*}{\partial q_k} = Q_k^* + \sum_{i=1}^{n} q_i \frac{\partial Q_i^*}{\partial q_k} - \sum_{j=1}^{m} q_j \frac{\partial X}{q_k} \quad \ldots\ldots\ldots\ldots\ldots (6.7)$$

However, from the first order conditions given in (6.2), (6.7) may be rewritten as:

$$\frac{\partial \pi^*}{\partial q_k} = Q_k^* - \lambda [\sum_{i=1}^{n} \frac{\partial f}{\partial Q_k^*} \cdot \frac{\partial Q_k^*}{\partial q_k} + \sum_{j=1}^{m} \frac{\partial f}{\partial X_j^*} \cdot \frac{\partial X_j^*}{\partial q_k}] \quad \ldots\ldots (6.8)^3$$

The expression inside the brackets on the right hand side of (6.8) is the derivative of $f(Q,X)$ with respect to q_k; but, by definition, $f(Q,X)$ is identical equal to zero, thus, $\dfrac{\partial F}{\partial q_k} = 0$, and we obtain:

$$\frac{\partial \pi^*}{\partial q_k} = Q_k^* \quad \ldots\ldots\ldots\ldots\ldots\ldots\ldots\ldots\ldots\ldots\ldots\ldots (6.9)$$

Thus, the Marshallian output supply and input demand functions given in equations (6.4) and (6.5) may be obtained directly from the profit function by partial differentiation:

$$Q_i^* = Q_i^*(q_i, q_j) = \frac{\partial \pi^*}{\partial q_i} \quad \ldots\ldots\ldots\ldots\ldots\ldots\ldots\ldots (6.10)$$

$$X_j^* = X_j^*(q_i, q_j) = \frac{\partial \pi^*}{\partial q_j} \quad \ldots\ldots\ldots\ldots\ldots\ldots\ldots\ldots (6.11)$$

This important property of the profit function, known as Hotelling's Lemma, is an example of a rule called the Envelop Theorem. Conversely, we can also deduce a profit function through solution of the constrained profit maximisation problem from the transformation function, via the output supply and input demand functions. Hotelling's Lemma means that it is possible to retrace these steps and retrieve the output supply, input demand and transformation functions from the profit function.

The output supply function (6.10) which was derived from the profit function (6.6) is

$$Q_i^* = Q_i^*(q_i, q_j) = \frac{\partial \pi^*}{\partial q_i} \quad \dots\dots\dots\dots\dots\dots\dots\dots (6.10)$$

This supply response function implies that supply has always a positive response to price changes. Using Hotelling's Lemma, partially differentiating equation (6.10) with respect to own output prices, it is possible to get output supply response as:

$$\frac{\partial Q^*}{\partial q_i} = \frac{\partial^2 \pi^*}{\partial q_i^2} \geq 0, \dots\dots (i = 1, \dots n) \quad \dots\dots\dots\dots\dots (6.12)$$

The supply curve for the ith output must be upward sloping, i.e. as output price increases, *ceteris paribus*, supply cannot decrease. Supply must be positive or zero.

Similarly, using Shepherd's Lemma, partially differentiating equation (6.11) with respect to input prices, it is possible to get factor demand response as:

$$\frac{\partial^2 \pi^*}{\partial q_j^2} = -\frac{\partial X_j^*}{\partial q_j} \geq 0$$

$$\therefore \frac{\partial X_j^*}{\partial q_j} \leq 0, \dots\dots (j = 1, \dots m)$$

$$\dots\dots\dots\dots\dots\dots\dots (6.13)$$

Input demand always has a negative response to price changes and the demand curve for the jth input must be downward sloping. If an input price increases, *ceteris paribus*, demand for that input cannot increase.

However, this supply response analysis in the neoclassical theory of profit maximisation relies on at least two assumptions about production. The first is that production is for commercial use and production and consumption are separated into two independent sectors. The second is that profit is only concerned with farm profit and the effect of non-farm income is excluded. If semi-commercial production (including substantial own-consumption) and external income effects are taken into account simultaneously, the profit maximising behaviour model may need to be modified; expected utility (full income) maximisation may be inconsistent with farm profit maximisation.

6.2.2   Supply response and subjective utility

In contrast to conventional profit maximisation theory, subjective utility theory, first formulated by Chayanov in the 1920s (Chayanov, 1966), takes demographic change in family structure into account using a peasant farm household model. Subjective utility maximisation is concerned with a farm

95

family's two opposing objectives: (a) an income objective required to meet the consumption needs of the household (utility of income); (b) a work-avoidance objective which may conflict with the first objective. Decision-making by the household seemed to involve a trade-off between the drudgery of farm work and utility of income. The equilibrium point in Chayanov's model is where the marginal product of labour is equal to the subjective wage. This differs from the neo-classical profit maximisation theory, in which the equilibrium point is where the marginal product of labour is equal to the market wage.

Subjective wage in Chayanov's theory is determined by the demographic structure of the household and is expressed as the so-called c/w ratio, i.e, the ratio of consumers to producers in the household. According to the Chayanov's theory, when the ratio of c/w is low, the subjective wage becomes high. For example, the household consists of just two adult workers without children, c/w ratio is 2:2. The household prefers leisure to income. On the contrary, when the ratio of c/w is high, the subjective wage tends to be low. For example, if the size of household grows, eg. three children are born and the children are small, the minimum consumption or the ratio of c/w is raised from 2:2 to 5:2. Under such a condition, the minimum consumption constraint is raised. The household has to work more hours and accept a smaller rise in income for the loss of leisure than before. So the marginal utility of income has increased, and the marginal utility of leisure has decreased. This means that the subjective wage will depend on changes in the demographic structure of a household. Thus, if the subjective wage falls, a new equilibrium point will be established at higher output and labour inputs for a given production function. This also implied that the marginal product of labour would be lower and would be consistent with optimisation at a lower subjective wage. The reverse would happen as children become producers and the c/w ratio changed. Thus, the family size and composition determine the subjective wage and subjective equilibrium point.

It should be noted that the marginal utility of income and leisure at two extreme conditions in Chayanov's theory may become zero. First, if an increased utility of leisure cannot compensate for a fall in income at the point of the minimum consumption level, the marginal utility of leisure may become zero. Second, the marginal utility of income may also tend to be zero if an increased utility of income cannot compensate for a fall in leisure at the point of minimum leisure consumption. Thus, although Chayanov's theory is not the same as a target income hypothesis, it does embody the notion that the disutility of additional work is relatively high when compared to the utility of additional income as the consumption norms of the family have been met. This implies that utility and profit (income) may

96

be separated into two independent sectors. Utility maximisation was not to be equated with income maximisation (profit maximisation). The peasant farmers' supply behaviour in Chayanov's theory may differ from the profit maximisation behaviour of the farm/firm in neo-classical theory, because output supply response in the peasant farm economy becomes unpredictable. This is because family labour in Chayanov's theory will be applied to meet subsistence requirements beyond the point where the marginal value product of labour equals the market wage rate. Therefore, if prices fall, peasant households who have no other means to meet their cash requirements may increase their production: this response will only happen in conjunction with changes in the structure of the farm family, which distinguishes this theory from a target income hypothesis. The key assumption in the Chayanov's subjective utility theory is that no labour market exists. However, if a labour market exists, this income effect will disappear. The total labour input on the farm (including hired labour) will decrease when output prices decline as farmers seek other income in the labour market.

Utility in Chayanov's theory was specified as a function of leisure (L) and income (M), and maximising utility is subject to labour (A) and land (B) input constraints. This utility function was expressed mathematically by Nakajima (1986) in the following way.

$$\text{Max } U=u(A,M)\dots\dots\dots\dots\dots\dots\dots\dots\dots\dots\dots\dots\dots\dots(6.14)$$

subject to a farm production or farm income constraint given as follows.

$$M = q_x F(A, B) \dots\dots\dots\dots\dots\dots\dots\dots\dots\dots\dots(6.15)$$

Where, A is the amount of family labour; M is the money income; q_x is product price; F is total output and; B is the amount and quality of land available.

It is assumed that there are no labour or land markets and all the produce is to be sold to the market. The subjective equilibrium condition is given by

$$q_A F_A = {-U_A}\big/{U_M} \dots\dots\dots\dots\dots\dots\dots\dots\dots\dots\dots\dots\dots(6.16)$$

In equation (6.16), the marginal utility of labour (U_A) is assumed to be negative because it gives direct disutility and it reduces the amount of leisure. The marginal utility of income (U_M) is, however, always positive. The trade-off between leisure and income can be measured by the term $-U_A\big/U_M$, which can be called the 'marginal rate of substitution of family labour for money' or the 'marginal value of family labour'.

Chayanov's subjective equilibrium theory was further developed within a neoclassical framework by many others such as Barnum and Squire (1979) and Low (1986).[4] It has been successfully incorporated into econometric studies by Lau and Youtopolous (1971) Strauss (1984). Barnum and Squire (1979) abandoned Chayanov's assumption of absence of labour markets and introduced labour markets in their models. Farm output was no longer determined by the subjective consumption preferences, rather by profit maximisation because the external opportunity cost of labour time was given by the market. They provided a framework for generating the prediction of the farm household's response to changes in demography (family size and structure) and market variables (output and input prices, wage rate and technology). However, their model mainly dealt with the conditions for hiring more labour for farm work. In contrast, Low (1986) dealt with a situation in which household demography is affected by off-farm work by household members. He introduced the ratio of off-farm wages to the retail food price (w/p) as a proxy variable to analyse peasant performance according to household size and structure. The effect of changes in the ratio (w/p) on the peasant farmers' options between on-farm and off-farm work in Southern Africa was examined by Low. He concluded that household members would engage in subsistence production only where the real opportunity cost of time (w/p) was lower than their Marginal Physical Product of Labour (MPP_L). If the real opportunity cost of time was higher than MPP_L, the household member would engage in off-farm work. Although these models re-introduced profit maximisation into their theoretical framework, they still failed to explain convincingly whether this objective was a factor in peasant farmers' production behaviour.

6.2.3   Alternative theoretical framework: full income maximisation

Is the assumption of profit maximisation appropriate to Chinese farm households? The validity of the profit maximisation assumption in estimating Chinese grain supply has been questioned by many researchers for example Chen and Buckwell (1991). In spite of the fact that Schultz (1960) hypothesised that farmers in developing economies are no less rational than their counterparts in industrial economies in terms of seeking maximum profit, and in spite of the fact that such a proposition has been supported by several pieces of evidence,[5] there are a number of studies which criticise Schultz's hypothesis (Ellis, 1988). The major concerns about the rationality assumption relate to the particular characteristics of the Chinese farm household and the highly regulated environment in which they operate. These have been alluded to earlier and include: the high level of subsistence farming; highly regulated markets for outputs and inputs;

institutional constraints etc. Nerlove (1979) argued that increased production in peasant agriculture is more dependent on non-price factors such as infrastructural development, technical progress and demographic change .... 'one might infer little supply response to price observed in central markets, for example, simply because such prices are largely irrelevant to the allocation problems which these farm households resolve' (Nerlove, pp 883-885).

However, if profit maximisation is rejected, what is a sound theoretical underpinning for analysing Chinese farmers' supply response behaviour? In order to examine this problem, we must explore the characteristics of Chinese farm households' supply behaviour in their specific economic environment.

Supply response in a relatively closed single agricultural economy The Chinese agricultural economy before rural reform, more precisely before 1984, was a relatively closed single agricultural economy. Farm income was the only source of farm households' income. The farm households' production was also dependent upon their level of consumption. The marketable surplus of grain was the principal source of cash income, which in turn was required for purchasing non-farm inputs such as electricity, machinery and fertilizer, and for purchasing non-farm consumer goods in satisfying their own production and subsistence requirements. Under such a circumstances, rural household income could be equated with farm income. The primary function of rural households was thought to be production of food, fibre and livestock for the household's consumption and for the market. Thus, researchers analysing the history of peasant farmers' supply behaviour unanimously agreed that the traditional Chinese farmer was an economically rational producer. Buck (1937) in his study of 16,786 farms in 168 localities and 38,256 farm families in 22 provinces in China, 1929-33, found that a rise in farm prices before 1931 stimulated agricultural production and increased the intensive use of land.

Even under complete administered planning and strict price controls Chinese peasant farmers also seemed to be economically rational producers. Perkins (1966) concluded that 'the first and most essential feature is that the Chinese peasant farmer, in a fundamental sense, has generally been economically rational. Within the scope of his limited knowledge and given the high risks involved in almost any agricultural undertaking in China... he has attempted to maximise his expected return' (p 24). Lardy (1983 a & b) held the same viewpoint as Perkins.

Chou (1984) pointed out that, as long as total farm revenue is larger than total cost, or grain price is larger than the average cost, farm households will provide more to the state or to the market. This implies that Chinese farmers will spend more time on farm production in order to increase their

99

income.

Supply response in a diverse agricultural economy Chinese farmers' behaviour, however, in terms of their production frontier choices, was changed dramatically by the process of economic reform. Before economic reform, Chinese farmers were largely restricted to growing a small number of crops, such as grain and cotton. Production expansion of cash crops and livestock products was not permitted except by the state plan. Furthermore, non-farm production was in general prohibited at that time. However, after 1984 the new rural economic policies encouraged farmers to engage in multiple production and to develop rural industry. This offered increasing opportunities for non-farm work for rural labour. In addition, as income from non-farm activities was generally much higher than that of farming, farming became relatively less attractive. As a result, peasants engaged partially in farm production and partially in non-farm activities. As farm households' income now consists of two parts-farm income and non-farm income- assumptions that the household pursues farm profit only, rather than full income, are likely to be unrealistic.

Under such circumstances, farmers' decision-making is more probably influenced by multiple goals. The priority objective of a farm household may be to meet the food requirements of the household members, i.e. immediate survival needs. In addition to subsistence production, farm profit is also an explicit goal: this reflects the requirement for commercial goods and for enhanced future commercial consumption. The third goal farm households pursue is that of other non-farm income. These three goals together reflect some desired utility or full-income maximisation outcome. Thus, decision making in grain production in such a multiple agricultural economy is influenced by the possible trade-offs among these three goals, e.g., between leisure and income, own-consumption and market supply, on-farm versus off-farm employment. These interactions obviously affect labour allocation decisions between farm and off-farm activities and will ultimately determine the level of marketable surplus supply.

6.2.4   Household utility maximisation

In what follows we explore household supply behaviour within a utility maximisation framework, under two broad situations.

Situation One: farm income is the only source of farm household income. Total income of the farm household will be a function of output price and on-farm labour input. Thus, farm household income (I) will rise along with an increase in the amounts of on-farm labour (H_1) input. A rise in output prices (q) will increase both labour input and marketable surplus

100

supply.

Utility maximisation of the farm household depends on farm income (I) and leisure (L), which can be written as:

$$U=u(I, L) \dots\dots\dots\dots\dots\dots\dots\dots\dots\dots\dots\dots\dots (6.17)$$

The relationship between income and leisure can be expressed as the relationship between income and labour input. The utility function can be written as:

$$U=u(I, H_1) \dots\dots\dots\dots\dots\dots\dots\dots\dots\dots\dots (6.17_a)$$

Where U is utility function; H_1 is the amount of on-farm labour input. As farm work brings about direct disutility due to physical and mental strains, and it generates indirect disutility by reducing leisure, the utility of labour is thus negative, i.e., $U_{H1}<0$.

Differentiating equation (6.17_a), the necessary condition for maximising the utility function is:

$$dU = U_{H_1} dH_1 + U_I dI = 0 \dots\dots\dots\dots\dots\dots\dots (6.17_b)$$

From (6.17_b), we can derive

$$\frac{dI}{dH_1} = \frac{-U_{H_1}}{U_I} \dots\dots\dots\dots\dots\dots\dots\dots\dots (6.18)$$

This implies that the marginal productivity of labour will equal the ratio of the marginal utility of leisure to the marginal utility of income.

On the other hand, the utility maximisation is subject to production (or income) and labour constraints, i.e.,

$$\text{Max } U=u(I, H_1) \dots\dots\dots\dots\dots\dots\dots\dots\dots (6.19)$$

Subject to

$$Q = g(H_1, \bar{B}, \bar{C}) \dots\dots\dots\dots\dots\dots\dots\dots (6.20)$$

$$I = qQ(H_1, \bar{B}, \bar{C}) \dots\dots\dots\dots\dots\dots\dots\dots (6.21)$$

Where, Q is output of grain; $\bar{B}$ is the amount of land; $\bar{C}$ is the amount of capital inputs; q is output prices; and $\bar{B}$ and $\bar{C}$ are assumed to be constant. The equilibrium values of H_1 and I are determined by the following simultaneous equations.

$$I = qQ(H_1, \bar{B}, \bar{C}) \dots\dots\dots\dots\dots\dots\dots (6.22)$$

$$q \cdot \frac{\partial Q}{\partial H_1} = \frac{-U_{H_1}}{U_I} (\equiv Z) \dots\dots\dots\dots\dots\dots (6.23)$$

Equation (6.23) also can be written as,

$$U_I(q \cdot \frac{\partial Q}{\partial H_1}) = -U_{H_1} \dots\dots\dots\dots\dots\dots\dots\dots\dots\dots (6.23_a)$$

This means that the equilibrium point the marginal utility of income equals the marginal disutility of labour. Assuming that the household produces a single output, the profit function for maximisation can be written as

$$Max \ qQ(H_1) - \sum_{i=1}^{N} P_1 H_1 \dots\dots\dots\dots\dots\dots\dots\dots\dots (6.24)$$

Where, P_1 is the wage of farm labour; H_1 is the amount of farm labour input. The necessary condition for maximising income is

$$q \cdot \frac{\partial Q}{\partial H_1} = P_1 \dots\dots\dots\dots\dots\dots\dots\dots\dots\dots (6.25)$$

which determines the equilibrium value of H_1 as well as the equilibrium value of production (Q) and income (I). This means that the marginal value product of labour equals the wage of labour. Differentiating equation (6.25) partially with respect to output price (q),

$$\frac{\partial H_1}{\partial q} = \frac{-\partial Q / \partial H_1}{q \cdot (\partial^2 Q / \partial H_1^2)} (> 0) \dots\dots\dots\dots\dots\dots (6.26)$$

$$\frac{\partial Q}{\partial q} = \frac{-(\partial Q / \partial H_1)^2}{q \cdot (\partial^2 Q / \partial H_1^2)} (> 0) \dots\dots\dots\dots\dots\dots (6.27)[6]$$

Equations (6.26) and (6.27) imply positive effects of price changes on both output and on-farm labour supply, i.e., an increase in output prices (q) will lead to increases in both labour input and marketable surplus supply.

Situation Two: farm income is only one source of the household's full income; non-farm income is also important. This means that the following will hold.

(1) *If the hourly return to off-farm labour rises relative to that of on-farm labour, there will be a reduction in farm labour and a rise in household full income*

As the full income of the household consists of both farm income and off-farm income, full income is a function of on-farm and off-farm labour inputs at given output prices (q) and market wage (P_2).

$$I = qQ(H_1, \bar{B}, \bar{C}) + P_2(H_2) \dots\dots\dots\dots\dots\dots\dots (6.28)$$

Where P_2 is wage rate of off-farm labour; H_2 is amount of off-farm labour.

We assume that the equilibrium point of farm production is still at the point where the marginal utility of income equals the marginal disutility of labour, i.e. as given in equation 6.23.

The equilibrium values of farm labour input (H_1) and full income (I) are determined at given output price (q) and non-farm wage (P_2). Each of the equilibrium values is a function of farm income (qQ) and off-farm income (P_2H_2). Thus, the effects of the off-farm wage on farm labour demand and marketable surplus supply can be derived.

Differentiating equation (6.28) partially with respect to P_2, we can obtain the effect of changes in the off-farm wage (P_2) on farm labour input and on full income respectively.

$$\frac{\partial H_1}{\partial P_2} = \frac{-1}{\Delta} \cdot \frac{\partial Z}{\partial I}(< 0) \ldots\ldots\ldots\ldots\ldots\ldots\ldots\ldots\ldots\ldots (6.29)$$

$$\frac{\partial I}{\partial P_2} = \frac{1}{\Delta} \cdot (\frac{\partial Z}{\partial H_1} - q \cdot \frac{\partial^2 Q}{\partial H_1^2})(> 0) \ldots\ldots\ldots\ldots\ldots (6.30)^7$$

Where,

$$\Delta = Z \cdot \frac{\partial Z}{\partial I} + \frac{\partial Z}{\partial H_1} - q \cdot \frac{\partial^2 Q}{\partial H_1^2} > 0 \ldots\ldots\ldots\ldots\ldots\ldots (6.31)$$

Equations (6.29) and (6.30) show a negative effect of off-farm wage (P_2) on farm labour input and a positive effect on the household full income. Here it should be noted, from equation (6.31), that the marginal value of labour is positive, i.e.,

$$\frac{\partial}{\partial H_1} \cdot (\frac{-U_{H_1}}{U_I}) = \frac{\partial Z}{\partial H_1} > 0 \ldots\ldots\ldots\ldots\ldots\ldots\ldots\ldots (6.32)$$

$$and \ \frac{\partial}{\partial I} \cdot (\frac{-U_{H_1}}{U_I}) = \frac{\partial Z}{\partial I} > 0 \ldots\ldots\ldots\ldots\ldots\ldots\ldots (6.33)$$

$$-q \cdot \frac{\partial^2 Q}{\partial H_1^2} > 0 \ldots\ldots\ldots\ldots\ldots\ldots\ldots\ldots\ldots\ldots (6.34)$$

(2) An increase in non-farm income will reduce the marketable surplus supply, but enhance the total utility of households.

As $\dfrac{\partial Z}{\partial I}$ in equation (6.29) is positive, hence $\dfrac{\partial H_1}{\partial P_2}$ in equation (6.29) must be negative. This implies that an increase in off-farm wage (P_2) will reduce the amount of farm labour input (H_1). Furthermore, we can obtain the effects of the off-farm wage on output and utility in equations (6.35) and (6.36).

$$\frac{\partial Q}{\partial P_2} = \frac{\partial Q}{\partial H_1} \cdot (\frac{\partial H_1}{\partial P_2})(< 0) \quad \ldots\ldots\ldots\ldots\ldots\ldots\ldots\ldots\ldots (6.35)$$

$$\frac{\partial U}{\partial P_2} = U_{H_1} \cdot (\frac{\partial H_1}{\partial P_2}) + U_I \cdot (\frac{\partial I}{\partial P_2}) = U_I (> 0) \quad \ldots\ldots\ldots (6.36)^8$$

Equations (6.35) and (6.36) show that an increase in the off-farm wage will reduce the marketable surplus supply, but enhance the total utility of households.

(3) The effect of changes in grain prices on farm labour input and marketable surplus supply become indefinite due to the effects of the non-farm wage.

We must further examine the effects of changes in output prices on farm labour input and marketable supply. Differentiating equation (6.28) partially with respect to output prices (q), we can obtain,

$$\frac{\partial H_1}{\partial q} = \frac{-Q}{\Delta} \cdot \frac{\partial Z}{\partial I} + \frac{1}{\Delta} \cdot \frac{\partial Q}{\partial H_1} \quad \ldots\ldots\ldots\ldots\ldots\ldots\ldots\ldots (6.37)$$

Substituting equation (6.29) into equation (6.37), we obtain,

$$\frac{\partial H_1}{\partial q} = \frac{-Q}{\Delta} \cdot \frac{\partial Z}{\partial I} + \frac{1}{\Delta} \cdot \frac{\partial Q}{\partial H_1} = Q \cdot (\frac{\partial H_1}{\partial P_2}) + \frac{1}{\Delta} \frac{\partial Q}{\partial H_1} \overset{>}{\underset{<}{(=0)}}$$

$$\ldots\ldots\ldots\ldots\ldots\ldots\ldots (6.37a)^9$$

Analogously, we can obtain the effect of changes in prices on output supply,

$$\frac{\partial Q}{\partial q} = \frac{\partial Q}{\partial H_1} \cdot (\frac{\partial H_1}{\partial P}) = \frac{\partial Q}{\partial H_1} \cdot [Q \cdot (\frac{\partial H_1}{\partial P_2}) + \frac{1}{\Delta} \cdot (\frac{\partial Q}{\partial H_1})] \overset{>}{\underset{<}{(=0)}} .$$

$$\ldots\ldots\ldots\ldots\ldots\ldots\ldots 6.38)$$

These results imply that on-farm labour and output supply response become unpredictable due to the effect of off-farm income.

6.3   Alternative empirical approaches

6.3.1   Some basic methodological considerations

There is an intimate, symbiotic relationship between theoretical and empirical studies. The development of a fully new economic analysis requires a new empirical approach.

The theoretical analysis above suggests that marketable surplus supply is influenced by many factors, including prices, income, consumption, on-farm and off-farm labour supply. Changes in the grain price will exert various different effects on these variables with implications for medium and long-run marketable surplus supply. An empirical model must seek to incorporate these effects. This is difficult to do using traditional *ad hoc* econometric modelling. What is required is the development of an integrated framework. From the scientific as well as from the policy point of view, this really challenges agricultural economists.

6.3.2   *Major issues in estimating supply response*

Early farm household models based on neo-classical economic theory assumed that production and consumption were separable: production and consumption responses are separated into two independent sectors. There has, however, been a sharp shift away over the past three decades towards more integrated models. There were a number of attempts as early as the 1960s to capture the specific features and cultural characteristics of semi-commercial peasant economies, in order to model peasant production taking farmers' own-consumption into account (Mathur, et al., 1961; Krishnan, 1965; Krishna, 1963; Behrman, 1966, 1968; Bardhan and Bardhan, 1971, see the review in the previous chapter). It was recognised that the neo-classical assumption of the separability of production and consumption may not hold for farm households in developing countries.

More recently, household models have been developed which combine producer, consumer and labour supply decisions (Singh et al. 1986). Essentially, they assume that farm households are producers, consumers and labour suppliers. Considering production, household behaviour is assumed the same as that of a profit-maximising. Considering consumer behaviour, this differs somewhat from the behaviour that would be expected under traditional demand theory. Following an increase in the price of a commodity, the traditional demand theory would predict an unambiguous decrease in the consumption of the commodity, assuming it is a normal good. However, in household models, it is hypothesised that households will tend to increase their demand for a commodity when their income is increased following such a price increase. With respect to the relationship between consumption and supply, the important point to note is that although households' consumption and labour supply decisions depend on production, the production decision is independent of the consumption (Singh et al. 1986). In these models, the household decision is considered to be 'recursive', i.e. a one way relationship is assumed to exist between production and consumption. Essentially, production determines farm profit (a component of household income). In turn, this profit influences consumption and labour supply decisions. In other words, consumption and labour supply depend on both prices and income. However, consumption does not influence production decisions. Recursivity is a common assumption in applied farm household supply analysis (Singh et al. 1986). Using this approach, Strauss (1984) explored household food consumption and production decisions in rural Sierra Leone.

However, it would be difficult to use a similar approach to analyse the Chinese situation. The recursivity assumption is theoretically inconsistent with the Chinese reality. There is a long history of subsistence farming in China and structural reform was slow to occur, even after the rural reforms. The majority of the crops are likely to be grown for own consumption. Only part of the total quantity produced will be traded in markets. At least 200 million rural households out of a total of 215 million are currently engaged in grain production in China, but on average only about 350 kg of grain marketable surplus is supplied by each household to be traded on the market in a year (Ke 1991). Contrary to Strauss's (1984) assumption that consumption does not influence production decisions, a minimum own-consumption for food grain is probably the starting point of production decision-making in Chinese farm households.

Empirically, the assumptions in recursive models are rather restrictive particularly in the Chinese situation. Firstly, all markets are competitive and perfect. Secondly, family and hired labour are perfect substitutes in the production function. Thirdly, the disutility of on-farm and off-farm activities is identical and on-farm and off-farm work are perfect substitutes in the utility function. Thus, we conclude that in order to model Chinese household grain supply behaviour we need to take household consumption into account within a non-recursive framework.

6.3.3   The alternative approach

Lopez (1984, 1986) examined farm households' production behaviour through a non-recursive model using a dual approach. Firstly, in contrast to traditional models, this model emphasises the interdependence between production and consumption. The main linkage between the production and consumption decisions lies in the endogeneity of labour used by the household, which is dependent on changes in output price and production technology. Lopez also showed that the farm household consumption decision (demand for consumer goods), production decision and the equilibrium supply of farm labour are all dependent on parameters derived from both the consumption and production equations of the model.

Secondly, this model examines the difference between utility maximisation and profit maximisation decisions. The theoretical assumption is the absence of perfect substitutability between on-farm and off-farm work. Unlike the recursive model where producers are indifferent between alternative allocations of their time to farm and off-farm activities, Lopez analysed the labour choice problem based on a different utility connotation. In the recursive model, the profit maximisation decision was subsumed as farm income maximisation only since the shadow price of on-farm work was regarded as equal to the off-farm wage rate. In contrast, Lopez emphasises that on-farm and off-farm labour are not perfect substitutes in production; thereby, a farm household's utility does not just depend on the total labour supply but also on the allocation between on-farm and off-farm work.

Thirdly, Lopez's model jointly estimated on-farm and off-farm labour supply, consumption and profit functions simultaneously. This model allows one to separate the effect of relative prices on income, consumption and production based on the functional relationships. Therefore, it overcame most of the problems prevalent in the recursive approach.

There are a number of advantages in using such an integrated approach over the *ad hoc* econometric method. Firstly, output supply and consumption (including input) demand can be estimated in an integrated way as both are derived from the same indirect utility function. Secondly, the effects of price and income can be disentangled; being derived through a comparison of compensated and uncompensated consumption price elasticities. Thirdly, partial elasticities and the total elasticities of marketable surplus can be derived based on the functional relationships in the estimated model; these cannot be obtained from a directly estimated *ad hoc* econometric model.

6.4 Other issues

Aggregate versus disaggregate analysis The estimation will be based on an aggregate econometric model. There are three main reasons for using the aggregate approach.

Firstly, although agricultural production is now organised in many small family production units (particularly after the establishment of HPRS), economic analysis generally focuses on the aggregate supply response behaviour of these farmers. Aggregate analysis provides the broadest indication of the outcome of the complex web of interactions between farmers and the political, economic and institutional settings in which they operate.

Secondly, aggregate analysis is more appropriate for policy purposes.

The aggregation usually provides a picture of the real system in which all of the minute detail disappears, but in which the broad outline, shapes and contours stand out more clearly.

A third reason is data availability. Research on Chinese agricultural development has always been hampered by data problems: particularly for research conducted from outside the country. The data available from the State Statistical Bureau (SSB), the Ministry of Agriculture (MOA), or the Ministry of Commerce (MOC) are high level aggregated data. The data collection procedure is characterised by a high degree of aggregation based on the 'table reporting system'. This system is based on the statistical forms reported by the bottom statistical agency (the village) to the top authority (the State Statistical Bureau). Each village completes uniform tables which are prepared by the SSB and submitted to the Township Statistical Office at fixed time intervals for the first stage of aggregation. Then the township submits its aggregated data to its upper authority, the County Statistical Bureau (CSB), then to Provincial Statistical Bureau (PSB), and finally to the SSB. There is a rather high degree of aggregation in every step. This procedure produces aggregated production, consumption, output, acreage, price etc. data which are published mainly at the national level (and partly at the provincial level). Sample data are rather piecemeal. Although sample surveying started in China in the 1950s, it had always been used as a supplement to the table reporting system, at least until the 1980s. The sample survey became rather expensive due to the disintegration of collective organisation in the early 1980s. The records kept by the collective were usually not maintained by Chinese farm households. Thus, survey data about Chinese farm households is only available for discrete years: for example, the living expenses of farmers in 1983; the output of crops in 1988 published by the SSB; and a sample survey of rural households in 1991 by the General Team of the Rural Economic Survey (Wu 1995). Thus, it is very difficult if not impossible to use such sample survey data to estimate supply response of Chinese farm households.

Aggregate analysis is possible and appropriate in this study for three reasons. (a) China's grain sector has been heavily intervened by the central government. Under such circumstances, where the nature of state policy is not much different from region to region, aggregate analysis at the sectoral level is a useful tool for capturing the underlying grain supply mechanism. (b) It is difficult to specify unified or representative producers at the grassroots level in particular years, as rural institutional changes were so complicated and took many years to complete. Aggregate modelling has no such requirement and can include the institutional factors in the analysis (Wang 1995). (c) Although China is a large country with substantial

108

differences in output and weather conditions among regions, there are two points worthy of attention: firstly, subsistence farming and patterns of own-consumption are not much different from region to region - own-consumption accounted for a large proportion of production in all regions; secondly, off-farm activities and the numbers in off-farm employment have increased, albeit at different rates, in both developed and undeveloped regions in rural China.

Thus, we would argue that it is possible to use aggregate analysis for assessing the impact of own-consumption and off-farm income on marketable surplus supply in China.

Selection of the study period.   This is usually subject to the following constraints: (a) the aims of the study; (b) the availability of the data required; (c) the expected uses and implications of the results. Taking these factors into account, the period 1978 to 1992 was selected. This was a period of fairly fundamental price and institutional change.

Another reason is that before 1978 many of the data series needed were either not available or were unreliable. However, after 1978, the statistical system in China was gradually improved and outputs, yield, marketable surplus, consumption and prices began to be surveyed more comprehensively at the provincial level.

Selection of data type The study uses panel data over the fifteen year period, i.e. it combines time-series with cross-sectional data. There are two important advantages for this particular study in using such data. The first is that panel data can provide multiple observations on each individual in the sample therefore improving the efficiency of econometric estimates. The second, and more important reason, is that it can overcome or lessen the problem of multicollinearity, thus allowing the influence of each explanatory variable to be more reliably estimated. Panel data usually give a large number of sample points and more information on individual attributes; therefore, it can offer more degrees of freedom and reduce the gap between the information requirements of the model and the information provided by the data (Cheng, 1986).

However, it also should be recognised that there are disadvantages involved in utilising panel data. For example, inconsistent estimates may arise due to parameter heterogeneity between time-series and cross-sectional elements.   Nevertheless, we selected panel data because the advantages seemed greater than the disadvantages. The quality of data improved over the period, for example, sample sizes used by the SSB were considerably increased (Fan et al. 1995). Also, if the sample size is large enough and time period long enough it is possible to obtain consistent estimates of the unknown parameters, as such estimates are asymptotically normally distributed.   Our panel data contained observations on 28 provinces over fifteen years, i.e. a total of 420 observations. This number should avoid serious specification bias and provide consistent estimates.

6.5   Summary

As most econometric models of Chinese grain supply response have been constructed rather loosely from a theoretical standpoint, and as the *ad hoc* econometric approach has various limitations, it is necessary to explore alternative theoretical and empirical approaches to study Chinese farm households' supply behaviour. This chapter has sought to clarify theoretical and empirical issues and to outline an appropriate alternative approach. In particular, we have sought to establish that farm profit maximisation is an inadequate portrayal of household behaviour where there is a high level of own-consumption and where off-farm income opportunities are rapidly increasing. In this context full income or utility maximisation is more appropriate. On the empirical side we have argued that a non-recursive approach is needed. This should take account of the interdependence between household production and consumption.   Output supply and consumption (including output) demand should be derived from the same indirect utility function. Finally, we have outlined the nature of the panel data set and the main reasons for selecting it.

Notes

1. For discussions of the regularity properties of the production function see Chambers, R.G., (1988). Applied Production Analysis: A Dual Approach, Cambridge University Press.

2. In addition to the first order condition given in (5.2), solution of the profit maximisation problem requires that a second order condition and a 'total' condition be satisfied as well. See for example, Gravelle, H. and Rees, R (1981), Microeconomics, Longman. p220-224.

3. From (6.2), we can derive: $q_i = -\lambda \dfrac{\partial f}{\partial Q_i}; q_j = \lambda \dfrac{\partial f}{X_j}$ (6.7$_a$).

   Equation (6.8) can be derived when (6.7$_a$) is substituted into (6.7).

4. Such a development of Chayanov's theory was well illustrated by Ellis (1988). See Ellis's Peasant Economy (1988).

5. There is considerable evidence about peasant response behaviour in

studies such as Bauer and Yamey (1959); Barber (1960); Stern (1962); Krishna, (1963); Bateman (1965); Dean (1966) and many research reports conducted by the World Bank recently. This evidence was derived from careful empirical studies, rather than simple observations of individual behaviour.

6. At the equilibrium point Q, $\dfrac{\partial Q}{\partial H_1} > 0, and \dfrac{\partial^2 Q}{\partial H_1^2} < 0$. As q_i is always

positive, so $-q \cdot \dfrac{\partial^2 Q}{\partial H_1^2} > 0$. Thus, both equations (6.26) and (6.27) are

positive.

7. From equations (6.32),(6.33) and (6.34), it can be seen that because

$\Delta > 0$, $\dfrac{\partial Z}{\partial I} > 0$, thus, $\dfrac{\partial H_1}{\partial P_2} < 0$; and because $\dfrac{\partial Z}{\partial H_1} > 0$, and

$-q \cdot \dfrac{\partial^2 Q}{\partial H^2} > 0$, thus, $\dfrac{\partial I}{\partial P_2} > 0$. For the detailed procedure for equations

(6.29) and (6.30), (see Appendix 6A).

8. Because $\dfrac{\partial Q}{\partial H_1} > 0$, and $\dfrac{\partial H_1}{\partial P_2} < 0$, thus, $\dfrac{\partial Q}{\partial P_2} < 0$. For the detailed

procedure of equations (6.35) and (6.36); and because

$$\Theta \quad \frac{\partial H_1}{\partial P_2} = \frac{-1}{\Delta} \cdot \frac{\partial Z}{\partial I} (< 0) \quad \dots \dots \dots \dots \dots \dots \dots .(6.29)$$

$$\frac{\partial I}{\partial P_2} = \frac{1}{\Delta} \cdot (\frac{\partial Z}{\partial H_1} - q \cdot \frac{\partial^2 Q}{\partial H_1^2})(> 0) \quad \dots \dots \dots \dots \dots \dots .(6.30)$$

(6.29) and (6.30) being substituted into (6.36), we have

$$\frac{\partial U}{\partial P_2} = U_{H_1} \cdot (\frac{-1}{\Delta} \cdot \frac{\partial Z}{\partial I}) + U_I \cdot \frac{1}{\Delta} \cdot (\frac{\partial Z}{\partial H_1} - q \cdot \frac{\partial^2 Q}{\partial H_1^2}) \quad \dots (6.36a)$$

$$\Theta \frac{-U_{H_1}}{U_I} \equiv Z \therefore U_{H_1} = -U_I \cdot Z \quad \dots \dots \dots \dots \dots \dots \dots . (6.36b)$$

(6.36b) being substituted into (6.36a), we have

111

$$\frac{\partial U}{\partial P_2} = -U_I Z \cdot (\frac{-1}{\Delta} \cdot \frac{\partial Z}{\partial I}) + U_I \cdot \frac{1}{\Delta} \cdot (\frac{\partial Z}{\partial H_1} - q \cdot \frac{\partial^2 Q}{\partial H_1^2})$$

$$= \frac{U_I \cdot (Z \cdot \frac{\partial Z}{\partial I} + \frac{\partial Z}{\partial H_1} - q \cdot \frac{\partial^2 Q}{\partial H_1^2})}{\Delta}$$

$$= U_I (> 0)$$

$$(\Theta \; \Delta = Z \cdot \frac{\partial Z}{\partial I} + \frac{\partial Z}{\partial H_1} - q \cdot \frac{\partial^2 Q}{\partial H_1^2})$$

Thus, equation (6.36) >0.

9. Because $\frac{\partial H_1}{\partial P_2} < 0$, and $\frac{\partial Q}{\partial H_1} > 0$, thus equation (6.37) become unpredictable. For the detailed procedure of equation (6.38), see Appendix 6A.

Appendix

The effect of output price on farm labour input
The necessary condition for maximising income is the marginal value product of labour equals the price of labour, i.e.,

$$q \cdot \frac{\partial Q}{\partial H_1} = p_1 \; \dots\dots\dots\dots\dots\dots\dots\dots\dots\dots\dots\dots\dots \; (6.25)$$

Differentiating equation (6.25) partially with respect to prices q, we can obtain the effect of output prices (q) on farm labour supply.

$$\frac{\partial Q}{\partial H_1} + q \cdot \frac{\partial^2 Q}{\partial H_1^2} \cdot \frac{\partial H_1}{\partial q} = 0$$

$$So \; \frac{\partial H_1}{\partial q} = \frac{-(\partial Q / \partial H_1)}{q \cdot (\partial^2 Q / \partial H_1^2)} (> 0)$$

$$\Theta \; \frac{\partial Q}{\partial H_1} > 0 \; and \; \frac{\partial^2 Q}{\partial H_1^2} < 0$$

q is always positive.

$$\therefore q \cdot \frac{\partial^2 Q}{\partial H_1^2} < 0$$

$$\therefore \frac{\partial H_1}{\partial q} = \frac{-(\partial Q / \partial H_1)}{q \cdot (\partial^2 Q / \partial H_1^2)} > 0 \quad \dots\dots\dots\dots\dots\dots\dots (6.26)$$

The effect of output price on output supply
Output supply is a function of grain price (q), on-farm labour input (H_1).
Supply function can be written as
$$Q = Q[q, H_1(q)] \quad \dots\dots\dots\dots\dots\dots\dots\dots\dots\dots\dots\dots (6.27a)$$
Differentiating (6.27a) partially with respect to grain price (q), we can obtain the effect of output prices on marketable surplus supply.

$$\frac{dQ}{dq} = \frac{\partial Q}{\partial q} + \frac{\partial Q}{\partial H_1} \cdot \frac{dH_1}{dq} \quad \dots\dots\dots\dots\dots\dots\dots\dots\dots\dots (6.27b)$$

The necessary condition for maximising the output supply function is

$$\frac{\partial Q}{\partial q} + \frac{\partial Q}{\partial H_1} \cdot \frac{dH_1}{dq} = 0 \quad \dots\dots\dots\dots\dots\dots\dots\dots\dots\dots (6.27c)$$

$$\therefore \frac{\partial Q}{\partial q} = -\frac{\partial Q}{\partial H_1} \cdot \frac{dH_1}{dq} \quad \dots\dots\dots\dots\dots\dots\dots\dots\dots\dots (6.27d)$$

(6.26) being substituted into (6.27d), we have

$$\frac{\partial Q}{\partial q} = -\left(\frac{\partial Q}{\partial H_1}\right) \cdot \left(\frac{-\partial Q/\partial H_1}{q \cdot \partial^2 Q/\partial H_1}\right) = \frac{-(\partial Q/\partial H_1)^2}{q \cdot (\partial^2 Q/\partial H_1^2)} > 0 \quad \ldots\ldots\ldots (6.27)$$

Thus, equation (6.27) being substituted into (6.27b) we have

$$\frac{dQ}{dq} = \frac{\partial Q}{\partial q} + \frac{\partial Q}{\partial H_1} \cdot \frac{dH_1}{dq} > 0$$

The effect of non-farm wage on farm labour supply

The full income (I) is a function of on-farm (H_1) and off-farm labour input (H_2), output prices (q) and market wage (P_2).

$$I = qQ(H_1, \bar{B}, \bar{C}) + P_2(H_2) \quad \ldots\ldots\ldots\ldots\ldots\ldots\ldots\ldots\ldots\ldots (6.28)$$

P_2: Off-farm wage

Assume that marginal utility of income equals the marginal disutility of labour, i.e.,

$$q \cdot \frac{\partial Q}{\partial H_1} = \frac{-U_H}{U_I} (\equiv Z) \quad \ldots\ldots\ldots\ldots\ldots\ldots\ldots\ldots\ldots (6.23)$$

Thus, Z is a function of full income and on-farm labour input H_1 and non-farm wage (P_2). i.e.,

$$Z = Z[I(P_2), H_1(P_2)]. \quad \ldots\ldots\ldots\ldots\ldots\ldots\ldots\ldots\ldots\ldots (6.23a)$$

and $Z \equiv q\dfrac{\partial Q}{\partial H_1} = \dfrac{-U_{H_1}}{U_I}$

Differentiating equations (6.28) and (6.23) partially with respect to P_2 (off-farm wage), we can obtain the effect of the off-farm-wage (P_2) on farm labour supply response.

$$\frac{\partial I}{\partial P_2} = q \cdot \frac{\partial Q}{\partial H_1} \cdot \frac{\partial H_1}{\partial P_2} + 1 \quad \ldots\ldots\ldots\ldots\ldots\ldots\ldots\ldots (6.29a)$$

$$\frac{\partial Z}{\partial P_2} = \frac{\partial Z}{\partial I} \cdot \frac{\partial I}{\partial P_2} + \frac{\partial Z}{\partial H_1} \cdot \frac{\partial H_1}{\partial P_2} \quad \ldots\ldots\ldots\ldots\ldots\ldots\ldots (6.29b)$$

$$\frac{\partial Z}{\partial P_2} = q \cdot \frac{\partial^2 Q}{\partial H_1^2} \cdot \frac{\partial H_1}{\partial P_2} \quad \ldots\ldots\ldots\ldots\ldots\ldots\ldots\ldots (6.29c)$$

(6.29_c) being substituted into (6.29_b), we have

114

$$q \cdot \frac{\partial^2 Q}{\partial H_1^2} \cdot \frac{\partial H_1}{\partial P_2} = \frac{\partial Z}{\partial I} \cdot \frac{\partial I}{\partial P_2} + \frac{\partial Z}{\partial H_1} \cdot \frac{\partial H_1}{\partial P_2} \quad \dots\dots\dots\dots\dots \text{(6.29d)}$$

(6.29$_a$) being substituted into (6.29$_d$), we have

$$q \cdot \frac{\partial^2 Q}{\partial H_1^2} \cdot \frac{\partial H_1}{\partial P_2} = \frac{\partial Z}{\partial I} \cdot (q \cdot \frac{\partial Q}{\partial H_1} \cdot \frac{\partial H_1}{\partial P_2} + 1) + \frac{\partial Z}{\partial H_1} \cdot \frac{\partial H_1}{\partial P_2}$$

$$q \cdot \frac{\partial^2 Q}{\partial H_1^2} \cdot \frac{\partial H_1}{\partial P_2} = \frac{\partial Z}{\partial I} + \frac{\partial Z}{\partial I} \cdot q \cdot \frac{\partial Q}{\partial H_1} \cdot \frac{\partial H_1}{\partial P_2} + \frac{\partial Z}{\partial H_1} \cdot \frac{\partial H_1}{\partial P_2}$$

$$\therefore -\frac{\partial Z}{\partial I} = \frac{\partial Z}{\partial I} \cdot q \cdot \frac{\partial Q}{\partial H_1} \cdot \frac{\partial H_1}{\partial P_2} + \frac{\partial Z}{\partial H_1} \cdot \frac{\partial H_1}{\partial P_2} - q \cdot \frac{\partial^2 Q}{\partial H_1^2} \cdot \frac{\partial H_1}{\partial P_2}$$

$$\therefore -\frac{\partial Z}{\partial I} = \frac{\partial H_1}{\partial P_2} \cdot (\frac{\partial Z}{\partial I} \cdot q \cdot \frac{\partial Q}{\partial H_1} + \frac{\partial Z}{\partial H_1} - q \cdot \frac{\partial^2 Q}{\partial H_1^2})$$

$$\therefore \frac{\partial H_1}{\partial P_2} = \frac{-(\partial Z / \partial I)}{\Delta} = \frac{-1}{\Delta} \cdot \frac{\partial Z}{\partial I} (< 0)$$

$$\Delta = \frac{\partial Z}{\partial I} \cdot q \cdot \frac{\partial Q}{\partial H_1} + \frac{\partial Z}{\partial H_1} - q \cdot \frac{\partial^2 Q}{\partial H_1^2}$$

$$\dots\dots\dots\dots\dots\dots\dots \text{(6.29}_E\text{)}$$

$$\Theta \quad \frac{\partial}{\partial H_1} \cdot (\frac{-U_{H_1}}{U_I}) = \frac{\partial Z}{\partial H_1} > 0 \qquad \dots\dots\dots\dots\dots \text{(6.32)}$$

$$and \; \frac{\partial}{\partial I} \cdot (\frac{-U_{H_1}}{U_I}) = \frac{\partial Z}{\partial I} > 0 \qquad \dots\dots\dots\dots\dots \text{(6.33)}$$

$$-q \cdot \frac{\partial^2 Q}{\partial H_1^2} > 0 \dots\dots\dots\dots\dots\dots \text{(6.34)}$$

$$\therefore \Delta = Z \cdot \frac{\partial Z}{\partial I} + \frac{\partial Z}{\partial H} - q \cdot \frac{\partial^2 Q}{\partial H_1^2} > 0^1 \dots\dots\dots\dots \text{(6.31)}$$

$$\therefore \frac{\partial H_1}{\partial P_2} = \frac{-1}{\Delta} \cdot \frac{\partial Z}{\partial I} < 0$$

The effect of non-farm wage on full income

Equation (6.29e) being substituted into (6.29a), we can obtain the effect of off-farm wage on full income.

$$\frac{\partial I}{\partial P_2} = q \cdot \frac{\partial Q}{\partial H_1} \cdot (\frac{-1}{\Delta} \cdot \frac{\partial Z}{\partial I}) + 1$$

$$= \frac{1}{\Delta} \cdot (-q \cdot \frac{\partial Q}{\partial H_1} \cdot \frac{\partial Z}{\partial I} + \Delta)$$

$$= \frac{1}{\Delta} \cdot (-q \cdot \frac{\partial Q}{\partial H_1} \cdot \frac{\partial Z}{\partial I} + \frac{\partial Z}{\partial I} \cdot q \cdot \frac{\partial Q}{\partial H_1} + \frac{\partial Z}{\partial H_1} - q \cdot \frac{\partial^2 Q}{\partial H_1^2})$$

$$= \frac{1}{\Delta} \cdot (\frac{\partial Z}{\partial H_1} - q \cdot \frac{\partial^2 Q}{\partial H_1^2}) > 0 \ldots\ldots\ldots\ldots(6.30)$$

$$[\Theta \ -q \cdot \frac{\partial^2 Q}{\partial H_1^2} > 0, \therefore \frac{1}{\Delta} \cdot (\frac{\partial Z}{\partial H_1} - q \cdot \frac{\partial^2 Q}{\partial H_1^2}) > 0]$$

The effect of the non-farm wage on marketable surplus supply

$$\frac{\partial Q}{\partial P_2} = \frac{\partial Q}{\partial H_1} \cdot (\frac{\partial H_1}{\partial P_2})(< 0) \ldots\ldots\ldots\ldots\ldots\ldots\ldots (6.35)$$

$$\Theta \ \frac{\partial H_1}{\partial P_2} < 0 \ldots\ldots\ldots\ldots\ldots\ldots\ldots\ldots .(6.29)$$

$$\therefore \frac{\partial Q}{\partial P_2} = \frac{\partial Q}{\partial H_1} \cdot \frac{\partial H_1}{\partial P_2} < 0$$

The effect of the non-farm wage on utility

$$\Theta \ U = u(H_1, I) \ldots\ldots\ldots\ldots\ldots\ldots\ldots\ldots\ldots\ldots .$$
.(6.16a)

$$I = q \cdot Q(H_1, \bar{B}, \bar{C}) + P_2(H_2) \ldots\ldots\ldots\ldots\ldots .(6.28)$$

Differentiating (6.16a) and (6.28) partially with respect to P_2, we have

$$\frac{\partial U}{\partial P_2} = U_{H_1} \cdot (\frac{\partial H_1}{\partial P_2}) + U_I \cdot (\frac{\partial I}{\partial P_2}) = U_I (> 0) \ldots\ldots\ldots\ldots .(6.36)$$

$$\Theta \quad \frac{\partial H_1}{\partial P_2} = \frac{-1}{\Delta} \cdot \frac{\partial Z}{\partial I}(< 0) \ldots\ldots\ldots\ldots\ldots\ldots (6.29)$$

116

$$\frac{\partial I}{\partial P_2} = \frac{1}{\Delta} \cdot (\frac{\partial Z}{\partial H_1} - q \cdot \frac{\partial^2 Q}{\partial H_1^2})(> 0) \quad \ldots\ldots\ldots\ldots\ldots\ldots (6.30)$$

(6.29) and (6.30) being substituted into (6.36), we have

$$\frac{\partial U}{\partial P_2} = U_{H_1} \cdot (\frac{-1}{\Delta} \cdot \frac{\partial Z}{\partial I}) + U_I \cdot \frac{1}{\Delta} \cdot (\frac{\partial Z}{\partial H_1} - q \cdot \frac{\partial^2 Q}{\partial H_1^2}) \ldots (6.36a)$$

$$\Theta \frac{-U_{H_1}}{U_I} \equiv Z \therefore U_{H_1} = -U_I \cdot Z \ldots\ldots \quad \ldots\ldots (6.36b)$$

(6.36b) being substituted into (6.36a), we have

$$\frac{\partial U}{\partial E} = -U_I Z \cdot (\frac{-1}{\Delta} \cdot \frac{\partial Z}{\partial I}) + U_I \cdot \frac{1}{\Delta} \cdot (\frac{\partial Z}{\partial H_1} - q \cdot \frac{\partial^2 Q}{\partial H_1^2})$$

$$= \frac{U_I \cdot (Z \cdot \frac{\partial Z}{\partial I} + \frac{\partial Z}{\partial H_1} - q \cdot \frac{\partial^2 Q}{\partial H_1^2})}{\Delta}$$

$$= U_I (> 0)$$

$$(\Theta \ \Delta = Z \cdot \frac{\partial Z}{\partial I} + \frac{\partial Z}{\partial H_1} - q \cdot \frac{\partial^2 Q}{\partial H_1^2})$$

The effect of output price on farm labour input

$$\Theta \ I = qQ(H_1, \bar{B}, \bar{C}) + P_2(H_2) \ \ldots\ldots\ldots \quad \ldots\ldots\ldots\ldots .(6.28)$$

$$q \cdot \frac{\partial Q}{\partial H_1} = \frac{-U_H}{U_I} (\equiv Z) \ \ldots\ldots\ldots\ldots\ldots\ldots\ldots\ldots (6.23)$$

Differentiating the equation (6.28) and (6.23) partially with respect to output prices q, we obtain

$$\frac{\partial I}{\partial q} = Q + q \cdot \frac{\partial Q}{\partial H_1} \cdot \frac{\partial H_1}{\partial q} \ \ldots\ldots\ldots\ldots\ldots\ldots\ldots\ldots .(6.37a)$$

$$\frac{\partial Z}{\partial q} = \frac{\partial Q}{\partial H_1} + q \cdot \frac{\partial^2 Q}{\partial H_1^2} \cdot \frac{\partial H_1}{\partial q} \ \ldots\ldots\ldots\ldots\ldots\ldots .(6.37b)$$

$$\Theta \ Z = z(H_1, I)$$

$$\therefore \frac{\partial Z}{\partial q} = \frac{\partial Z}{\partial I} \cdot \frac{\partial I}{\partial q} + \frac{\partial Z}{\partial H_1} \cdot \frac{\partial H_1}{\partial q} \ \ldots\ldots\ldots\ldots\ldots\ldots .(6.37c)$$

(6.37a) and (6.37b) being substituted into (6.37c), we have

117

$$\frac{\partial Q}{\partial H_1} + q \cdot \frac{\partial^2 Q}{\partial H_1^2} \cdot \frac{\partial H_1}{\partial q} = \frac{\partial Z}{\partial I} \cdot \frac{\partial I}{\partial q} + \frac{\partial Z}{\partial H_1} \cdot \frac{\partial H_1}{\partial q}$$

$$= \frac{\partial z}{\partial I} \cdot (Q + q \cdot \frac{\partial Q}{\partial H_1} \cdot \frac{\partial H_1}{\partial q}) + \frac{\partial Z}{\partial H_1} \cdot \frac{\partial H_1}{\partial q}$$

$$= \frac{\partial Z}{\partial I} \cdot Q + \frac{\partial Z}{\partial I} \cdot q \cdot \frac{\partial Q}{\partial H_1} \cdot \frac{\partial H_1}{\partial q} + \frac{\partial Z}{\partial H_1} \cdot \frac{\partial H_1}{\partial q}$$

$$\Theta \frac{\partial Z}{\partial I} \cdot q \cdot \frac{\partial Q}{\partial H_1} \cdot \frac{\partial H_1}{\partial q} + \frac{\partial Z}{\partial H_1} \cdot \frac{\partial H_1}{\partial q} - q \cdot \frac{\partial^2 Q}{\partial H_1^2} \cdot \frac{\partial H_1}{\partial q} = \frac{\partial Q}{\partial H_1} - \frac{\partial Z}{\partial I} \cdot Q$$

$$\therefore \frac{\partial H_1}{\partial q} \cdot (\frac{\partial Z}{\partial q} \cdot q \cdot \frac{\partial Q}{\partial H_1} + \frac{\partial Z}{\partial H_1} - q \cdot \frac{\partial^2 Q}{\partial H_1^2}) = \frac{\partial Q}{\partial H_1} - Q \frac{\partial Z}{\partial I}$$

$$\therefore \frac{\partial H_1}{\partial q} = -\frac{Q}{\Delta} \cdot \frac{\partial Z}{\partial I} + \frac{1}{\Delta} \cdot \frac{\partial Q}{\partial H_1} = Q \frac{\partial H_1}{\partial E} + \frac{1}{\Delta} \cdot (\frac{\partial Q}{\partial H_1}) \underset{<}{\overset{>}{(=0)}} \dots\dots\dots\dots\dots\dots (637_e)$$

$$(\Theta \frac{-1}{\Delta} \cdot \frac{\partial Z}{\partial I} = \frac{\partial H_1}{\partial E})$$

(b) The effect of output prices on marketable surplus supply

$$\frac{\partial Q}{\partial q} = \frac{\partial Q}{\partial H_1} \cdot (\frac{\partial H_1}{\partial q}) = \frac{\partial Q}{\partial H_1} \cdot [Q \cdot (\frac{\partial H_1}{\partial P_2}) + \frac{1}{\Delta} \cdot (\frac{\partial Q}{\partial H_1})] \underset{<}{\overset{>}{(=0)}} \dots. (6.38)$$

$$(\Theta \frac{\partial H_1}{\partial P_2} < 0)$$

118

7 Household own-consumption and grain marketable surplus

7.1 Introduction

The previous chapter pointed to the importance of an integrated theoretical and empirical framework which takes account of the interdependence between household production and consumption. The main aim of this chapter is to explore the effect of household own-consumption on grain marketable surplus supply in China. The analytical section explores the different effects of farm income and household full income on consumption and marketable surplus supply; this is done by estimating and comparing uncompensated and compensated consumption price elasticities. The effects of own-consumption on marketable surplus supply are then considered through a comparison of conditional and unconditional supply price elasticities. Before proceeding to the model specification and estimation we briefly review some salient features of the farm household sector in China.

7.2 Chinese farm households

Distinctive features of Chinese farm households are: (a) a significant proportion or usually the totality of their labour input is supplied by family members; (b) the return from family farming is only one source of a household's full income, non-farm income may also be an important factor; (c) in many cases a substantial part of the family farm output is orientated to satisfy directly the household's own consumption necessities. In1992, over 65 per cent [1] of the total grain output was consumed by producers themselves as a staple food (China Statistical Yearbook, 1993, p609). Thus, grain production and marketing are influenced by own-consumption, labour supply and income choices made by households seeking to maximise utility.

These features have important implications for modelling Chinese farm households. Firstly, farm labour input (supply) is provided by farm family members. Labour use (demand) is also decided by the farm household. Hence, there exists a farm labour supply and demand schedule for the farm household. The internal equilibrium shadow price of family labour is given by the intersection of these two schedules. The demand schedule for family labour is dependent on production technology, output and labour prices. The supply schedule is dependent on household's preferences, on-farm income, other non-farm income, output and input prices faced by the household. Changes in any of these variables will affect the labour supply schedule. Thus there exists a fairly complex set of relationships between output prices, returns to farm and non-farm labour, farm production, own-consumption and marketable surplus supply. Even if a household does not trade any grain in the market, the price of grain will nevertheless signal the opportunity cost of own-consumption. The reader is referred to Strauss (1984a) who used a Slutsky-type compensation framework to isolate a pure price effect on own-consumption from the indirect (income) effect of the price change. In what follows we develop a modelling framework which seeks to analyse and disentangle some of these effects and interdependencies.

7.3   Model specification

7.3.1   Outline of the model

The underlying model is intended to analyse the effects of output prices, own-consumption and labour supply on grain marketable surplus supply. In order to capture better the complexity of household supply behaviour, the model integrates household production and consumption decisions into a unified framework.

The theoretical model starts by considering a utility function which includes three consumer goods, i.e. grain own-consumption, leisure and other non-farm goods. The household's consumption is dependent upon the household's preference, prices of consumer goods and family income. It is subject to budget and time constraints. Income obtained from farm work is linked to farm profit, which is a function of output price and farm labour input. The profit function is defined as a conditional profit function, i.e., conditional on the household's labour use. Thus, the model consists of two functional forms, namely, a utility function and a profit function. The utility function represents the consumption side of the model and the conditional profit function represents production side. As leisure consumption is directly related to labour supply, the household's labour supply behaviour can be analysed through the utility function.

The major linkage between production and consumption in the model lies in the endogeneity of the labour used (leisure consumption as well as own-consumption) by households. Changes in output prices (exogenous) would lead to changes in labour used (and own-consumption) by the household in both the utility function and the conditional profit function.

In order to derive demand equations for leisure and consumption goods, the utility function is replaced by an indirect utility function based on standard duality theory. The indirect utility function reflects the fact that utility depends indirectly on prices and income via the maximisation process. The indirect utility function is subject to the same budget constraint as in the utility function. In the budget constraint, output price (rather than the retail price) is used as the own-consumption price. The daily net return per unit of on-farm family labour is used to represent a leisure price (opportunity cost). The total expenditure on consumption goods, including leisure, cannot be larger than the household's full income, using Becker's concept of full income. A set of consumption equations for leisure and consumer goods can then be derived from the indirect utility function by using Roy's identity. Meanwhile, a set of conditional output supply and input demand equations can be derived from the conditional profit function by using Hotelling's lemma.

The distinctive feature of this model is that both consumption and production responses are derived from the same indirect utility function by differentiating production and consumption behaviour equations. Therefore, the model captures the interdependence of production and consumption decisions.

In the estimated model, the Gorman Polar Form (GPF) is chosen as an indirect utility function and the Generalised Leontief Form is chosen as a conditional profit function. These equations are jointly estimated and the various supply and demand responses can then be derived.

In order to facilitate the theoretical analysis and empirical estimation, three assumptions are made.

Assumption One: In order to isolate the net effect of changes in labour supply, an assumption of no fixed inputs in production was made. This is mainly for simplicity of analysis. Farm profit is defined as a function of output price and on-farm labour input, i.e., $\pi = \pi(q;H_1)$. Thus, capital and land factors are omitted from the profit function. Farm return ($\bar{\pi}$) can be viewed as a daily net return per unit of on-farm family labour. If the assumption of no fixed inputs is relaxed, farm profit will be a function of output price (q), on-farm labour input (H_1), capital (K) and land (L), i.e.,

$\pi = \pi(q;H_1, K, L)$. Farm return ($\bar{\pi}$) would then be a gross profit i.e.

a return to all factors (labour, capital and land). π could no longer be treated as a daily net return per unit of on-farm family labour, which would make the analysis of labour effects rather difficult.

Assumption Two: In order to obtain a linear budget constraint for the household's utility maximisation problem, an assumption of constant returns to scale is made. If both the objective function and the budget constraints are non-linear, then standard duality theory cannot be applied. This assumption is rather restrictive, but it is necessary.[2] The assumption of constant returns to scale with no fixed factors of production means that the profit function is homogeneous of degree one in H_1, i.e., $\pi(q;H_1)=H_1\bar{\pi}(q)$. Thus, labour use decides the scale of production. This allows us to isolate the net effect of prices on farm labour, and the net effect of farm labour supply on-farm production (supply).

Assumption Three: The theoretical analysis is based upon the tacit assumption that prices of consumer goods including the leisure 'commodity' are constant. This is mainly for the purpose of simplifying the empirical estimation. If these prices are not assumed to be constant, the whole analysis and estimation would become rather complex. A detailed discussion about the assumption of a constant price (wage) for leisure will be given later.[3]

These simplifications have the advantage of substantially reducing the difficulties in empirical estimation of the model; they also facilitate comparative statics analysis. We now specify the model in detail.

7.3.2 The theoretical model

Assume for simplicity that there is no off-farm employment in this model and that the household maximises its utility which is a function of consumer goods (X_i) and farm income: the latter is related to labour input (H_1). The utility function can be written as follows.[4]

$$U=U(X_i, H_1) \dots\dots\dots\dots\dots\dots\dots\dots\dots\dots\dots\dots\dots\dots(7.1)$$

It is assumed that the household maximising such a utility function is subject to budget (7.1_a) and time (7.1_b) constraints.

$$P_iX_i \leq \bar{\pi} H_1 + r \dots\dots\dots\dots\dots\dots\dots\dots\dots\dots\dots\dots(7.1_a)$$
$$H_1 \leq H \dots\dots\dots\dots\dots\dots\dots\dots\dots\dots\dots\dots\dots\dots(7.1_b)$$

Where U is a utility function; P_i are prices of consumer goods consumed by the household; X_i are commodities including agricultural staples and non-agricultural goods consumed by households; $\bar{\pi}$ is the 'daily net return per unit of on-farm family labour', i.e., gross farm return per unit of labour minus total cost (excluding farm labour) per unit of labour.[5] H_1 is time spent on farm work; r is other non-labour income; $\bar{\pi} H_1$ is on-farm income;[6] H is total activity time available.

The budget constraint (7.1_a) says that total expenditure (P_iX_i) cannot be larger than the total revenue (farm income $\bar{\pi} H_1$ and other non-labour income, r). The time constraint (7.1_b) means that the household cannot allocate more time to on-farm work than the total time available to the household.

As income obtained from farm work is related to farm profit, the utility function (7.1) also is subject to a production constraint. For the sake of simplicity, capital and land factors in the production function are omitted, and the farm profit is conditional on farm labour input. The conditional profit can be expressed as a function of output price (q) and on-farm labour input (H_1), i.e., $\pi=\pi(q; H_1)$. The profit function is defined as follows:

$$\pi(q; H_1) \equiv \text{Max} \{q^T, Q:(Q;H_1) \in \bar{T}\} \dots\dots\dots\dots\dots\dots(7.2)$$

where $q \equiv (q_1, q_2,...q_n)$ is a vector of output and input prices; $Q \equiv (Q_1, Q_2,...Q_n)$ is a vector of outputs and inputs; and $\bar{T}$ are the production possibilities set, i.e., the set of all output and input combinations which the household can produce given the state of knowledge.

Furthermore, the assumption that the production technology exhibits Constant Returns to Scale (CRS) and that there are no fixed factors of production, means that the profit function is homogeneous of degree one in H_1. The profit function can be decomposed as follows.

$$\pi(q; H_1)=H_1 \bar{\pi} (q) \dots\dots\dots\dots\dots\dots\dots\dots\dots\dots\dots(7.2a)$$

Where π (q) is linear homogeneous in q.[7]

The utility maximisation (7.1) can be expressed in a more convenient form as a function of consumer goods (X_i) and leisure (H-H$_1$), i.e.,

$$\text{Max } U(H\text{-}H_1; X_i) \dots\dots\dots\dots\dots\dots\dots\dots\dots\dots\dots\dots\dots\dots(7.3)$$

subject to

$$P_iX_i + \overline{\pi}\,(H\text{-}H_1) \leq \overline{\pi}\,H + r \equiv Y \dots\dots\dots\dots\dots\dots\dots\dots\dots\dots\dots(7.3_a)$$
$$H\text{-}H_1 \geq 0,\ X_i \geq 0 \dots\dots\dots\dots\dots\dots\dots\dots\dots\dots\dots\dots\dots\dots\dots\dots(7.3_b)$$
$$(H\text{-}H_1) \leq H \dots\dots\dots\dots\dots\dots\dots\dots\dots\dots\dots\dots\dots\dots\dots\dots\dots(7.3_c)$$

Where (H-H$_1$) is leisure which replaces labour input (H$_1$) in the model (7.3). In the constraint equation (7.3$_a$), the left-hand side shows total household 'expenditure' on consumer goods: P_iX_i is the expenditure on consumption commodities (including grain and other non-farm goods) consumed by the household and $\overline{\pi}$ (H-H$_1$) is the expenditure on leisure (the household's 'purchase' of its own time). The right hand side is full income (Y).[8]

It should be noted that leisure (H-H$_1$) in the utility function (7.3) is treated as a 'consumer good' (not utility) which in this sense is just like any other consumer commodity (X_i). Thus, $\overline{\pi}$ may be seen as a price of leisure consumed by family members.[9]

Introducing leisure into the utility function (7.3) has two main advantages over the specification in (7.1). Firstly, (7.3) is defined over the non-negative orthant and thus the corresponding budget constraint may be defined using non-negative prices and positive income. Secondly, (7.3) is a standard maximisation problem with a linear constraint provided that $\overline{\pi}$ (q) is known and that constraint (7.3$_c$) is not binding. Thus, standard duality theory can be applied in order to derive equations for commodity demand and labour supply.

The 'full income' used in this model is Becker's (1965) concept of household full income. Full income equals the value of its time endowment, plus the value of farm profit and any other non-labour income. In the concept of full income used here, the value of the stock of time ($\overline{\pi}$ H) owned by the household is explicitly recorded[10]. As long as the commodity price (p) and the wage rate for farm work ($\overline{\pi}$)[11] are constant, full income (Y) would have a meaningful interpretation. This is because Y gives the monetary income achievable if all the time available were devoted to work.

This achievable income is 'spent' on the commodities either directly through expenditures on goods or indirectly through the foregoing of income (leisure).

The full income approach provides a meaningful resource constraint as it combines goods and time constraints into a single overall constraint. It also incorporates a unified treatment of all substitutions of non-pecuniary for pecuniary income because time can be converted into goods through monetary income. If full income is denoted by Y and if the total earnings foregone are denoted by $\bar{\pi}$ (H-H$_1$), how much is earned or foregone depends on the consumption set chosen in the utility function. For example, the less leisure chosen the larger the monetary income (See Becker, 1976, p92-93, 117).

The household's utility maximisation in the utility function (7.3) is clearly focused on the consumer choice of a given bundle of consumer goods at a given income constraint. As to leisure itself an increase implies a rise in utility. In other words, leisure may always have a positive effect on utility, i.e., $\dfrac{\partial U}{\partial L} > 0$. The more leisure, the more utility you have. On the other hand, labour input (income) also always has a positive effect on utility as an increase in work days implies an income rise, therefore an increase in utility. However, either leisure or labour utility (or total utility) is subject to total time available constraints. Any increase in one side (leisure) implies a decrease in the other (labour input). Total utility analysis must take these constraints into account simultaneously. If income is more important than leisure, a decrease in leisure will mean an increase in utility. In mathematical terms, $dU = \dfrac{\partial U}{\partial L} dL + \dfrac{\partial U}{\partial H_1} dH_1$, $\dfrac{\partial U}{\partial L} < 0$. Thus, in this situation, utility maximisation behaviour was reflected in a consumption choice by the household. The household can choose the level of consumption of agricultural and non-agricultural goods, as well as consumption of the leisure 'commodity' which is related to the total labour input into agricultural production.[12]

The use of a constant farm wage rate to value leisure is mainly for the purpose of simplifying the empirical applications. The question is whether the commodity price (p) and farm wage rate($\bar{\pi}$) can be regarded as constant in the theoretical and empirical models.

If the production technology exhibits diminishing return to scale, i.e., the production function is a curve rather than linear, it may not make sense to use a constant wage to value leisure because a reduction in labour input may not imply a decline in profit. Pollack and Watcher (1975) have shown that commodity shadow prices and leisure prices are endogenous to the levels of commodity and leisure demand. This is because the shadow prices of commodities are not only dependent on input prices, but also on household production technology and consumption preferences.

Thus, the price of leisure, in theory, should be a marginal wage rather than an average, as the marginal, not average wage rate (or prices) is more relevant to behaviour. Therefore, the causality between wage and labour supply can be better captured. Moreover, using the average wage rate rather than the marginal rate might overstate full income in (7.3_a) if the marginal wage was below the average wage.

One possible approach to resolving this problem is that we could define the marginal wage rate, i.e., $\bar{\pi}^* \equiv \dfrac{\partial \pi(q, H_1)}{\partial H_1}$, as the shadow price of labour expressed as $P_i X_i + \bar{\pi}^*(H - H_1) \leq \bar{\pi}^* H + r \equiv Y$ in the budget constraint of equation (7.3a), rather than the average wage rate. The estimating technique should, however, take care of the endogeneity of $\bar{\pi}^*$ and Y by estimating H-H$_1$(p$_i$, $\bar{\pi}^*$, r, Y) and X(p$_i$, $\bar{\pi}^*$, r, Y) simultaneously since Y is dependent on r and $\bar{\pi}^*$. There are several problems in following this approach. Firstly, the marginal wage ($\bar{\pi}^*$) is unobservable and we can derive them only through indirect estimation using the profit function $\pi(q; H_1)$. Secondly, indirect estimation of the marginal wage ($\bar{\pi}^*$) must be done under the condition that the production technology has constant returns to scale, i.e., $\pi(q; H_1) = H_1 \bar{\pi}(q)$. Only under this assumption, can full income be calculated. Otherwise the 'full income' (Y) would not be calculated correctly. Thirdly, even if it is possible to calculate the marginal wage rate ($\bar{\pi}^*$), its value would not correspond to the 'true' value which the household actually considered in its utility maximising decisions. For example, the level of H$_1$ actually chosen by households may reflect possible errors of optimisation. Under such a circumstance, the marginal wage ($\bar{\pi}^*$) variable, which depend on the levels of H$_1$, may also be incorrectly measured. Thus, the relevant shadow prices considered by households are also unknown.

It is virtually impossible to use the marginal wage rate in estimating demand for leisure and commodities in equation (7.3) due to the complexity

126

of the budget constraint. Under such circumstances, these functions could only be arbitrarily specified and hence the linkage between the theoretical and estimating equations would be lost.

However, if the production technology has constant return to scale, using a constant wage to value leisure does make sense. Lancaster (1966) and Becker (1965) concluded that, if the assumption of constant returns to scale was made, the prices of commodities faced by the household as consumers were exogenous to the level of commodities demanded. Thus, Becker (1965) used the average wage rate to value 'time income'. In the utility model (7.3) , it is assumed that the production technology has no fixed factors of production and constant returns to scale.[13] It is also assumed that producers are price takers, and that the wage rate received by household members working on farm is given by the market (an assumption made in all farm household models); the wage rate as the price of leisure is exogenous to the model.[14] This implies that the budget constraint would be linear rather than a curve. Thus, farm income is dependent on on-farm labour input (H_1) as the farm profit function is homogeneous of degree one in H_1. On-farm labour use determines the scale of production. It is possible, therefore, to use the wage rate to value leisure.

As the assumption of constant returns to scale and no fixed inputs holds, the standard duality theory can be introduced. An indirect utility function

$G(p, \bar{\pi}, r, Y)$ is defined as follows.

$$G(p, \bar{\pi}, r, Y) \equiv MaxU(H-H_1, X_i) \dots\dots\dots\dots\dots\dots\dots\dots (7.4)$$
$$i=1,2.$$

Where p is prices of consumer goods; $\bar{\pi}$ is leisure prices; r is other income and Y is full income. The advantage of the indirect utility function is that the explanatory variables, originally quantities (X_i) in the utility function, are now replaced by prices and income $(\bar{\pi}, p, r, Y)$ variables. The optimal solution in equation (7.4) can be viewed equivalently as resulting from minimising expenditure subject to a given utility level or maximising utility subject to a given expenditure level.

$$Max\ U(H-H_1, X_i) \equiv Min\{G(\bar{\pi}, p, r, y)\} \dots\dots\dots\dots\dots\dots (7.5)$$

subject to

$$P_iX_i + \bar{\pi}\ (H-H_1) \leq \bar{\pi}\ H+r \equiv Y \dots\dots\dots\dots\dots\dots\dots\dots (7.5_a)$$
$$H-H_1 \geq 0,\ X_i \geq 0 \dots\dots\dots\dots\dots\dots\dots\dots\dots\dots\dots\dots (7.5_b)$$
$$(H-H_1) \leq H \dots\dots\dots\dots\dots\dots\dots\dots\dots\dots\dots\dots\dots\dots (7.5_c)$$

Where G is continuous, quasi-convex in p, $\bar{\pi}$ and Y, non-increasing in p, non-increasing in Y and homogeneous of degree zero in p, $\bar{\pi}$ and Y.

From (7.5) it is possible to derive Marshallian demand functions for leisure (H-H$_1$,) and consumer goods (X$_i$) using Roy's identity ($X = -\dfrac{\partial G \big/ \partial p}{\partial G \big/ \partial Y}$).

$$H - H_1 = -\frac{\partial G \big/ \partial \bar{\pi}}{\partial G \big/ \partial Y} = \Phi(p,\bar{\pi},r,Y)^{15} \quad \dots\dots\dots\dots\dots\dots\dots\dots \quad (7.6)$$

$$X_i = -\frac{\partial G \big/ \partial P_i}{\partial G \big/ \partial Y} = \omega(p,\bar{\pi},r,Y) \quad \dots\dots\dots\dots\dots\dots\dots\dots \quad (7.7)$$

Meanwhile, a set of conditional supply and factor demand equations can be derived from the conditional profit function (7.2a). Using Hotelling's Lemma, the output supply function is:

$$Q_i(q_i;H_1) = H_1 \frac{\partial \bar{\pi}(q_1)}{\partial q_1} \quad \dots\dots\dots\dots\dots\dots\dots\dots\dots\dots\dots\dots \quad (7.8)$$

i=1,....n.

If there are n outputs in (7.8), there are n output supply equations Q$_n$(p, q, r, Y). When a commodity is an input, then -Q$_i$ is defined as inputs.

7.3.3   The limitations of using a constant price (wage) to value leisure

Theoretically, causality between the wage rate and labour supply runs not only from the net wage to hours worked, but also in reverse. However, constant prices cannot of course reflect causality between prices and supply. Thus, there are certainly limitations in using a constant price (wage) to value leisure in capturing farm labour supply behaviour.

Firstly, the use of a constant price must be done under a strict assumption of constant returns to scale. If this is not the case, then it becomes a strong assumption.

Secondly, if this assumption is relaxed there would be problems with this approach as the relationship between wage and labour supply is mutually dependent. For example, if prices increase, labour's marginal revenue product will increase, which will lead to an increase in labour input. Meanwhile, a rise in labour input would reduce labour's marginal physical (revenue) product given diminishing (or increasing) returns to scale. This leads to a decline (or increase) in labour input. Using a constant rate may not capture such a mutually dependent relationship.

Thirdly, using a constant wage to estimate labour supply may not reflect the household's labour supply preference. For example, if individuals with low income prefer work to leisure, they will accept work at a relatively low wage rate. Hence, using observed data on labour supply to estimate the effect of wages on farm work may be biased downwards (Deaton and Bauer, 1989).

More recently, some researchers have used marginal wages instead of constant wages to estimate labour supply. The marginal wage was based on an estimated marginal product through estimating a production function. Once marginal products are estimated, they can be used as proxies for shadow wages to estimate labour supply. For example, Jacoby (1993) used shadow wages for men and women in the Peruvian Sierra to estimate a labour supply function. The shadow wages were derived from the estimated marginal products of a farm production function. Using data from rural India, Skoufias (1994) estimated the marginal productivities (shadow wages) of family labour by using the Cobb-Douglas production function. The estimated shadow wages and income were then used as variables in a structural model of labour supply. Using the Peruvian Living Standards Survey data, Newman and Gertler (1994) extended Lopez's (1986) model to estimate labour supply responses, taking account simultaneously of labour flow between the on-farm and off-farm sectors. Three types of equation were modelled: (a) the marginal rate of substitution between leisure and other goods consumption; (b) a market wage function; and (c) the marginal return to farm work function. The latter is derived from a restricted farm profit function (conditional on family labour use) under the assumption that family farm labour, output price and quasi-fixed inputs are constant. The marginal farm returns functions were estimated without using farm income data. This marginal return provides an estimate of the shadow wage of an individual's farm labour. If the individual also works off-farm then the shadow wage equals the market wage.

The important difference between the use of the marginal wage and the use of the observed market wage (constant) is that the marginal (shadow) wage and income are endogenous variables in the model. Any changes in the exogenous variables in the system will lead to new optimal values for the Lagrange multiplier (λ) and that in turn leads to a new optimal value for the marginal (shadow) wage rate. On the empirical side, the reason for using the marginal wage rate is that causality between wage and labour supply can be better captured.

However, as mentioned above, the marginal approach to estimate labour supply is not without its problems: (a) identifying this marginal wage (unobservable) is not easy; (b) the results of the estimated marginal wage may be questionable due to the difficulties in measuring input and input quality accurately; (c) estimating marginal products directly raises the data requirements considerably; and (d) it may not actually make any sense if the estimated marginal wage is much different from the observed market wage. Given these difficulties, one might well be suspicious of estimated results of marginal productivity studies. Perhaps this is one of the reasons why this approach has not been more widely used.

7.3.4   The estimating model

Functional forms for the indirect utility function and for the conditional profit function Using the indirect utility function G (p, $\bar{\pi}$, r, Y) and farm profit function $\pi(q;H_1)$, one can obtain the household's demand for consumption goods (X_i), as well as the net output supply response as discussed above. Thus, it is necessary to postulate appropriate functional forms for G(p, $\bar{\pi}$, r, Y) and $\pi(q; H_1)$. A Gorman Polar Form (GPF) indirect utility function is specified as an appropriate functional form from which the on-farm labour supply, own-consumption and marketable surplus supply elasticities can be derived. The GPF was introduced by Gorman (1953), explicated by Blackorby et al. (1978) and further applied by Lopez (1984). The GPF indirect utility function can be written as

$$G(p,\bar{\pi},r,Y) = \frac{Y - \Lambda(p,\bar{\pi},r,Y)}{\varphi(p,\bar{\pi},r,Y)} \quad \dots\dots\dots\dots\dots\dots\dots (7.9)$$

Where, Λ and φ are continuous, concave, non-decreasing and positively homogeneous of degree one in $\bar{\pi}$, and Y (Blackorby et al, 1978). Blackorby and Lopez proposed a Constant Elasticity of Substitution (CES) form for the $\varphi(p,\bar{\pi}$, r,Y) function and Generalised Leontief form for the $\Lambda(p,\bar{\pi}$, r,Y) function. The component $\Lambda(.)$ in (7.9) belongs to the class of flexible functional form that may be interpreted as a second order approximation to any arbitrary function.

130

$$G = \frac{Y - \sum\limits_{i=1}^{3}\sum\limits_{j=1}^{3} \delta_{ij} P_i^{\frac{1}{2}} P_j^{\frac{1}{2}}}{[\sum\limits_{i=1}^{3} \alpha_i P_i^{\rho}]^{\frac{1}{\rho}}} \quad\dots\dots\dots\dots\dots\dots\dots\dots (7.10)$$

Using Roy's identity ($X = -\dfrac{\partial G / \partial p}{\partial G / \partial Y}$), we can derive the demand equations in expenditure form as follows.

$$S_i = \frac{\alpha_i P_i^{\rho}[Y - \sum\limits_{i=1}^{3}\sum\limits_{j=1}^{3} \delta_{ij} P_i^{\frac{1}{2}} P_j^{\frac{1}{2}}]}{\sum\limits_{i=1}^{3} \alpha_i P_i^{\rho}} + P_i[\sum\limits_{j=1}^{3} \delta_{ij}(\frac{P_j}{P_i})^{\frac{1}{2}}] \quad\dots\dots\dots (7.11)$$

Where i=1,...3; $S_1 \equiv P_1(H-H_1)$; $S_2 \equiv P_2 X_2$; $S_3 \equiv P_3 X_3$; S_i are functions of a set of prices; Y is full income; p_1, p_2 and p_3 represent daily net return per unit of on-farm family labour ($\bar{\pi}$) and prices of own-consumption for food grain and other non farm consumption goods respectively; X_1 X_2 and X_3 represent leisure (H-H_1), amount of own-consumption for food grain, and for non-farm consumption goods respectively; and where $\delta_{ij} = \delta_{ji}$, for all i≠j. α_i δ_{ij} and ρ are parameters that need to be estimated. From (7.11), we can derive three demand equations, i.e., leisure consumption (S_1), own-consumption for food (S_2) and other non-farm goods consumption (S_3).

At the same time, output supply and input demand equations can be derived. These are based on the assumption that profit is a function of output price (q_1) and on-farm labour input (H_1), i.e. $\pi = \pi(q_1; H_1)$ and that the profit function is homogeneous of degree one in H_1 i.e., $\pi = H_1 \pi (q_1)$. The Generalised Leontief form is chosen as a conditional profit function as follows.

$$\pi(q, H_1) = H_1(\sum\limits_{i=1}^{3}\sum\limits_{j=1}^{3} b_{ij} q_i^{\frac{1}{2}} q_j^{\frac{1}{2}}) \quad\dots\dots\dots\dots\dots\dots\dots\dots (7.12)$$

The effect of output prices on farm profit is derived by differentiating equation (7.12) partially with respect to the output price (q_i). Thus, net profit response is:

$$\frac{\partial \pi}{\partial q_i} = H_1 [\sum_{j=1}^{3} b_{ij} (\frac{q_j}{q_i})^{\frac{1}{2}}] \quad \dots\dots\dots\dots\dots\dots\dots\dots\dots\dots\dots (7.12_a)$$

Using Hotelling's Lemma $\dfrac{\partial \pi}{\partial q_i} = Q_i$, the output supply and input demand functions (Q_i) per unit of family labour can be obtained from equation (7.12_a).

$$\frac{Q_i}{H_1} = \sum_{j=1}^{3} b_{ij} (\frac{q_j}{q_i})^{\frac{1}{2}} \quad \dots\dots\dots\dots\dots\dots\dots\dots\dots\dots\dots\dots (7.12_b)$$

where, Q_1, Q_2, and Q_3 represent respectively marketable surplus supply, labour demand and capital inputs; q_1, q_2 and q_3 are prices of output, labour and capital input respectively; and $b_{ij} = b_{ji}$ for all $i \neq j$. b_{ij} are parameters which need to be estimated.

The GPF is chosen as it is consistent with the use of aggregate data.[16] The Generalised Leontief form for the profit function has been arbitrarily selected from a number of alternative flexible functional forms. Thus, using Blackorby et al. (1978) and Lopez's (1984) approach, it becomes possible to examine the effect of changes in grain prices and income on own-consumption, and the effect of own-consumption and farm labour supply on marketable surplus supply. The advantage of this approach is that the interdependence of production and consumption decisions is emphasised and both consumption and supply responses are derived from the same indirect utility function (7.10).

7.3.5 The econometric model

In order to estimate the parameters of the indirect utility function and profit function, it is necessary to assume a stochastic structure for (7.11) and (7.12). It is assumed that the disturbances are additive and normally distributed with zero means and a positive semi-definite variance-covariance matrix sum. Thus, if (7.11) and (7.12) are written in a more compact notation and if the disturbance terms are added, the econometric model is

(1) $S_1 = f_1(p_1, p_2, p_3, Y) + \mu_1$
(2) $S_2 = f_2(p_1, p_2, p_3, Y) + \mu_2$
(3) $S_3 = f_3(p_1, p_2, p_3, Y) + \mu_3$
(4) $Q_i = H_1 \phi^i (q) + v_i \quad i = 1...3 \quad \dots\dots\dots\dots\dots\dots (7.13)$

132

The expenditure equations (S_i) in (7.13) are assumed to be dependent on the actual profit per day of work (p_1), rather than on the optimal or expected price level[17]. Under the assumptions used (constant returns to scale and no fixed factors of production), it should be noted that p_1 ($\equiv \bar{\pi}$) is now used as a variable rather than a function. As the variable p_1 is exogenous independent of household's preferences (independent of H_1), its use as an explanatory variable represents no inconvenience. The interpretation of p_1 as an explanatory variable in the expenditure equations is that households are able to estimate the returns to their labour time spent on the family farm based on information about output prices, input prices and knowledge of the production technology they have available. Based on their estimation of the returns to their work on their own farm, a cost of living index (p) and households full income (Y), they decide upon their optimal expenditures i.e. to maximise their utility.

The demand and supply equations in (7.13) need to be jointly estimated despite the fact that there are no parameter restrictions across them. The theoretical model discussed in section 7.3 above recognises the fact that both production and consumption decisions are taken by one individual or household. A logical implication of such a model is that the errors made by farmers in their production decisions will be correlated with their utility maximisation errors. Given the non-recursive nature of the model, the estimates of the demand equations would not only be asymptotically inefficient but also inconsistent if the production and consumption sectors are not jointly estimated. This represents an important difference from the conventional model which ignores the interactive effects between production and consumption, based on the hypothesis of independent production and consumption decisions. Thus, three net supply equations (Q_1, Q_2, Q_3), together with three consumption demand equations (S_1, S_2, S_3) derived from equation (7.13) are jointly estimated using a Full Information Maximum Likelihood (FIML) method.

7.3.6 Some comparative statics

Using model (7.13) the interdependence between the consumption and production sides of the model is now examined by considering the effects of changes in output prices, farm income and full income on the household's own-consumption and on-farm labour supply. Furthermore, the effects of changes on the consumption side eg. own-consumption and leisure (on-farm labour supply) on marketable surplus supply can be examined. Thus, having estimated parameters in the system of equations (7.13) it is possible to estimate various elasticities and the standard comparative statics results can be derived in the usual manner.

The effect of changes in grain price and income on consumption   In order to measure the effect of own-consumption of grain on marketable surplus, it is necessary to examine the effect of price and income changes on own-consumption.

The uncompensated consumption price elasticities (η^*) reflect the direct effect of price changes on consumption under the assumption that income is constant. They can be derived directly by differentiating the demand function (7.11) partially with respect to grain prices. The full income elasticities ($\dfrac{\partial X_i^c}{\partial Y} \cdot \dfrac{Y}{X_i^c}$) of own-consumption are also derived directly from equation (7.11).

The compensated consumption price elasticities (η) assume that full income is allowed to vary. They can be derived from the values for η^* obtained from the (7.11) by inserting the income effects as follows (Barnum and Squire 1979 a & b).

$$\frac{\partial X_i^c}{\partial q_j} = \frac{\partial X_i^c}{\partial q_j}\Big|_{dY=0} + \frac{\partial X_i^c}{\partial y} \cdot \frac{\partial y}{\partial q_j} \quad \dotsfill \quad (7.14)$$

In elasticity terms, we have

$$\frac{\partial X_i^c}{\partial q_j} \cdot \frac{q_j}{X_c^c} = \frac{\partial X_i^c}{\partial q_j} \cdot \frac{q_j}{X_i^c}\Big|_{dy=0} + \frac{\partial X_i^c}{\partial y} \cdot \frac{\partial y}{\partial q_j} \cdot \frac{q_j}{X_i^c} \quad \dotsfill \quad (7.14_a)$$

The first term is the usual uncompensated elasticity of consumption of goods (i) with respect to the price (j). The second term is the income effect in elasticity form. $\dfrac{\partial Y}{\partial q_j}$ expresses the effect of output price on income.

This can be calculated by using Hotelling's Lemma $\dfrac{\partial \pi}{\partial q_j} = X_i$.[18] Following a price rise, the effect of income on own-consumption can be seen by comparing the elasticities η^* and η.

The effects of on-farm labour supply and own-consumption on marketable surplus supply   Having estimated own-consumption price elasticities, it is then possible, in two stages, to explore the effects of on-farm labour supply and own-consumption on marketable surplus.

In stage one, marketable surplus supply response with respect to grain prices is examined under the assumption that on-farm labour supply is constant; this is defined as the 'net supply response'. Then, the effect of on-farm labour supply on marketable surplus is introduced; this is defined as the 'conditional supply response' because own-consumption is assumed to be constant. The effects of on-farm labour on marketable surplus supply can be examined through a comparison between the 'net' and 'conditional' elasticities. In stage two, the effects of own-consumption are taken into account through estimation of 'unconditional marketable surplus supply elasticities', i.e., own-consumption is allowed to vary. The net effect of own-consumption can be examined through a comparison between the 'conditional' and 'unconditional' elasticities.

Thus, the 'net' supply elasticities are examined first with on-farm labour supply held constant. They can be derived directly from equation (7.12$_b$) as follows.

$$\frac{\partial Q_i}{\partial q_1}\frac{q_i}{Q_i} = \frac{\partial \left(Q_i/H_1\right)}{\partial q_1}\frac{q_1}{\left(Q_i/H_1\right)} \quad\dots\dots\dots\dots\dots (7.15)$$

The conditional marketable surplus supply elasticities allow on-farm labour to vary, but own-consumption of food grain holds constant. They can be derived directly by differentiating equation (7.12$_b$) partially with respect to the output prices (q_i) as follows.

$$\frac{\partial Q_i}{\partial q_1}\frac{q_i}{Q_i} = \frac{\partial \left(Q_i/H_1\right)}{\partial q_1}\frac{q_1}{\left(Q_i/H_1\right)} + \left(\frac{\partial H_1}{\partial p_1}\frac{p_1}{H_1}\right)\frac{q_iQ_i}{p_1H_1} \quad\dots\dots\dots (7.16)^{19}$$

The first term on the right hand side is the net supply response and the second term is the effect of labour on output supply.

If the effect of own-consumption is taken into account simultaneously, supply response is 'unconditional'; this is reflected in unconditional marketable surplus supply elasticities. It is possible to derive such an elasticity from the relationship between total output and marketable surplus, i.e. S=Q-C. Where S is marketable surplus; Q is total output and C is own-consumption.

As noted before, the conditional output supply is a function of output price (q), farm return ($\bar{\pi} = p_1$) and on-farm labour force (H$_1$).

135

$$Q_i = f(q, H_1) = H_1 \cdot \frac{\partial p_1}{\partial q_1} \dots\dots\dots\dots\dots\dots\dots\dots\dots\dots (7.17_a)$$

The own-consumption is a function of output prices (q_1), income (y) and rural population (H).

$$C_i = g(q, y(q), H) \dots\dots\dots\dots\dots\dots\dots\dots\dots\dots (7.17_b)$$

The total output supply (Q_i) is the sum of marketable surplus (S_i) and own-consumption (C_i).

$$Q_i = S_i + C_i \dots\dots\dots\dots\dots\dots\dots\dots\dots\dots\dots\dots (7.17_c)$$

or, $S_i = Q_i - C_i \dots\dots\dots\dots\dots\dots\dots\dots\dots\dots\dots (7.17_d)$

Thus, the effect of output price on the marketable supply can be derived by differentiating equation (7.17_d) partially with respect to output prices (q_1). The effect of output prices on the marketable supply is written as

$$\frac{\partial S_i}{\partial q_j} = \frac{\partial Q_i}{\partial q_j} - \frac{\partial C_i}{\partial q_j} = H_1 \cdot \frac{\partial(\frac{\partial p_1}{\partial q_i})}{\partial q_j} + \frac{\partial p_1}{\partial q_1}\frac{\partial H_1}{\partial p_1}\frac{\partial p_1}{\partial q_1} - H \cdot (\frac{\partial C}{\partial q_1} + \frac{\partial C}{\partial Y}\cdot\frac{\partial Y}{\partial q_1})$$

$$\dots\dots\dots\dots\dots\dots\dots\dots\dots\dots\dots (7.17_e)$$

The marketable surplus supply response is expressed in elasticity terms as

$$\frac{\partial S_i}{\partial q_j}\cdot\frac{q_j}{S_i} = \frac{\partial(\frac{Q}{H_1})}{\partial q_j}\cdot\frac{q_j}{(\frac{Q}{H_1})}\cdot\frac{Q}{S_i} + \frac{\partial H_1}{\partial p_1}\frac{p_1}{H_1}\frac{q_1 Q}{p_1 H_1} - (\frac{\partial C}{\partial q_1}\cdot\frac{q_j}{C})\cdot\frac{C\cdot H}{S_i} - (\frac{\partial C}{\partial Y}\frac{Y}{C})\frac{C\cdot H}{S_i}\frac{q_j}{Y}\cdot\frac{\partial Y}{\partial q_1}\cdot$$

$$\dots\dots\dots\dots\dots\dots\dots\dots\dots\dots\dots (7.17_f)$$

The first two terms on the right hand side of (7.17_f) are conditional elasticities. The second two terms are the effect of own-consumption. Thus the effect of own-consumption on marketable surplus can be seen by comparing the conditional and unconditional elasticities.

7.4 The data

Aggregated time series data were available over a relatively short time period of 15 years, therefore it was felt that the data set should be augmented with cross sectional data. As a result, pooled data for twenty-eight provinces over a period of 15 years was used. There were approximately 420 observations for each variable. The use of purely cross-sectional data was precluded due to lack of price variation. The main variables required to estimate the model were: (a) the number of days of on-farm work; (b) the farm net income; (c) the amount of own-consumption of food grains and their prices; (d) the amount of consumption of non-farm goods and their prices; (e) the amount of marketable surplus supply and inputs together with their prices. There were no data available for days of on-farm work, input price and on-farm labour prices. However, it was possible to use indirect procedures to calculate these variables from other information. The sources for the major variables are outlined below.

The number of days of on-farm work, on-farm income and on-farm labour prices The SSB provided the average net return to on-farm work per person per year, the number of days on-farm work was calculated by dividing average net return to on-farm work per person per year by labour price per day.

The annual data on farm return per capita in farm households derived from sample surveys carried out by the SSB. The main advantage of this data is the full coverage of the incomes of rural households.

There are no data available on labour price and number of days on farm work in China's statistical census. Census data for total labour costs and total number of days of labour used in production were available. Hence, the average labour price per day could be derived, i.e., the total labour cost per tonne divided by the number of days of farm labour used per tonne.

Price data The mixed average purchase price, rather than the retail price, was used to represent the own-consumption price for food grain. Grain price in China can be broadly divided into two categories: the free market price and the state purchase price. The state purchase price took several forms during the reform period. These were: (a) quota purchase price; (b) above quota purchase price; (c) proportional price; and (d) negotiated price i.e. the price paid by the government to buy grain from the free market. There are major problems in obtaining and using free market price data. These prices at provincial level were never published by the SSB or the MOA. Data on free market prices at the national level obtained from different sources were not consistent as there are many government organisations involved in collecting data (Wu and Kirke, 1994). Compared to the total amount of grain marketed, the amount traded through the free market is quite low. Indeed free market sales typically have been below 20 per cent of the total traded grain. The government itself purchases the majority of marketable surplus. Furthermore, the sellers of grain in the free market are usually not the farmers themselves but dealers. The latter collect grain from farm households at a lower price and sell in the free markets in towns and cities. Therefore the published free market prices are usually not farm gate prices (Du, 1995). Thus, the grain price used in this study was the mixed average purchase price at the national level[20]. This weighted average producer price was based on the state contract, negotiated and free market prices and reflected a range of standards, varieties and grades for each commodity. We believe it was an appropriate variable to reflect price trends and changes over the reform period.

Expenditure on own-consumption of food grain, other non-food consumer goods and their prices   Own-consumption of grain in this study refers to the quantity of direct household consumption of food grain per capita excluding that grain used for feeding animals and for seed. The per capita measure adjusts for population changes. The own-consumption data came from the Chinese Statistical Yearbooks. The expenditure on food consumption per capita was calculated as the quantity of consumption of food grain per capita multiplied by grain purchase prices.

There are no data available on the quantity and prices of individual items of non-farm commodities purchased by households. However, it was possible to derive a total non-farm consumer expenditure per capita by deducting per capita food expenditure from total expenditure. This non-farm expenditure was used to replace the non-farm consumer price in the model. [21]

Inputs and input prices   There were also no data available for individual input items and input prices. However, cost-of-production data were available on aggregate capital and current inputs per hectare: these provided the necessary data on inputs. Input prices used were the capital and current input unit cost. i.e. aggregate total capital and current input cost per hectare divided by total output per hectare.

Marketable surplus   The marketable surplus is the amount of grain sold in markets. It includes the quantity of grain purchased by the state commercial agencies i.e. the state quota (before 1984) contract purchases (after 1984), above-quota purchases (before 1984) and negotiated purchases (after 1984). It also includes the amount traded by farmers directly to non-agricultural households. Thus, the total marketable surplus was the sum of the government purchase and non-government trade in the free market, i.e. the total amount of social purchase.

In order to remove the influences of inflation during the period 1978-92, prices and income data related to both supply and consumption were deflated based using the rural consumption price index (1978=100).

The data used in the study are summarised in Table 7.1.

Table 7.1
Summary of the data used in the model

	Unit	Mean	Standard deviation	Minimum	Maximum
On farm return (p_1)	Yuan/Day/ Capita	1.35	0.49	0.68	3.38
Own-consumption price (p_2)	Yuan/Kg	0.34	0.15	0.26	3.45
Non-farm goods expenditure (p_3)	Yuan/Day/ Capita	0.28	0.17	0.00	1.35
Output prices (q_1)	Yuan/Tonne	339.93	153.57	263.00	3445.00
Labour cost prices (q_2)	Yuan/Tonne	156.01	74.00	51.99	535.53
Capital and current input cost (q_3)	Yuan/Tonne	125.29	71.90	43.52	493.63
Expenditure on leisure ($H-H_1$) (L_5)	Yuan/Year/ Capita	287.34	155.20	46.53	889.41
Expenditure on own-consumption for food grain (L_6)	Yuan/Year/ Capita	87.77	48.17	61.37	1040.73
Expenditure on non-farm goods (E_5)	Yuan/Year/ Capita	102.56	62.20	1.11	487.69
Net marketable supply for grain (S_1)	Tonne/Year/ Capita	0.44	0.50	0.59	2.99
Net labour demand (S_2)	Year/Capita	0.16	0.18	0.02	1.15
Net capital and current input demand (S_3)	Yuan/Year/ Capita	1.32	1.41	0.07	8.21
Full income (Y)	Yuan/Year/ Capita	574.95	213.04	276.83	1404.04
Own consumption of food per capita (OC)	Tonne/Year/ Capita	0.25	0.03	0.19	0.37
Net output of grain (Q_1)	Tonne/Year/ Capita	1.66	3.55	0.63	70.62
Net labour demand (Q_2)	Year/Capita	0.51	0.75	0.08	14.26
Net capital and current input demand (Q_3)	Yuan/year/ Capita	5.22	6.12	0.66	97.04

Data limitations   Research on Chinese agricultural development has always been hampered by data problems. This is particularly so for research conducted outside the country. Data issues have been given close attention in this work as these can have important influences on the specification and estimation of the empirical model.

The main data used in this study relate to households' income, consumption, expenditure, grain production, marketable surplus and other non-agricultural commodities. These were obtained from various issues of the Chinese Statistical Yearbook and Rural Statistical Yearbook of China published by the SSB in the period 1978-92. In the past these data were collected for a few key years only. However, it was possible to make up any short-fall using data published by the United States Department of Agriculture (USDA) in 1993.[22] The USDA source provides a relatively complete national as well as provincial data series for major grain production and consumption in China. These data mainly come from Chinese official data.

The data on peasant consumption, income and expenditure used in this study come primarily from surveys of households conducted by the SSB. A wide variety of survey data is collected by the SSB every year. The quality of survey data has improved due to the fact that the number of households surveyed has increased over time. A nation-wide unified survey system was organised in the middle 1950s, but was suspended during the Cultural Revolution; it commenced again in 1978. In 1982, China began to publish provincial aggregate per capita data from these surveys. Since then, the number of rural households surveyed has increased each year; the 1990 sample included 66,960 households (Fan et al. 1995). The SSB directs the surveys, prints the survey forms and trains the survey staffs. The surveys are used to collect data on rural population, labour force, grain production, commodity prices, household income, consumption and expenditures. For example, output estimates are compiled at local levels (county and prefecture) to enable the SSB to compile provincial and national totals.

However, not all agricultural data are reported by the SSB, for example provincial level cost-of-production data. The SSB only provided national-level cost data in the Rural Statistical Yearbook. The provincial level data used in this study are from sources in China's Ministry of Agriculture (MOA): this is also survey data. The major potential weakness of these data is accuracy because the size of samples used is not very clear. Furthermore, it is not clear whether the sample selection was random. In most cases, where there are overlaps the MOA data (for example population, income etc) corresponded closely to the SSB data. Therefore the MOA was considered acceptable as a secondary source. This may be a source of error.

Output data used in this study were those published by the SSB. Output data from other sources are not always consistent with the data published by the SSB. For example, Ministry of Commerce (MOC) are approximately 1.5 per cent higher than those published annually in recent years by the SSB (Wu, 1995). The data published by the SSB have traditionally been regarded as the official source.

Marketable surplus data were also obtained from the SSB. However, the data published by the SSB exclude grain trade among farmers, due to difficulties of collection. The marketable surplus grain defined by the SSB includes purchases by the State Grain Bureau, the State Commercial Department, the Rural Supply and Marketing Co-operatives, firms and sales from between farmers to urban residents. It does not include grain trade among farmers, which has become more important. Precise estimates are not available but the Rural Household Survey shows average grain

140

purchases from non-state sources (including trade in rural areas) to be 3 per cent of grain output in 1986 (Wu, 1995).

Clearly, there are considerable data limitations imposed on this study. Some of the data have had to be calculated indirectly as they simply did not exist in the required form. All of this can, of course, introduce errors into the estimation procedure. Nevertheless, we have endeavoured to minimise this problem through very careful scrutiny of the data and their sources. We concluded that the data used were the best available and were acceptable for the purposes of this study.

7.5   Results

7.5.1   Model estimation

The parameters for marketable surplus and the total output were obtained through joint estimation of the consumption equation (7.11) and the supply equation (7.12$_b$). There is one degree of freedom for the parameters of the CES function which can be exhausted by any suitable normalisation (Blackorby et al. 1978, Lopez 1984). The normalisation chosen is that the share parameter α_2 is equal to one. The results are given in Table 7.2 (a) and (b) respectively.

In the marketable surplus case, eleven of the fifteen parameters were significant at the 1 per cent level. Four of the parameters were not significant. In the total output case, eleven of the fifteen parameters were significant at the 1 per cent level and two at the 5 per cent level of significance. Two of the parameters were not significant. As there are no intercepts in this model system, the conventional R^2 may no longer be

appropriate. Instead a generalised $\bar{R}^2$, proposed by Baxter and Cragg (1970), was adopted to test the goodness-of-fit of the model. This coefficient is defined as follows:

$\bar{R}^2 = \{1 - \exp[2*(L_o - L_{max})/N]\}$. Where L_o is the value of the logarithm of the likelihood function when all parameters are constant to zero; L_{max} is its maximum value when all coefficients are allowed to vary and N is the total

number of observation. The generalised $\bar{R}^2$ was 0.99 in both the marketable surplus case and the total output case, indicating a high goodness-of-fit in both these cases.

Table 7.2

Estimated parameters of marketable surplus and total output

(a) The Marketable Surplus Model		
Coefficient	Estimate	T-Statistic
α_1	2.94	26.14 **
α_2	1	(-)
α_3	-0.06	-24.81**
δ_{11}	184.48	57.25 **
δ_{12}	-12.56	-0.58
δ_{13}	4.22	10.23 **
δ_{22}	332.04	12.24 **
δ_{23}	-7.86	-7.80 **
δ_{33}	357.30	400.10 **
Rho	-0.05	-2.16 **
b_{11}	0.08	0.99
b_{12}	-0.13	-13.71**
b_{13}	0.70	15.05 **
b_{22}	0.37	11.98 **
b_{23}	-0.93e-02	-0.55
b_{33}	0.06	0.34
Value of likelihood function	-4626.11	
Number of observations	420	
Generalised $\bar{R}^2$	0.99	

Table 7.2 (cont.)

(b) The Output Supply Model		
Coefficient	Estimate	T-Statistic
α_1	2.77	19.23 **
α_2	1	-
α_3	0.25	19.77 **
δ_{11}	198.33	35.77 **
δ_{12}	-10.56	-1.22 *
δ_{13}	-5.64	-2.06 **
δ_{22}	296.81	36.72 **
δ_{23}	32.45	15.67 **
δ_{33}	360.20	145.97 **
Rho	0.02	1.15 *
b_{11}	-0.18	-0.12
b_{12}	-0.55	-31.21 **
b_{13}	3.52	18.57 **
b_{22}	1.27	4.22 **
b_{23}	0.08	2.22 **
b_{33}	-1.96	-0.91

Value of likelihood function	-7065.45
Number of observations	420
Generalised $\bar{R}^2$	0.99

** and * denote significance at the 1 per cent and 5 per cent levels respectively

The null hypothesis of symmetry model, i.e., ($\delta_{ij} = \delta_{ji}$,) for all i≠j imposed on the model was tested by estimating restricted ($\delta_{ij} = \delta_{ji}$) and unrestricted models. Using a likelihood ratio test, the calculated χ^2 was 14.42 in the marketable surplus case and 13.56 in the total output case. Both of them were higher than the critical value 5 per cent at the level of significance (12.59) and lower than the 1 per cent value (16.81) with six degrees of freedom. Thus, the null hypothesis of symmetry ($\delta_{ij} = \delta_{ji}$) for all i≠j was rejected at the 5 per cent level but not at the 1 per cent level of significance. The reader should note that regional dummies were used in an early run of the model. However, the parameters were not significant and the dummies were dropped from the final run.

The estimated parameters from the model were used to calculate various elasticities to analyse the effects of changes in prices and income on labour supply and own-consumption. We then proceed to examine, amongst other things, the effects of own-consumption on farm labour demand and marketable surplus supply.

7.5.2   Uncompensated consumption elasticities

If we assume that household's full income is constant, the effects of changes in grain prices and farm income on consumption can be observed by estimating uncompensated consumption elasticities (η^*), using the analytical procedure outlined in section (7.3). These elasticities are presented in Table 7.3.

The effects of grain price on on-farm labour supply are positive in both the marketable surplus and the total output cases. Farm income also has positive effects on on-farm labour supply. The effects of both grain price and farm income on own-consumption are negative. This suggest that farm households' own-consumption of food grain declined as the opportunity cost of own-consumption increased. Thus, an increase in grain price led to a decrease in own-consumption. The results also suggest that on-farm labour supply increased as a result of increases in grain prices and farm incomes.

Table 7.3
Uncompensated on-farm labour supply and own-consumption elasticities at the sample mean

(a) The Marketable Surplus Case		Farm income	Own-consumption grain prices	Other non-farm consumption price
On-farm labour supply	η^*	1.026	0.379	0.356
Own-consumption	η^*	-0.070	-0.802	-0.328
(b) The Total Output Case				
On-farm labour supply	η^*	0.987	0.362	0.370
Own-consumption	η^*	-0.751	-0.133	-0.246

7.5.3 Full income elasticities of consumption and labour supply

Full income, however, had a different impact on both the farm labour supply and own-consumption. The elasticities of own-consumption and farm labour supply with respect to full income are derived directly from equation (7.11). The results are presented in Table 7.4.

Table 7.4
The elasticities of on-farm labour supply and own-consumption with respect to full income at the sample mean

	Full Income	
	(Marketable Surplus Case)	(The Total Output Case)
On-farm labour supply	-1.020	-0.516
Own-consumption	0.886	0.717

In contrast to the effects of farm income, full income had quite a different impact on farm labour supply and own-consumption. The effect on farm labour supply was negative, i.e., farm labour supply declined as full income increased. In the marketable surplus case, the impact of full income on labour supply was strong (elasticity of -1.02). The effect of full income on food own-consumption was also quite strongly positive, which is consistent with observed increases in household consumption from relatively low levels in the early years of the study.

7.5.4 Compensated labour and consumption elasticities

In estimating the compensated elasticities we relax the assumption that full income is constant and allow it to vary. The elasticities, which are based on equation (7.14a) are shown in Table 7.5.

Table 7.5
Compensated on-farm labour and own-consumption elasticities at the sample mean

(a) The Marketable Surplus Case		Farm income	Own-consumption grain prices	Other non-farm consumption price
On-farm labour supply	η	0.912	0.266	0.243
Own-consumption	η	0.030	-0.704	-0.230
(b) The Total Output Case				
On-farm labour supply	η	0.588	-0.037	-0.029
Own-consumption	η	-0.417	0.202	0.090

By comparing the compensated and uncompensated values, i.e. Tables 7.3 and 7.5 it seems clear that if we allow for full income changes we see a positive effet on own-consumption. Firstly, the negative effects of farm income on own-consumption were reduced. In the marketable surplus case, the own-consumption income elasticity changed sign from negative (-0.07) to positive (0.03). In the case of total output, the negative elasticity was reduced from -0.75 to -0.42. This is due to the fact that an increase in full income leads to a rise in own-consumption which weakened the negative effect of the farm income change alone on own-consumption. Secondly, the negative effect of prices on own-consumption responses also declined. The two negative consumption price elasticities in the marketable surplus case were reduced from -0.80 to -0.70 and from -0.33 to -0.23 respectively. In the total output case, these consumption elasticities actually changed signs from -0.13 to 0.20 and from -0.24 to 0.09. These results indicate that own-consumption of both food grain and other non-farm goods by the Chinese farm household increased following increases in household full income.

Comparing the values for labour supply responses η^* and η in Tables (7.3) and (7.5), shows the negative effect of full income on on-farm labour supply. In the marketable surplus case, labour supply elasticity with respect to farm income reduced from 1.03 to 0.91. Labour supply elasticity with respect to grain price and other consumer price also reduced from 0.38 to 0.27 and from 0.36 to 0.24 respectively. In the total output case, labour supply elasticity with respect to farm income reduced from 0.99 to 0.59.

These results imply that on-farm labour supply declined as farm households' full income increased. Farm labour supply response with respect to grain price and non-farm consumption price (total output case) actually changed signs from 0.36 to -0.04 and from 0.37 to -0.03 respectively as a result of the full income effect..

7.5.5   Net supply and demand elasticities

In order to explore the impact of on-farm labour changes on marketable surplus and output supply, the net supply and demand responses can be examined as a first step. The net supply and demand elasticities assumed that farm labour supply is held constant following changes in prices. These elasticities were defined in equation (7.15) and estimates are presented in Table 7.6.

Table 7.6
The net supply and demand elasticities at the sample mean

(a) The Marketable Surplus Case	Output Price	Labour Price	Capital and Current Input Cost
Marketable surplus supply	-0.381	-0.102	0.484
Family labour demand	-0.616	0.642	-0.026
Capital and current input demand	0.437	-0.004	-0.433
(b) The Total Output Case			
Output supply	-0.531	-0.111	0.643
Family labour demand	-0.787	0.721	0.066
Capital and current input demand	0.555	0.008	-0.563

The net supply elasticities in both the marketable surplus and total output cases are negative (-0.38 and -0.53 respectively); however, it should be remembered that farm labour supply is being held constant in this estimating procedure.

The labour demand elasticities with respect to output price in both the marketable surplus and total output cases are also negative. This is consistent with the negative supply price elasticities as a decline in marketable surplus and total output would result in a decrease in on-farm labour demand. The effect of capital and current input cost on marketable supply is positive. It is difficult to explain this result. This may have

147

arisen because unit input cost was used rather than input prices as these were not available. Thus, the positive relationship may have been due to an increase in the volume of input usage.

7.5.6   The conditional supply and demand elasticities

The conditional supply and demand elasticities are presented in Table 7.7. These take account of changes in farm labour but hold own-consumption of grain constant. They were defined in equation (7.16).

Table 7.7
The conditional supply and demand elasticities at the sample mean

(a) The Marketable Surplus Case	Output Price	Labour Price	Capital and Current Input Cost
Marketable surplus supply	0.334	-0.224	-0.325
Family labour demand	1.331	0.521	-0.834
Capital and current input demand	0.278	-0.125	-1.241
(b) The Total Output Case			
Output supply	2.122	-0.487	-2.432
Family labour demand	1.866	0.345	-3.009
Capital and current input demand	3.208	-0.368	-3.638

As expected, the effect of output prices on both marketable surplus and total output supply are positive, but the supply price response in the total output case (elasticity 2.12) is much stronger than that in marketable surplus case (elasticity 0.33). The possible explanation for this is the nature of grain production in rural China. Generally, farm households can only provide a rather small proportion of total grain output to the market; the rest is for their own-consumption. The farm household is both a grain producer and consumer. It may respond positively in total grain production to output price changes. A rise in output results in an increase in household income, which in turn may lead to higher own-consumption of grain. Thus, compared with total output response, marketable surplus response is much less elastic.

The effects of output prices on family farm labour demand, in both the marketable surplus and total output cases, are also positive and strong (elasticities 1.33 and 1.87 respectively). This reflects the fact that an increase in output and marketable surplus supply depends, to a large extent,

148

upon a rise in labour input. This result is consistent with a positive marketable surplus price elasticity. Similarly, capital and current input demand responses with respect to output prices in both the marketable surplus and the total output cases are positive although much stronger in the total output case. Both the family labour and the capital and current demand elasticities with respect to capital input prices are negative and relatively strong (-3.01 and -3.64 respectively in the total output case). In contrast, the capital and current demand elasticity with respect to labour price is relatively small (only -0.37) in the total output case. This suggests a complementary rather than a substitute relationship between capital and labour during the period of the study.

7.5.7   *The unconditional supply and demand elasticities*

The conditional and unconditional supply and demand elasticities are presented for comparative purposes in Table 7.8.   The unconditional elasticities allow own-consumption of grain to vary and were defined in equation (7.17).

Table 7.8
The conditional and unconditional supply and demand elasticities at the sample mean

	Marketable surplus supply	Family labour demand	Capital and current input demand
Output Prices γ^*	0.334	1.331	0.278
γ	-0.838	-0.240	-0.045

γ^* denotes conditional and γ unconditional elasticities

The differences in signs and magnitude between the conditional and unconditional cases indicate the significant effects of own-consumption. The unconditional price elasticity of marketable surplus is negative and relatively large (-0.84), after taking simultaneous account of own-consumption. This may be compared with the positive conditional value (0.33). The unconditional farm labour demand and capital input demand also changed their signs from positive to negative. These results suggest a strong negative effect during the study period of own-consumption on marketable surplus in Chinese households' responses to output price changes. Thus, is spite of the fact that production and marketing have become increasingly commercialised in the reform era, the subsistence nature of production and own-consumption behaviour remain fundamental factors determining Chinese grain producers' supply behaviour.

7.6   Summary

In this chapter we have mainly examined the effects of own-consumption on the marketable surplus of food grain while grain prices were rising. The theoretical analysis showed the significance of an integrated framework that takes changes in full income, own-consumption and marketable surplus into account simultaneously.   A set of empirical supply and consumption responses were obtained from such an integrated model.   The results indicate the value of such models in reflecting the complex linkages between the production and consumption behaviour of households; and in assessing the impact of changes in grain prices and income on marketable surplus supply in rural China.   The integrated approach also highlighted the direction and quantitative significance of the effects of changes in prices and income on marketable surplus.

We have used a compensation framework to explore and quantify the effects of household full income changes on farm labour supply and household own-consumption.   This demonstrated the positive effect of full income on own-consumption.   The comparison of conditional and unconditional elasticities allowed us to demonstrate the substantial impact of household own-consumption on grain marketable surplus.   Thus, in spite of the improved market environment and the trend of increasing output prices during the period of study, we cannot rule out the possibility of a negative marketable surplus supply response where own consumption of grain represents a relatively large proportion of production.

We turn now to explore the effects of off-farm income opportunities on grain marketable surplus supply using a similar integrated modelling framework.

Notes

1.   This figure is obtained from China Statistical Yearbook, 1993. It is different from the data cited from Rural Statistical Yearbook of China (1994, p241). The net social purchase based on Rural Statistical Yearbook of China (1994, p241) is 25 per cent of the total grain output in 1992. Therefore, the real own-consumption including grain for stock and feed may be 75 per cent if the re-selling of grain to the deficient rural areas by the state was taken into account.

2.   The constant return to scale is almost invariably assumed in the household production literature (Deaton and Bauer, 1989). In fact, many of the advanced economic models cannot be solved unless linear homogeneity of the production function is assumed (Gould et al. 1980). The assumption of constant returns to scale is not unrealistic for China. In recent studies by Lin (1988, 1992), Wen (1989) the hypothesis of constant returns to scale was not rejected. It also should be noted that the assumption of constant returns to scale is only for the purpose of obtaining a linear constraint condition for the utility maximisation problem. It does not mean that the utility function itself is a linear homogeneous function. It is clearly not permissible to directly use a linear homogeneous function in the case of utility function since utility is not measured cardinally.

3.   This assumption is also frequently used in the utility analysis in Microeconomics (See Gravelle, et al. 1992. p151) The assumption of constant prices of consumption goods (including leisure) implies that the individual producer's production and demand do not affect prices (See Gould and Ferguson, 1980. p233). In this sense, the price is given at the market and could be regarded as an exogenous variable. Thus, constant prices cannot of course reflect causality between prices and supply. A detailed discussion about the use of a constant price of leisure and its limitations will be given later. It should be noted that a constant price only refers to price determination in a static sense. It does not mean that price is fixed in a dynamic sense.

4.   It is assumed that there is no off-farm employment. This assumption will be relaxed and the effect of off-farm labour will be discussed in detail in the next chapter.

5.   This is similar to the concept of 'farm wage rate' (w_1). However, it may be inappropriate to use the term wage since it is related to self-employed rather than hired farmers. Thus, using 'daily net return per unit of on-farm family labour' may be a more suitable term as it includes return to family labour and management. Please note that $\bar{\pi}$ does not include return to capital and land: it is gross farm return per unit of labour minus total cost (excluding farm labour).

6.   As '$\bar{\pi}$' is the 'daily net return per unit of on-farm family labour' and H_1 is total on-farm work days per year, $\bar{\pi} H_1$ is on-farm income (farm

151

income= daily net return per unit of on-farm family labour × total on-farm work days per year). It is essential to distinguish π and $\bar{\pi}$ used in this study. (1) $\pi(q; H_1)$ is a profit function, but $\bar{\pi}$ (q) is daily net return per unit of on-farm family labour which is a function of prices (q). (2) It should be noted that in the empirical model, $\bar{\pi}$ is not treated as a function, but is an explanatory variable. If $\bar{\pi}$ is a function rather than a variable, the whole estimation will become very complex. For a detailed explanation about this, see 7.3.5.

7. 'Constant return to scale', 'linear homogeneity' and 'homogeneous of degree one' are interchangeable when used to describe a production function. See Gould and Ferguson (1980). The assumption of constant return to scale shows that the budget constraint is linear.

8. It should be noted that here 'full income' is Becker's (1965) concept.

The concept of full income ($\bar{\pi} H_1 + r$) in (7.1$_a$) was developed into the concept of 'full wealth' in (7.3a) in which the value of the stock of time owned by the household is recorded. Thus, adding the value of leisure, $\bar{\pi}(H - H_1)$, to both sides of (7.1a), we have equation (7.3a).

$$P_i X_i \le \bar{\pi}(H_1) + r.....(7.1_a).$$
$$\Downarrow$$

$$P_i X_i + \bar{\pi}(H - H_1) \le \bar{\pi} H + r \equiv Y.....(7.3_a)$$

The concept of 'full wealth' in (7.3a) is an extension of the definition of 'full income' given earlier. The term on the left shows how this full wealth is 'spent': either on goods (X_i) or on the forgone earnings associated with time consumption (leisure). The right hand side expresses full income (or 'full wealth').

9. See Gravelle, H and Rees, R. (1992), p150. Using constant wage rate to value leisure may be controversial. In order to avoiding misunderstanding, five points should be made. (1) leisure (H-H$_1$) in the utility function (7.3) is treated as a 'consumer good' (not utility).

(2) $\bar{\pi}$ (H-H$_1$) expresses a valuation of the leisure commodity (more precisely it is an expenditure of leisure), rather than a valuation of leisure utility. This is similar to the case of expenditure on consumer

152

goods (px) in equation 7.3a, where px means the valuation of consumer goods (expenditure) consumed by the consumers, rather than a measure of the utility of consumer goods. (3) The utility of commodity cannot be directly determined by its value (or its price). Thus, the concepts of commodity utility and its valuation (or its price) should be regarded as separate. That is, although the utility of leisure is diminishing, the price of leisure (the opportunity cost of work) could be constant. (4) In this sense, using the constant price (or wage) to value a consumer commodity (or leisure) does not imply a constant utility of commodities (or leisure). Thus, the assumption of constant

returns to scale made in the theoretical model only implies that $\bar{\pi}$ (the price) is constant, but not that leisure utility is constant.

10. $\bar{\pi} H$ is a value of the stock of time, i.e., $\bar{\pi} \times H$ (H is the total activity time available).

11. Here the term farm wage rate is used to refer to hourly (or daily) net farm returns ($\bar{\pi}$) earned by the household members' on farm activities.

12. The theoretical analysis is mainly focused on consumer choice, rather on the measurement of utility. As the magnitude of utility cannot directly be expressed by either absolute monetary income (or its price) or absolute quantity, the household's utility maximisation in the utility function (7.3) is clearly focused on the consumer choice of a given bundle of consumer goods at a given income constraint. In this sense, the use of $\bar{\pi}(H - H_1)$ is to express the expenditure of leisure at a given income constraint, therefore, the optimal points of utility maximisation can be examined. Indeed it is very difficult to measure utility either in terms of 'valuation' or 'quantity' as utility is subjective. Most economists analyse utility by examining changes in the quantity of a given bundle of consumer goods at a given income constraint and discuss how these changes in the quantity reflect changes in utility (see Gravelle, H. G. and Rees, R. 1992).

13. If technology has a constant return to scale, the budget constraint would be linear. The price of leisure would be treated as exogenous. See Deaton, (1989) for a detailed explanation.

14. This approach is frequently used in household's models (see, for

example, Lau, Lin and Yotopolous, 1976; Becker, 1976; Barnum and Squire, 1979 a & b; Strauss, 1984 a & b, Singh, et al, 1986; Schnepf and Senauer, 1989; Adelman and Taylor, 1991) as well as in Gravelle and Rees (1992) p 149-152). Also this assumption that producers are price takers is not unrealistic to China since family farming is a major feature of agricultural production and millions of households as independent production units compete in the grain markets after establishment of HPRS in China.

15. The marginal utility of leisure can be examined through the leisure demand function (7.6). In order to avoid misunderstanding, three points should be made. (1) $\dfrac{\partial G}{\partial Y}$ expresses 'the marginal utility of income' and ($-\dfrac{\partial G}{\partial \underline{\pi}}$) intuitively expresses the idea that as the price ($\overline{\pi}$) of the leisure goods increases the leisure consumed by the individual will decline. The ratio of the two marginal utilities (rather than 'an absolute valuation itself') can be used to judge the utility of leisure (See Gravelle and Rees 1992, p112 for a detailed explanation). (2) Equation (7.6) itself does not express the marginal utility of leisure. However, it can be seen that the optimum point (utility maximisation) for leisure demand in the model is dependent on the ratio of two marginal utilities, i.e., $\dfrac{\partial G}{\partial Y}$ and ($-\dfrac{\partial G}{\partial \underline{\pi}}$). Thus, the solution of the model based on the demand function for leisure (7.6) can be regarded as the optimum point at a given budget constraint. It also reflects the fact that utility of leisure is not directly expressed through its valuation, $\overline{\pi}(H - H_1)$.

154

16. For the detailed explanation about the properties of GPF form, see Blackorby et al. (1978).

17. If $\bar{\pi}$ used here is as a function rather than a variable, the expenditure equations would be: $S_i = f_i(\phi(q;H_1), w_2, p, Y) + \mu_i$, Although it may be better to capture the causality between wage rate and labour flow, it is infeasible to estimate such an equation due to econometric difficulties. Thus, (7.13) was used instead.

18. Note: Y is full income, rather than farm profit (π). So Hotelling's Lemma cannot be used to calculate $\dfrac{\partial Y}{\partial q}$ directly. This is similar to Strauss's (1984b) problems. The real relationship between the full income and output prices should be written as $\dfrac{\partial Y}{\partial \pi} \cdot \dfrac{\partial \pi}{\partial q}$. Hotelling's Lemma could be used to calculate $\dfrac{\partial \pi}{\partial q}$ directly. It is necessary to make some assumptions about $\dfrac{\partial Y}{\partial \pi}$. Considering that the farm profit (π) and the full income (Y) have the same direction and proportion in changes, we adopt Strauss's method to deal with it, i.e., assume that the full income and the farm profit are proportional. (see Strauss, 1984)

19. It should be noted that the model is not involved in analysing the marginal productivity of labour. As the assumption of constant return to scale was made, the conditional profit function is homogeneous of degree one in H_1. The output function derived from the profit function was defined as $Q_i = H_1 \dfrac{\partial \bar{\pi}(q)}{\partial q}$, and differentiating output with respect to output price, we can derive an output supply response to price as

$$\frac{\partial Q}{\partial q} = \frac{\partial^2 \bar{\pi}}{\partial q^2} + \frac{\partial H_1}{\partial \bar{\pi}} \frac{\partial \bar{\pi}}{\partial q}.$$ Clearly it is not necessary to find a marginal productivity of labour $\left(\dfrac{\partial Q}{\partial H_1}\right)$ in the elasticity estimation.

155

20. The output price data refer to the national level whereas other data were obtained at the provincial level. The national mixed average price takes account of the free market price. A similar method has been used by Lin (1992), Rural Reforms and Agricultural Growth in China, American Economic Review (82): 34-51.

21. Considerable difficulties were encountered in collecting price data for inputs and the specific consumer goods in this study. The input price was replaced by input cost per unit. The price for non-farm consumer goods was replaced by average daily consumption expenditure. Clearly this is not entirely satisfactory as an increase in unit input cost or in expenditure may reflect a combination of volume and price changes.

22. USDA, (1993). Agricultural Statistics of the People's Republic of China, 1949-90.

23. In a large sample the maximum likelihood estimates are asymptotically normally distributed so that statistical significance can be tested with standard t statistics (William, et al., 1993, p453; Benjamin and Guyomard, 1994)

24. Although the main focus in this Chapter is on the marketable surplus supply response, in order to estimate unconditional supply response, we also give total output supply responses.

25. It should be noted that farm labour demand used here is different from labour supply which we assumed was constant.

8 Off-farm income and grain marketable surplus

8.1 Introduction

The farm and non-farm economies became increasingly integrated during the economic reforms, particularly after 1985. The Chinese rural economy has been much more flexible and free to adjust its economic structure in response to changes in its economic environment. Factor movements, resource relocation and production adjustment have all occurred, though not perfectly. This economic integration is an important factor for the analysis of farm households' supply response behaviour. In a highly closed agricultural economy, indirect policy effects do not play a significant role in influencing farmers' supply behaviour since there is not much room for sector interactions. However, in the current relatively open Chinese rural economy, farmers' behaviour is not only subject to sector specific policies, such as procurement prices and state quota policies, but is also affected by non-farm policies.

The difficulties in estimating the effects of non-farm income on marketable surplus supply using an *ad hoc* approach were discussed in Chapter 6. A single equation for output supply is unable to capture feedback effects. In order to overcome this problem, this chapter investigates empirically such non-farm impacts on grain marketable surplus supply using an integrated model. It is mainly concerned with the possible impacts of labour flows between the farm and non-farm sectors. The main purpose of the chapter is to clarify how off-farm income affects labour supply through a comparison of cross-income effects on the farm and off-farm labour supply. The effects on farm households' grain supply response behaviour are then studied through a comparison of conditional and unconditional marketable surplus supply elasticities.

In section 8.2, some important features of labour supply and their implications for modelling are discussed. In section 8.3, the model specification and the estimation procedure for marketable surplus supply and factor demand responses are outlined. In section 8.4, the data used in the model are described and some data problems are discussed. Results are discussed in section 8.5. Finally, conclusions drawn from the empirical study are made in section 8.6.

8.2   Labour supply features and modelling implications

More and more people have recognised that, after the rural economic reform in 1978, Chinese farmers increasingly have comparative advantages in off-farm work. Four distinct features of China's farming are worth mention. These are: (1) weather, as an important production condition, is stochastic and its effects during the course of production are unpredictable; (2) the technology of production is traditional and has remained virtually unchanged: it is rather backward and still mainly depends upon manual work in many rural areas; (3) the conditions of work are hard and the length of time spent on farming is longer than in non-farm work: the rule of eight hours work per day does not exist in rural areas; (4) the on-farm wage is lower than the off-farm wage due to the large differences in labour productivity between farm and non-farm industries. These characteristics may be strong enough to induce a farmer to migrate from rural to urban to seek an alternative income source.

The recognition of these features is rather important for modelling Chinese farm households' supply response behaviour. Apart from using the same assumptions as in Chapter 7, i.e., constant returns to scale and no fixed inputs, the theoretical model in this chapter also makes the following two assumptions.

Assumption One: On-farm return is not equal to the off-farm wage rate,

i.e., $\pi \neq w_2$. There are two wage rates relevant to the household: one is the wage rate for off-farm work and the other is the wage rate for on-farm work which is dependent on production technologies and output prices. This can be justified by the following two reasons. Firstly, as discussed in Chapter 4 and above, disparity of wage income between farm and non-farm industries can be frequently observed in China due to large differences in labour productivity between these two sectors. Disparity of wage rate between these two sectors may be a long run phenomenon in China. Secondly, if there exists free entry and exit in the on-farm and off-farm labour markets, the shadow price of on-farm work is equal to the off-farm wage rate from the point of view of the long-run equilibrium. However, many on- and non-farm activities are subject to rather important institutional restrictions and free entry is certainly far from reality as discussed in Chapter 4. Thus, the shadow prices of on- and off-farm work cannot be treated as identical. This allows the use of two wage rates to estimate the household's labour supply response in the model.

Assumption Two: In contrast to the conventional model, on-farm and off-farm work are considered to be two different 'commodities' in the model, from the point of view of the household as a utility maximiser. This assumption can be justified by the following two reasons. Firstly, on-farm and off-farm labour are not perfect substitutes in production. It has long been recognised that utility may have a different connotation in relation to on-farm and off-farm work (Diewert, 1971, Lopez, 1984). Utility differences associated with different working activities are likely to be even greater in the semi-commercial rural economy in China. This can be seen particularly in certain traditional social concepts such as salaried work which is regarded as more noble than rural farm work; farmers are proud of working in off-farm activities in contrast to farm work. Thus, household members show different preferences towards on-farm and off-farm work. Secondly, as on-farm return is lower than the off-farm wage rate, farm households face two different family labour choices due to the different income opportunities. This is particularly so after liberalisation of the labour market. The Chinese farmers responded to these opportunities, thus, time spent on farming activities relative to off-farm activities tended to decline.

Assumptions One and Two imply that households' utility will depend on the allocation of labour supply between on-farm and off-farm work, rather than on total labour supply. Thus, utility maximisation by Chinese farm households will be related to a full income maximisation objective, including farm income and non-farm income. The amount of family labour remaining on-farm may be only for family survival and subsistence. These assumptions imply that there could be different labour supply behaviour towards on-farm and off-farm work in Chinese farm households.

8.3   Model specification

The characteristics of the model used in this study, as well as the linkages between theoretical and empirical models, were discussed in detail in the previous chapter. In this chapter, the effect of off-farm activities is introduced. The utility function is extended by introducing off-farm activities; the function is little different from the model represented by equation (7.3).

8.3.1 *Supplementary specification of the theoretical model*

Lopez (1984) developed a microeconomic model which integrated production and consumption into a unified theoretical framework. The theory starts from a utility function which includes consumption of goods and leisure. These two variables are linked through the definition of income and profit functions. The approach in this chapter is similar to that of Lopez: however, it differs in that we focus on the effect of off-farm income on marketable surplus.[1] If off-farm activities were taken into account, the household's utility can be expressed as a function of farm income, off-farm income and commodity consumption. As income is related to labour input, the utility function can be written as follows.

$$\text{Max } U(H_1, H_2; X) \dots \dots \dots \dots \dots \dots \dots \dots \dots (8.1)$$

subject to budget (8.1_a) and time (8.1_b) constraints,

$$PX \leq \bar{\pi} H_1 + w_2 H_2 + r \dots \dots \dots \dots \dots \dots \dots (8.1_a)$$
$$H_1 + H_2 = H \dots \dots \dots \dots \dots \dots \dots \dots (8.1_b)$$
$$H_1 > 0, H_2 > 0, X > 0 \dots \dots \dots \dots \dots \dots (8.1_c)$$

Where U is household's utility function; $P=(p_1,...,p_i)$ is a price vector of commodities consumed by the household members; $X=(x_1,..., x_i)$ is the i dimensional vector of consumption goods; H_1 is the time spent on farm work; H_2 is the time spent on off-farm work; H is total work time that household members spend on on- and off-farm work;[2] $\bar{\pi}$ is daily net return per unit of on-farm family labour, i.e., gross farm return per unit of labour minus total cost (excluding farm labour) per unit of labour; πH_1 is, therefore, the farm income; w_2 is off-farm wage rate received by household members when they engage in off-farm work; $w_2 H_2$ is off-farm income; r is non-labour income. The constraint condition (8.1_a) implies that the total expenditure (px) cannot be larger than the total revenue: on-farm income $(\bar{\pi} H_1)$, off-farm income $(w_2 H_2)$ and non-labour income (r). The constraint condition (8.1_b) implies the on-farm and off-farm work cannot exceed the total work time available.

As the farm income is related to farm production, the farm profit

160

function $\pi(q;H_1)$ is a function of output price (q) and on-farm labour input (H_1). The same assumption as in the previous chapter was made, i.e., production technology exhibits a constant return to scale. As the profit function is homogeneous of degree one in H_1, i.e.,

$\pi(q; H_1)= \bar{H_1} \pi(q)$ ....(8.2), the farm income is dependent on on-farm labour input (H_1).

The utility maximisation model (8.1) allows household members to have different preferences for the different types of work that they can provide (on-farm or off-farm work). Changes in the parameters of the model will induce changes in the distribution of labour supplied to on-farm and off-farm activities. Following the same procedure used in the previous chapter, utility maximisation can be expressed in a more convenient form as follows:

$$U(H-H_1, H-H_2; X) \equiv U^*(H_1, H_2; X) \dots\dots\dots\dots\dots\dots\dots (8.3)$$

Where X is consumption goods; $H-H_1$ is non-on-farm work time; $H-H_2$ is non-off-farm work time. The reason we use (8.3) rather than (8.1) is that the utility function is defined over the non-negative orthant and that the corresponding budget constraint may be defined using non-negative prices and positive income. This is also emphasising the fact that each individual has an opportunity cost of on-farm and off-farm work regardless of whether he or she is in the wage market. Thus, the work time allocation between on-farm and off-farm activities by the household can be examined. The utility function can be formulated as:

$$\text{Max } U(H-H_1, H-H_2; X) \dots\dots\dots\dots\dots\dots\dots\dots\dots (8.4)$$

subject to

$$PX \leq \bar{\pi} H_1 + w_2 H_2 + r \equiv Y \dots\dots\dots\dots\dots\dots\dots\dots (8.4_a)$$
$$H_1 + H_2 = H \dots\dots\dots\dots\dots\dots\dots\dots\dots\dots (8.4_b)$$
$$H_1 \geq 0, \ H_2 \geq 0, \ X \geq 0 \dots\dots\dots\dots\dots\dots\dots\dots (8.4_c)$$

The constraint (8.4_a) shows total household 'expenditure' on marketed-purchased commodities (PX) cannot be greater than total household income including on-farm income $(\bar{\pi} H_1)$, non-farm income $(w_2 H_2)$ and other non-labour income (r). The utility function (8.4) is a standard maximisation problem with a linear constraint provided that $\bar{\pi}(q)$ is known. Assuming that constraint (8.4_c) is not binding, this implies that it is an internal

161

solution.[3] Thus, the standard duality theorem can be applied in order to derive equations for commodity demand, on-farm and off-farm labour supply. The indirect utility function $G(P, \bar{\pi}, w_2, Y)$ can be defined in the standard manner.

$$G(P, \bar{\pi}, w_2, Y) \equiv \max u\{(H-H_1), (H-H_2), X\} \dots\dots\dots\dots\dots (8.5)$$

subject to

$$PX \leq \bar{\pi} H_1 + w_2 H_2 + r \equiv Y \dots\dots\dots\dots\dots\dots\dots\dots (8.5_a)$$
$$H_1 + H_2 = H \dots\dots\dots\dots\dots\dots\dots\dots\dots\dots (8.5_b)$$
$$H_1 \geq 0,\ H_2 \geq 0,\ X \geq 0 \dots\dots\dots\dots\dots\dots\dots\dots (8.5_c)$$

Where, G will be continuous, quasi-convex in P, $\bar{\pi}$ and w_2, non-increasing in P, non-decreasing in Y and homogeneous of degree zero in P, $\bar{\pi}$, w_2 and Y. From (8.5) it is possible to derive the Marshallian demand functions for $H-H_1$, $H-H_2$ and X using Roy's identity:

$$H - H_1 = -\frac{\partial G \big/ \partial \bar{\pi}}{\partial G \big/ \partial y} = \Phi(p, \bar{\pi}, w_2, r, Y) \dots\dots\dots\dots (8.6_a)$$

$$H - H_2 = -\frac{\partial G \big/ \partial w_2}{\partial G \big/ \partial y} = \omega(p, \bar{\pi}, w_2, r, Y) \dots\dots\dots\dots (8.6_b)$$

$$X = -\frac{\partial G \big/ \partial p}{\partial G \big/ \partial y} = \Omega(p, \bar{\pi}, w_2, r, Y) \dots\dots\dots\dots (8.6_c)$$

Furthermore, marketable surplus supply is a function of farm profit which can be expressed as follows.

$$Q_i(q_i; H_1) = H_1 \left(\frac{\partial \bar{\pi}(q_1)}{\partial q_1}\right) \dots\dots\dots\dots\dots\dots\dots\dots (8.7)$$

i=1,....n.
Where Q is the conditional supply or demand for production factor i. When

the commodity is an input then Q_i is defined as input. As the assumption of constant returns to scale is made, on-farm labour input (H_1) determines a scale of production.

8.3.2 The major features of the model

The most important feature of this model is that it distinguishes two different labour choices, i.e., between on-farm and off-farm activities made by household members. In most of the previous studies, there is no distinction between time allocation made to on-farm and off-farm activities. For example, Lau, Lin and Yotopoulos (1978) estimated a system of expenditure functions (including leisure, agricultural commodities and non-agricultural commodities) for households in Taiwan using a utility maximisation approach. But it only related to a sector where agricultural producers predominate. Using a profit function estimated by Yotopoulos et al.(1976) for the same Taiwan case, they estimated the household marketable surplus. The only source of interrelations between the consumption and production sides of the model was the effect of farm profit on households' income. It was assumed that the price of labour (or leisure) was unique and equal to the prevailing (exogenous) wage rate. Using a unique exogenous price of labour (or leisure) implies that households are indifferent among alternative allocations of their working time to on-farm and off-farm work. A similar approach was adopted by Barnum and Squire (1979) in analysing consumption and production responses of farm households in Malaysia. However, these studies failed to consider the labour choice problem. They imply an assumption that household utility depends on total labour supply not on the allocation among different working activities. In particular, on-farm work and off-farm work as wage earners are perfect substitutes in their models. The salaried off-farm working activities performed by households are treated the same as the farm work activities. It is also assumed that households provided only one type of labour service, i.e., either farm work or off-farm work. Thus, most previous studies have either estimated total labour supply or they concentrated on the estimation of the off-farm labour supply only.

If we consider the introduction to the model of labour choices about on-farm and off-farm activities, the use of a unique price of labour, either an on-farm return or off-farm wage rate, to estimate labour supply response has a serious theoretical weakness in capturing Chinese farm household's actual response behaviour. Firstly, this assumption implies that on-farm return ($\bar{\pi}$) is equal to off-farm wage (w_2), i.e., $\bar{\pi} = w_2$. This has been rejected in our discussion in 8.2.2.

163

Secondly, if the shadow price of on-farm and off-farm work was not identical, it would not be valid to use the on-farm wage (or off-farm wage) rate as a unique price of labour. If household members are involved in on-farm work as well as off-farm work, using on-farm return as a unique price of labour implies that off-farm labour supply will be a function of on-farm return. However, the relevant price of labour is not the farm wage rate because some household members did not engage in farm work. In this situation, the price of labour may no longer be the on-farm labour wage rate, rather the off-farm wage rate. Similarly, using the off-farm wage rate as a unique price of labour in the model implies that the input price to household members' work on-farm is a function of off-farm wage rate received by the household's members. If so, the profit function will become a function of the off-farm wage rate and, thereby, the indirect utility function will depend on the off-farm wage rate only.

Thirdly, using a unique price of labour to estimate labour supply response implies that on-farm and off-farm labour are perfect substitutes. However, this is also not the case in China as discussed in sections 8.2.1 and 8.2.2. Thus, using a unique price of labour may be misleading since it cannot distinguish two different labour supply choices. Clearly, this approach cannot reflect the real relationship between income and labour supply, therefore, it cannot capture the reality of farm household's response behaviour.

The use of two different wage rates to estimate labour supply is based on the idea that we can distinguish the different utility connotations between on-farm and off-farm activities. This allows the characteristics of labour supply response behaviour in the Chinese households to be better captured. Furthermore, the cross income effect of on-farm and off-farm labour supply can be examined.

8.3.3   The estimated model

The model to be estimated is the one described by the conditional profit function defined by equation (8.2) and by the indirect utility function defined by equation (8.5). To estimate the model represented by equations (8.2) and (8.5), the indirect utility functional form of G, and conditional profit functional form of (π) used in this study are the same as the one (GPF) in the previous chapter.

The indirect utility function is:

$$G = \frac{Y - [\sum_{i=1}^{3}\sum_{j=1}^{3}\delta_{ij}p_i^{\frac{1}{2}}p_j^{\frac{1}{2}}]}{[\sum_{i=1}^{3}\alpha_i p_i^{\rho}]^{\frac{1}{\rho}}} \qquad \dots\dots\dots\dots\dots\dots\dots\dots\dots\dots\dots\dots(8.8)$$

Where $\delta_{ij} = \delta_{ji}$, for all $i \neq j$; α_i, ρ δ are parameters to be estimated; p_1, p_2 and p_3 represent daily net return per unit of on-farm family labour ($\bar{\pi}$), off-farm wage rate and daily consumption expenditure respectively. Using Roy's identity, one can derive the consumption demand equations in expenditure form.

$$S_i = p_i X_i = \frac{\alpha_i p_i^{\rho}(Y - \sum_{i=1}^{3}\sum_{j=1}^{3}\delta_{ij}p_i^{\frac{1}{2}}p_j^{\frac{1}{2}})}{\sum_{i=1}^{3}\alpha_{ij}p_i^{\rho}} + p_i[\sum_{j=1}^{3}\delta_{ij}(\frac{p_j}{p_i})^{\frac{1}{2}}].(8.9)$$

Where
$$S_1 \equiv p_1 x_1 \equiv p_1(H - H_1); \quad S_2 \equiv p_2 x_2 \equiv p_2(H - H_2); \quad S_3 \equiv p_3 x_3.$$
Three consumption demand equations (S_1, S_2 and S_3) are derived from equation (8.9). S_1 and S_2 are actually the household's two labour (on- and off-farm) supply equations. The consumption decisions are constrained by production, time and labour available.

In order to estimate the production side of the model, it is necessary to estimate the conditional farm profit function. The conditional farm profit function is dependent on a vector of output prices (q_1) and on the amount of family labour used by farm household. The prices considered are aggregate data: output prices (q_1), on-farm labour price (q_2) and current and capital input price (q_3).

Assuming constant return to scale and specifying a Generalised Leontief conditional profit function, which is a flexible functional form in the sense that it provides second order approximations to any local function, the conditional farm profit function is:

$$\pi(q_i, H_1) = H_1 \left(\sum_{i=1}^{3} \sum_{j=1}^{3} b_{ij} q_i^{\frac{1}{2}} q_j^{\frac{1}{2}} \right) \quad \dots\dots\dots\dots\dots\dots\dots\dots\dots (8.10)$$
$$i = 1,..3.$$

Where $b_{ij} = b_{ji}$ for all i≠j; b_{ij} are parameters to be estimated. Given (8.10), the output supply response can be obtained using Hotelling's Lemma.

$$Q_i = H_1 \left[\sum_{j=1}^{3} b_{ij} \left(\frac{q_j}{q_i} \right)^{\frac{1}{2}} \right] \quad \dots\dots\dots\dots\dots\dots\dots\dots\dots\dots (8.11)$$

Thus, the output supply responses per unit of family labour are:

$$\frac{Q_i}{H_1} = \sum_{j=1}^{3} b_{ij} \left(\frac{q_j}{q_i} \right)^{\frac{1}{2}} \quad \dots\dots\dots\dots\dots\dots\dots\dots\dots\dots\dots (8.11_a)$$
$$i = 1,...3.$$

Where Q_1 is output supply; Q_2 is demand for labour on farm; and Q_3 is demand for current and capital input. In order to estimate the conditional profit function, one can proceed directly to estimate (8.10), or equivalently to estimate the supply equation system (8.11a). It is arbitrarily chosen to estimate the net supply function (8.11a).

8.3.4   The econometric model

The econometric model is

(1) $S_1 = f_1(p_1, p_2, p_3, Y) + \mu_1$
(2) $S_2 = f_2(p_1, p_2, p_3, Y) + \mu_2$
(3) $S_3 = f_3(p_1, p_2, p_3, Y) + \mu_3$
(4) $Q_i = H_1 \phi^i(q) + v_i$ i=1...3 $\quad \dots\dots\dots\dots\dots\dots\dots (8.12)$

Under the assumptions used (constant returns to scale and no fixed factors

of production), the variable p_1 ($\equiv \pi$) is exogenous independent of household's preferences (independent of H_1) and hence its use as an

explanatory variable represents no inconvenience. Note that p_1 ($\equiv \overline{\pi}$) is now used as a variable rather than a function. The expenditure equations (S_i) in (8.12) are assumed to be dependent on the actual profit per day of work (p_1), rather than on the optimal or expected price level, $\phi(q)$. As to this point, it has been explained in the previous chapter, therefore, it is

166

unnecessary to go into details here.

The equations in (8.12) need to be jointly estimated for the same reasons discussed in the previous chapter. Thus, three output supply and factor demand equations (Q_1, Q_2, Q_3), together with three consumption demand equations (S_1, S_2, S_3) derived from equation (8.12) are jointly estimated using a Full Information Maximum Likelihood method (FIML).

8.3.5   Labour and marketable surplus supply responses

Labour supply elasticities with respect to on-farm return and off-farm wage
As the on-farm labour supply is a function of on-farm return (p_1), grain output price (q_1) and off-farm wage (p_2), i.e., $H_1 = \Phi(q_1, p_1(q_1), p_2)$, the effect of on-farm return on the labour supply can be examined by analysing the elasticity of labour supply with respect to on-farm return. The on-farm labour supply elasticity with respect to on-farm return (p_1) is $\dfrac{\partial H_1}{\partial p_1} \cdot \dfrac{p_1}{H_1}$ and off-farm labour supply elasticity with respect to off-farm

wage (p_2) is $\dfrac{\partial H_2}{\partial p_2} \cdot \dfrac{p_2}{H_2}$. These elasticities can be derived directly from

equation (8.9). The cross income elasticities, $\left(\dfrac{\partial H_1}{\partial p_2} \cdot \dfrac{p_2}{H_1}\right)$ and

$\left(\dfrac{\partial H_2}{\partial p_1} \cdot \dfrac{p_1}{H_2}\right)$, also can be derived from equation (8.9) in a similar manner.

Labour supply elasticities with respect to output price   The effect of changes in output price (q_i) on-farm labour supply and off-farm labour supply can be examined using equations (8.7) and (8.9).

$$Q_i(q_i; H_i) = H_i \frac{\partial p_i(q_i)}{\partial q_i} \dots\dots\dots(i = 1, \dots 3) \dots\dots\dots\dots (8.7)$$

The effect of output price q_i on labour supply H_i is

$$\frac{\partial H_i}{\partial q_i} = \frac{\partial H_i}{\partial p_i} \cdot \frac{\partial p_i}{\partial q_i} \dots\dots\dots\dots\dots\dots\dots\dots\dots\dots\dots (8.13)$$

Using Hotelling's Lemma, we have

167

$$\frac{\partial p_i}{\partial q_i} = \frac{Q_i}{H_i}$$

Hence, labour supply elasticities with respect to output price (q_i) can be expressed as

$$\frac{\partial H_i}{\partial q_i} \cdot \frac{q_i}{H_i} = \frac{\partial H_i}{\partial p_i} \cdot \frac{\partial p_i}{\partial q_i} \cdot \frac{q_i}{H_i} = \frac{\partial H_i}{\partial p_i} \cdot \frac{Q_i}{H_i} \cdot \frac{q_i}{H_i} = \frac{\partial H_i}{\partial p_i} \cdot \frac{p_i}{H_i} \cdot \frac{q_i Q_i}{p_i H_i}$$

$$\dots\dots\dots\dots\dots\dots\dots\dots\dots\dots\dots\dots\dots\dots\dots\dots\dots\dots\dots\dots\dots (8.13_a)$$

Conditional marketable surplus supply and factor demand elasticities
In order to explore the effect of on-farm labour on marketable surplus supply, the 'net' supply responses are firstly examined under the assumption that on-farm labour supply is held constant. Then, the effect of on-farm labour supply on marketable surplus is introduced; this is defined as the 'conditional supply responses' because off-farm work is assumed to be constant. The effects of on-farm labour changes on marketable surplus supply can be examined through a comparison between the 'net' and 'conditional' elasticities. If the effect of off-farm work is taken into account simultaneously, marketable surplus supply response is 'unconditional'. The net effect of off-farm work can be examined through a comparison between the 'conditional' and 'unconditional' elasticities.

Thus, the 'net supply responses' are examined with on-farm labour supply held constant. They can be derived directly from equation (8.11a) as follows.

$$\frac{\partial Q_i}{\partial q_j} \frac{q_j}{Q_i} = \frac{\partial (Q_i/H_1)}{\partial q_j} \cdot \frac{q_j}{(Q_i/H_1)} \dots\dots\dots\dots\dots\dots\dots\dots\dots\dots (8.14)$$

For the conditional marketable surplus supply responses, it is assumed that on-farm labour is allowed to vary, but off-farm labour assumed to be constant after output price has been changed. Differentiating equation (8.7) partially with respect to the output (or input) prices (q_i), we can derive conditional supply elasticities. These elasticities are defined as follows.

$$\frac{\partial Q_i}{\partial q_j}\frac{q_j}{Q_i}=\frac{\partial(Q_i/H_1)}{\partial q_j}\cdot\frac{q_j}{(Q_i/H_1)}+(\frac{\partial H_1}{\partial p_1}\frac{p_1}{H_1})\frac{q_iQ_i}{p_1H_1}\quad\dots\dots\dots(8.15)$$

The first item of the right hand side of (8.15) is the effect of prices on marketable surplus supply assuming that on-farm labour supply is constant, and the second item is the effect of changes in prices on farm labour input.

Unconditional marketable surplus supply and factor demand elasticities If the effect of off-farm income was taken into account simultaneously, supply responses will be so-called 'unconditional'. The unconditional marketable surplus supply elasticities take account of changes in on-farm and off-farm labour simultaneously. The output supply function in (8.7) is

defined as $Q_i(q_i;H_i)=H_i\dfrac{\partial p_i(q_i)}{\partial q_i}$ which is dependent on on-farm

labour input. The on-farm labour supply is a function of on-farm return (p_1), grain output price (q_1) and off-farm wage (p_2), i.e., $H_1=\Phi(q_1,p_1(q_1),p_2)$. On-farm labour input will be affected by off-farm labour changes. The unconditional supply elasticities can be derived form the output and labour supply functions. Differentiating equation (8.7) with respect to output price q_1, we have

$$\frac{\partial Q_i}{\partial q_i}=(\frac{\partial^2 p_1}{\partial q_i\cdot\partial q_j})\cdot H_1+(\frac{\partial p_1}{\partial q_i})\cdot(\frac{\partial H_1}{\partial q_j}+\frac{\partial H_1}{\partial p_2}\cdot\frac{\partial p_2}{\partial p_1}\cdot\frac{\partial p_1}{\partial q_1})\quad\dots(8.16)$$

Thus, the unconditional marketable surplus supply elasticities are:

$$\frac{\partial Q_i}{\partial q_j}\cdot\frac{q_j}{Q_i}=\frac{\partial(Q_i/H_1)}{\partial q_i}\cdot\frac{q_j}{(Q_i/H_1)}+(\frac{\partial H_1}{\partial p_1}\cdot\frac{P_1}{H_1})\frac{q_jQ_i}{p_1H_1}+(\frac{\partial H_1}{\partial p_2}\cdot\frac{p_2}{H_1})\frac{q_jQ_i}{p_1H_1}$$

$$\dots\dots\dots\dots\dots(8.16_a)$$

The first two items on the right hand side of (8.16a) are conditional supply elasticities and the third item is the effect of changes in off-farm income on on-farm labour supply. It should be noted that if i=j, the effect of output price (q_i) on output (Q_i) will not be unambiguously positive as it depends on the second and third term's sign and magnitude, i.e. it depends on

169

whether $\dfrac{\partial H_1}{\partial p_1}$ and $\dfrac{\partial H_1}{\partial p_2}$ are positive or negative and their magnitude. The possibility of downward sloping supply or upward sloping input demand functions cannot be ruled out when the effect of changes in on-farm and off-farm income are taken into account simultaneously. Thus, marketable surplus supply could decline due to the reduction of on-farm labour input by households. Equation (8.16a) also can be expressed in elasticity terms.

$$\varepsilon_{ij} = S_{ij} + \varepsilon_{H_1 p_1} \cdot \dfrac{Q_i q_i}{p_1 H_1} + \varepsilon_{H_1 P_2} \cdot \dfrac{Q_i q_i}{P_1 H_1}$$

Where ε_{ij} is the marketable surplus supply elasticity with respect to output price (q_i). S_{ij} is the elasticity of conditional marketable surplus supply (Q_i/H_1) with respect to output price (q_i), $\varepsilon_{H_1 p_1}$ is the elasticity of on-farm labour (H_1) with respect to farm return (p_1) and $\varepsilon_{H_1 p_2}$ is the elasticity of on-farm labour supply (H_1) with respect to off-farm wage (p_2). Thus, the unconditional marketable surplus supply responses reflect the effect of off-labour changes on marketable surplus supply.

8.4   The data

The data used were obtained from various issues of the Chinese Statistical Yearbook published by the China State Statistical Bureau (the SSB). As aggregated time series data were available over a period of only 15 years, it was decided to use pooled data for 28 provinces over the same period. This generated 420 observations for each variable. The use of cross-sectional data was precluded due to lack of price variation. The main variables required to estimate the model were: (1) labour data on the number of days of on-farm and off-farm work; the amount of workers on-farm and off-farm; the on-farm return and the off-farm wage per person per day; (2) production data which are the amount of input, marketable surplus supply, output and input prices; (3) consumption data which includes consumption amounts and their prices. However, some of the data are not collected by the SSB. For example, there are no data available for the number of days of on-farm and off-farm work, prices for labour and other inputs. Thus, some of the data are derived through an indirect procedure using related variables. Those variables which had to be calculated from related data in this study are specified as follows.

(1) On-farm return, on-farm work and farm labour prices   The data on the

170

farm return per capita per year of farm households were available from sample surveys carried out by the SSB. However, there were no data available on labour price and the number of days on farm work in China's statistical census. There were census data on the total labour cost and the total number of days of labour used in unit production. Hence the labour price was obtained by calculating the average labour cost. This was derived from the labour cost per tonne divided by the number of days of farm labour used per tonne, i.e.,

$$\text{On-farm labour price/day} = \frac{\text{labour cost per tonne}}{\text{number of days of farm labour used per tonne}}$$

Likewise no data were available on the number of days of on-farm work from China's statistical census. Observations for these variables were obtained by dividing the average net return to on-farm work per person per year by labour price per day, i.e.,

$$\text{Days on farm work} = \frac{\text{average net return to on-farm work per person per year}}{\text{labour cost per tonne}}$$

(2) Off-farm work and off-farm wage   The total rural labour force reported by the SSB was divided into on-farm and off-farm work. The latter was related to rural industry, construction, transportation, commerce and miscellaneous occupations. However, the off-farm labour originally reported by the SSB excluded that rural industrial labour at and below the village-level. Beginning in 1985, rural industrial labour at and below the village-level was shifted from agriculture to industry and these new definitions were used to compile rural labour statistics. The original old data were adjusted back to 1978 based on this new definition and was used in this study.

The Chinese Statistical Yearbook provided data on average on- and off-farm income per capita per year sharing his/her effort between on- and off-farm work. There are no data available on off-farm wage and the number of days of off-farm work per capita within a year. In view of the fact that the ratio of on-farm labour to off-farm labour reflects, to some extent, the trend of changes in the allocation of work time between on-farm and off-farm for farm household members, the number of days of off-farm work per capita within a year were calculated based on the ratio of on-farm labour to off-farm labour, which was based on assumption that the ratio of on-farm

171

work time to off-farm work time equals to the ratio of on-farm labour to off-farm labour, i.e.,

Days of off-farm work =

$$\text{days of on-farm work} \times \frac{\text{the amount of off-farm workers}}{\text{the amount of on-farm workers}}$$

As the number of days of on- and off-farm work used in this study reflects the average worker sharing his/her effort in his/her total work time available, the total work time available by a household member was divided into two parts: time spent on farm work and on off-farm work. Thus, time spent on on-farm work and time on off-farm activities in the total work time available per household member per year can be derived.

Given the data on off-farm income and the number of days of off-farm work, the off-farm wage per day was derived by dividing off-farm income by the number of days of off-farm work, i.e.,

$$\text{Off-farm wage/day} = \frac{\text{off-farm income per person per year}}{\text{number of days of off-farm work per person per year}}$$

(3) Output and Input prices   Output price has been discussed in the previous chapter. With respect to input prices, there are no data available on amounts of input or input prices. In addition, input data used in the model is an aggregate value, i.e., all inputs are aggregated into one category. No data were available on aggregate input price. However, like labour cost price data, there exists census information on total capital and current input cost. Thus, we can obtain a unit average cost of capital and current inputs by dividing total capital cost into the total output, i.e.,

$$\text{Average unit cost/per tonne} = \frac{\text{total capital and current input cost per hectare}}{\text{total output per hectare (tonne)}}$$

It should be noted that the input price in this model was an average unit cost of capital and current inputs, rather than unit price. Thus, it should be borne in mind that there may be some difference between these two variables in the interpretation of the results as will be seen later.

4) Provincial data   Both capital and current input cost prices and labour

172

cost prices are calculated based on the cost of production data published by Ministry of Agriculture (MOA). This is only source for cost of production data available for major grains at the provincial level. However, provincial data for certain years and certain individual crops were missing. Thus, the labour price and the average unit cost of capital and current input were calculated based on weighted average value of individual crop price and cost. The main data used in the model are presented in Table 8.1

The data source and limitations have been discussed in detail in the previous chapter. The same problem regarding data limitations also existed in this model. Thus, the results obtained from the analysis must be interpreted with this caveat in mind.

8.5   Empirical estimation

The parameters for marketable surplus are obtained through the joint estimation of consumption functions (equation 8.9) and supply functions (equation 8.11). There is one degree of freedom for the parameters of the CES function which can be exhausted by any suitable normalisation. The normalisation chosen is that the share parameter α_2 is equal to one. The results estimated in the model are given in Table 8.2.

In the demand equations, six of the nine parameters are significant at the 1 per cent level and two at the 5 per cent level of significance.[4] Only one of the parameter was not significant. In the supply equations, four of the six parameters were significant at the 1 per cent level of significance. As there is no intercepts in this model system, the conventional R^2 may no longer be

appropriate. Instead a generalised $\bar{R}^2$, which was proposed by Baxter and Cragg (1970), was adopted to test the goodness-of-fit of the model. This

coefficient is defined as follows: $\bar{R}^2 = \{1-\exp[2*(L_o-L_{max})/N]\}$. Where L_o is the value of the logarithm of the likelihood function when all parameters are constant to zero; L_{max} is its maximum value when all coefficients are allowed to vary and N is the total number of observations. The

generalised $\bar{R}^2$ was 0.82 indicating a high goodness of fit.

The null hypothesis of symmetry, i.e., $\delta_{ij}=\delta_{ji}$, for all $i \neq j$ imposed on the model was tested by estimating restricted ($\delta_{ij}=\delta_{ji}$) and unrestricted models. Using a likelihood ratio test, the calculated χ^2 is 5.76 which is below the critical value of 12.59 at the 5 per cent of level of significance with six degrees of freedom. Thus, the null hypothesis of $\delta_{ij}=\delta_{ji}$ for all $i \neq j$, was not rejected.

173

Table 8.1
Description of the data from 1978-92

	Unit	Mean	Standard deviation	Minimum	Maximum
Family labour on farm (H_1)	Thousand persons	10633.86	8388.35	834.38	38809.72
Family labour off-farm (H_2)	Thousand persons	2420.34	2422.91	95.62	16657.75
On-farm return (p_1)	Yuan/per capita/ day	1.35	0.49	0.68	3.39
Off-farm wage rate (p_2)	Yuan/per capita/day	3.04	1.84	0.08	7.90
Daily expenditure on consumption (p_3)	Yuan/per capita/day	0.84	0.12	0.19	1.46
Output price (q_1)	Yuan/tonne	339.93	153.57	263.00	3445.00
Labour cost price (q_2)	Yuan/tonne	156.02	74.00	51.99	535.54
Capital and current input cost (q_3)	Yuan/tonne	125.29	71.90	43.53	493.64
Days of on-farm (D_1)	Days/year	155.78	58.34	66.56	401.02
Days of off-farm (D_2)	Days/year	33.91	20.99	11.20	182.73
Expenditure on non-farm work (L_5)	Yuan/year	287.34	155.20	46.53	889.41
Expenditure on non-off-farm work (L_6)	Yuan/year	505.53	260.17	135.78	1485.60
Expenditure on consumption (e_1)	Yuan/year	238.46	103.66	23.00	857.18
Net marketable supply for grain (S_1)	Tonne/year /per capita	0.439	0.50790	0.05980	2.99338
Net labour demand (S_2)	Year/ per capita	0.159	0.17616	0.02231	1.15287
Net capital and current input (S_3)	Yuan /year/ per capita	1.321	1.41236	0.07150	8.21177

In order to remove the influences of inflation during the period 1978-92, prices and income data related to both supply and demand were deflated based on the 1978 rural consumption price index (1978=100).

174

Table 8.2
Estimated parameters of the consumption and supply equations

Parameter	Estimate	T-Statistic
α_1	-0.55	-11.25**
α_2	1	(-)
α_3	2.09	8.59**
δ_{11}	-37.09	-1.78*
δ_{12}	39.91	5.68**
δ_{13}	70.59	2.30**
δ_{22}	-7.88	-2.26**
δ_{23}	-151.95	-4.95**
δ_{33}	-19.56	-0.26
Rho	0.09	1.71*
b_{11}	0.04	0.91
b_{12}	-0.23	-10.90**
b_{13}	0.64	21.28**
b_{22}	0.48	7.80**
b_{23}	-0.13	-2.35**
b_{33}	0.16	0.85
Value of likelihood function	-8107.65	
Number of observations	420	
Generalised $\bar{R}^2$	0.82	

Notes: (1) The parameters are estimated by the joint estimation of consumption equations of (8.9) and supply equations (8.11a) of the model using a Full Information Maximum Likelihood method (FIML).
(2) Two stars (**)and one star (*) in the Table indicate the statistical significance of the parameters at the 1 per cent , 5 per cent levels respectively.

Having estimated these parameters, labour supply elasticities, conditional and unconditional supply and demand elasticities can be derived using the analytical procedures outlined in section 8.3.4. The effect of farm return and off-farm wage on family labour supply are measured based on equation (8.9). These elasticities are presented in Table 8.3.

Table 8.3
On-farm and off-farm labour supply elasticities at the sample mean

	On-farm return	Off-farm wage	Consumption expenditure
On-farm labour supply	0.864	-0.872	0.098
Off-farm labour supply	-0.063	2.786	0.519

The results in Table 8.3 indicate that both on-farm and off-farm labour supply respond positively to their respective income. However, the off-farm wage effect (elasticity 2.79) is much stronger than the effect of on-farm return (elasticity 0.86). Moreover, the off-farm wage effect on the on-farm labour (elasticity -0.87) is rather strong whereas the impact of on-farm return on off-farm labour is negligible (elasticity -0.06). These results suggest Chinese farm households respond more strongly to off-farm wage than that to on-farm return. The elasticities with respect to consumption expenditure in Table 8.3 are both positive, demonstrating that households reduce their leisure and allocate labour to both on-farm and off-farm works in order to maintain or increase their living standard. However, the off-farm effect (0.52) is much stronger than the on-farm effect (0.10). This reflects the fact that the off-farm income may be a main source of income pursued by farm households while the consumption expenditure is rising.

The effects of changes in output price and labour price on labour supply are estimated from equation (8.13). Table 8.4 presents the estimated labour supply elasticities with respect to output price and labour price respectively.

Table 8.4
Labour supply elasticities with respect to output price
and labour price at the sample mean

	Output price	On-farm labour price
On farm labour supply	0.602	0.220
Off-farm labour supply	-0.044	-0.016

The farm labour supply elasticity with respect to output price displays the same sign as that for farm return: a 1 per cent increase in output price is associated with a 0.60 per cent increase in the number of days worked on farm, but 0.04 per cent decline in the number of days worked off-farm.

Thus, output price had little influence on off-farm work. Farm labour price has a positive influence on farm labour supply (0.22) but little influence (-0.02) on off-farm labour supply. These various elasticities at aggregate level show that such results are consistent with the theoretical framework.

In order to examine the impact of on-farm labour supply on marketable surplus, the net supply and demand responses are firstly estimated. Table 8.5 presents the net supply and demand elasticities which are derived directly from equation (8.14), i.e., assuming that on-farm labour supply remains constant while grain price has been changed.

Table 8.5
Net marketable surplus supply and factor demand elasticities
at the sample mean

	Output price	On-farm labour price	Capital and current input cost
Marketable supply	-0.267	-0.181	0.448^5
On-farm labour demand	-0.496	0.668	-0.171
Capital and current input demand	0.403	-0.056	-0.347

The net marketable surplus elasticity with respect to output prices (q_1) in Table 8.5 is negative at -0.27. This result is consistent with the sign of the net marketable surplus supply elasticity in the previous chapter. The labour demand elasticity with respect to output price (q_1) is negative at -0.50 which is also consistent with the negative marketable surplus price elasticity above. These results are not surprising. Apart from the reasons given in the previous chapter, i.e., data problems and own-consumption, the main reason for this is that the net supply and demand elasticities did not consider the effect of output prices on farm labour input, thereby, on marketable surplus supply simultaneously. Indeed, this is a very special case. However, if the effect of farm labour changes on supply and demand was taken into account, which is the so-called conditional supply and demand responses in section 8.3.4, the sign of elasticities will be quite different from 'net' elasticities in Table (8.5). The conditional supply and demand responses were defined based on equation (8.15), i.e., taking the effect of output prices on farm labour input into account, but ignoring the effect of changes in off-farm income on supply and demand. These results are presented in Table 8.6.

177

Table 8.6
Conditional marketable surplus supply and factor demand elasticities
at the sample mean

		Output price	On-farm labour price	Capital and current input cost
Marketable supply	η	0.221	-0.359	-0.095
On-farm labour demand	η	1.071	0.490	-0.715
Capital and current input demand	η	0.891	-0.234	-0.890

Marketable surplus supply response has become positive in relation to output price as expected. A 1 per cent increase in output price increases the marketable surplus supply by 0.22 per cent. Both on-farm labour and capital input demand respond positively to the output price and elasticities are relatively large (1.07 and 0.89 respectively). The marketable surplus supply responded (as expected) negatively to input prices (on-farm labour and capital input). This implies that an increase in input prices may lead to a decrease in marketable surplus supply. The cross price elasticities between farm labour and capital and current inputs are negative, indicating these two production factors were complements rather than substitutes during the period of study. The capital input demand responded negatively to its own prices, indicating that an increase in capital input prices will lead to decrease in demand for capital and current inputs. However, labour input demand responded positively to its own price. This is due to the fact that labour used here is family labour rather hired labour.

As an important issue discussed in this chapter is concerned with the impact of off-farm activities on marketable surplus supply; thus the unconditional marketable surplus supply elasticities will be the main focus of concern. The conditional supply and demand elasticities in Table 8.6 assume that off-farm labour is constant. The unconditional supply and demand responses take off-farm activities into account simultaneously while output price has been changed. The effect of off-farm income on marketable surplus supply can be examined through a comparison of conditional and unconditional supply response elasticities. In connection with the marketable surplus supply sector, it is important to note that the marketable surplus supply response was linked with changes in on-farm labour supply, and the latter is closely related to changes in off-farm activities. The unconditional supply and demand elasticities are presented in Table 8.7.

Table 8.7

Unconditional marketable surplus supply and factor demand elasticities at the sample mean

		Output prices	On-farm labour price	Capital and current input cost
Marketable supply	η^*	-0.272	-0.538	0.454
On-farm labour demand	η^*	0.578	0.669	-0.166
Capital and current input demand	η^*	0.398	-0.054	-0.341

Note: Elasticities (η) are conditional, i.e., hold off-farm labour supply constant. Elasticities (η^*) are unconditional, i.e., allow off-labour supply to vary.

The unconditional supply and demand elasticities in Table 8.7 are calculated using equation (8.16$_a$). The conditional and unconditional supply and demand responses in Tables (8.6) and (8.7) provide interesting comparisons. Firstly, the sign of the marketable supply price elasticity has changed from positive (0.22) to negative (-0.27). This is because the negative effects of off-farm employment on farm labour input tends to lead to a decline in marketable supply. Secondly, the magnitudes of the demand elasticities for farm labour and capital inputs are also reduced from 1.07 to 0.58 and from 0.89 to 0.40 respectively. Other elasticities also show significant changes. The negative response of marketable supply response to on-farm labour price became stronger, from -0.36 to -0.54. The response of capital and current input demand to farm labour price weakened, from -0.23 to -0.05; which implies that the demand for capital and current inputs may increase due to the fact that on-farm labour input is reduced. Thirdly, the marketable supply elasticity with respect to capital and current input prices changed from negative (-0.10) to positive (0.45). This implies that marketable supply became more dependent on capital inputs as on-farm labour input is reduced.

The difference in sign and magnitude between the conditional and unconditional supply and demand responses are substantial and indicate the impact of off-farm employment on farm labour supply and its negative effect on marketable supply. These results also demonstrate that labour migrants from the farm sector in China cannot any longer be regarded simply as zero value surplus labour. Most migrants are the stronger younger members of the labour force. Their age typically is in the range 15 to 34 years and, in many areas, males accounted for 75 to 85 per cent of the total (World Bank, 1993). Moreover, most off-farm migrants from rural to urban areas are educated young people. Thus, a large number of the male labour force was employed in the non-farm sector leaving a disproportionate number of old and female workers in farm work. In addition, increasing off-farm job opportunities not only cause more rural qualified labour force to move from farming to wage employment, but also reduced the time spent on farm by those remaining at home.[6]

8.6   Summary

This chapter examined the effect of off-farm income on marketable surplus supply while grain prices were rising in China. In contrast to the conventional subjective equilibrium model which emphasises the household's structure through its demographic structure changes (number, age, and sex of family members), this study highlights the demographic social changes due to changes in income and employment structure. The theoretical framework demonstrated that the farm households' supply behaviour depends not only on the profitability of farm production, but also on alternative off-farm wage opportunities for household members. The following main conclusions emerge from the empirical study.

Firstly, in the Chinese rural economy during the reform period, on-farm labour input was an important factor influencing marketable surplus supply response. A link can be seen between the positive effect of grain prices on farm labour input (elasticity 0.6) and the conditional marketable surplus supply elasticity (0.22) with respect to grain prices.

Secondly, to understand labour supply response, it is particularly important to understand the forces influencing farm household labour allocation decisions. This study showed that on-farm and off-farm labour responded positively to their respective incomes. However, off-farm labour supply was much more elastic with respect to the off-farm wage than was on-farm labour to farm return. This may indicate different labour supply responses between on-farm and off-farm work under two different income opportunities. The much higher off-farm labour supply elasticity with respect to consumption expenditure is consistent with the diversification of household labour in favour of off-farm work. These also show the possible impact of off-farm employment on on-farm labour input.

Thirdly, the growth of off-farm employment during the reform period has been a key factor influencing marketable surplus supply. The strong negative effect of this employment was demonstrated by the difference in the conditional marketable supply elasticity (0.22) and the unconditional value (-0.27).

Finally, as the Chinese rural economy continues to diversify and becomes more integrated with the wider economy, the tendency to allocate more farm household labour towards the non-farm sector will continue. Price incentives for grain in themselves may not be adequate to counter this trend and ensure sustained growth in marketable surplus supply. More capital intensive methods will be required and thus incentives to promote technical progress and capital investment will be needed alongside grain price incentives.

Notes

1. Lopez's used two leisures in his model. One major problem is that an overlap between $H-H_1$ and $H-H_2$ may occur. As the total activity time available is H, and total on-farm and off-farm activities cannot be larger than total time available, it implies that farm households will consume some leisure (L_3) at a given price and income, i.e., $H=H_1+H_2+L_3$. Thus, after dividing two leisures, the leisure 1 ($H-H_1$) is H_2+L_3 and leisure 2 ($H-H_2$) is H_1+L_3. This would mean that part of time (L_3) would be spent twice. In order to overcome this problem, we define H as a 'total work time available per year' (excluding leisure time L_3). So we use two labours in the model.

2. This assumption is plausible as the total work time each day or total work time in a year can be treated as constant. Therefore, ($H-H_1$) and ($H-H_2$) reflect how the household allocates its total work time between on-farm and off-farm work.

3. The reason why the model does not simply generate a corner solution, in which all labour is either in H_1 if $\bar{\pi} > w_2$ or all in H_2 if the reverse is the case, is for the following three reasons. (1) Theoretically, as labour supply was analysed through the utility function, behaviour can be explained in the context of utility maximising behaviour rather than profit maximising behaviour. That is, labour supply behaviour depends not only upon prices and the wage rate, but also upon preferences. (2) As the constraint condition (8.4c) has indicated that $H_1 \geq 0$, $H_2 \geq 0$, this means that (8.4_a) is not binding; thus, this is an internal solution. If constraint (8.4_c) is binding then for some households $H_1=0$ or $H_2=0$; and there are rather serious econometric difficulties associated with corner solution (3). Given that the data used in the empirical study are aggregated, both H_1 and H_2 are greater than zero at all sample points and

hence constraint (8.4_c) is not binding at any of the observations, therefore, it does not simply generate corner solutions.

4. In a large sample the maximum likelihood estimates are asymptotically normally distributed so that statistical significance can be tested with standard t statistics (William, et al., 1993, p453; Benjamin and Guyomard, 1994)

5. It should be noted that the elasticity of net market supply with respect to capital and current input cost in Tables 8.5 and 8.6 are positive. The reason for this is that the variable used here is unit cost of capital and current input rather than input prices. This is because no input prices are available. As an increase in capital and current input cost could be the results of either the rise of its prices or the rise of its amount used. Thus, if an increase in cost is caused by the latter, the supply elasticity with respect to cost will be positive.

6. One drawback of the model was that it was unable to reflect qualitative changes in labour supply due to the lack of household education data.

9 Résumé

9.1 Contribution of the study

This study is the first attempt to investigate systematically the linkages between grain prices and farm households' supply response behaviour in China during the period 1978-92. It is also the first attempt to develop and implement a comprehensive theoretical and empirical model for this purpose. Efforts were made to investigate grain price policies and Chinese farm household supply behaviour within economy-wide perspectives.

The most important feature of the work is its theoretical and empirical analysis, linking the effects of own-consumption, grain prices, farm income and other non-farm income on marketable surplus supply. The empirical results are consistent with the predictions of the theoretical model and demonstrate the complexity of these relationships within farm households at this stage in the development of Chinese rural economy. Prices undoubtedly exert influences on farm households' decision-making but the non-farm economy is seen to be increasingly influential.

9.2 Summary and conclusions

9.2.1 The core issues

Agriculture in China remains relatively traditional and is characterised by small scale units, labour intensive methods and high levels of subsistence production. Alongside this the rural reforms have resulted in a much more diversified rural economy and considerably expanded labour choices for farm household members. All of this has greatly increased the complexity of the rural economy: the choices available to farm household members have greatly increased and incentive structures have changed. All of this has made the modelling of grain production by farm households, especially marketable surplus supply, a much more difficult task. Our challenge was to develop a theoretical and empirical approach which could capture some of these complex interdependencies, especially as they might affect grain marketable surplus, and which would be consistent with economic theory. We believe we have made some progress along that road.

9.2.2   Main characteristics of the rural reforms

The most important characteristic of the Chinese rural economy is that it is neither a mature market economy nor a typical centrally-planned economy. It is in an economic transition process from a planning system to a market system, from a subsistent or semi-subsistent rural economy to a commercial economy. Thus, the entire rural economy has dual characteristics.

Market systems have developed rapidly but the state still relies heavily on administrative measures for output supply and input distribution in the grain sector. The market system is far from being mature: it is characterised by regional isolation, poor communications of the relevant market information, with most grain being traded through the state marketing channel.

Although commercial agricultural production has grown during the rural reform, the commercial grain sector is still relatively undeveloped. The traditional pattern of labour intensive production and grain own-consumption characterised the agricultural sector over the period of study. Farm households' own-consumption still accounts for a large proportion of their total production. This situation is likely to persist well into the future.

Price reform was the most important step towards a market oriented system. State intervention, however, is still extensive in grain markets. This has resulted typically in: (a) a disparity between the state purchase price and the free market price, as well as between the domestic and world market grain prices; (b) as a result dual price signals have existed in the grain market. Thus, we can say that price adjustments had more to do with the levels of prices rather than on creating a truly integrated grain market system and price.

The rapid growth of township, village and private enterprises in rural China was a notable outcome of the reforms. Choices for farm households have expanded and non-farm employment has become an important option in labour allocation. Although farmers are still restricted to some degree from participating in urban industries, they have, nevertheless, more opportunities to engage in various rural non-farm activities as a means of maximising household income. It should also be said that there is a traditional view that holding a salaried job is more noble than farm work: undoubtedly this has also been influential in employment choices.

9.2.3   A focus on the farm household

The growing complexity of the rural economy had implications for the way in which farm households' grain supply behaviour should be modelled. Household full income maximisation was regarded as a more appropriate behavioural assumption for the modelling exercise than farm profit maximisation.

Following the assumption of full income maximisation, an integrated non-recursive modelling framework was adopted.   This attempted to capture, in a theoretically appropriate manner, the complex linkages between marketable supply, grain prices, household consumption and labour allocation.   A set of household supply and consumption responses was derived from the same indirect utility function: this principally quantified the relationships between, on the one hand, grain prices, marketable surplus supply and households' own consumption and, on the other, grain prices, marketable surplus supply and off-farm income.

9.2.4   Some important results

The most important finding of the empirical study was that grain marketable surplus supply of farm households' was significantly affected by the levels of their own-consumption and off-farm work. These factors can make marketable supply somewhat unpredictable. The following more specific findings should be highlighted.

* *The effect of output price on own-consumption and farm labour supply in the absence of the full income effect (uncompensated own-consumption and labour supply responses)*   Output price has, as expected, a negative effect on own-consumption (elasticities of -0.80 in the marketable surplus case and -0.13 in the total output supply case) and a positive effect on farm labour supply (elasticities of 0.38 in the marketable surplus case and 0.36 in the total output supply case). This indicates that own-consumption will decline due to an increase in its opportunity cost after a grain price rise. Meanwhile, an increase in grain price will lead to an increase in farm labour supply due to an income effect.

* *The effect of farm income on own-consumption and farm labour supply in the absence of the full income effect (uncompensated own-consumption and labour supply responses)*   Associated with the effect of

185

output price, farm income has a dual effect on own-consumption: it will tend to decline due to an increase in farm income, since increased farm income following a grain price rise implies an increase in opportunity cost of own-consumption. On the other hand, own-consumption will tend to increase due to an increase in real income. The final effect of farm income on own-consumption depends on the magnitude of these two effects. The empirical results in this study show that farm income has a negative effect on own-consumption (elasticities of -0.07 in the marketable surplus case and -0.75 in the total output case). Meanwhile, farm income has a positive effect on farm labour supply (elasticities of 1.03 in the marketable surplus case and 0.99 in the total output case).

    * *The effect of full income on own-consumption and labour supply* However, full income has a positive effect on own-consumption. This is consistent with observed increases in household consumption from the relatively low levels in recent years. On the other hand, on-farm labour supply will tend to decline following a rise in full income. This is most likely due to the link between increases in household income and off-farm employment.

    * *Compensated own-consumption and labour supply responses* Taking the effects of full income into account, the compensated own-consumption price elasticities further indicated that full income has a positive effect on own-consumption. The negative effects of output prices on own-consumption were reduced from -0.8 to -0.7 in the marketable surplus case and from -0.13 to 0.20 in the total output case. This suggested that the own-consumption of grain among rural farm households is likely to be increased marginally due to the full income effect. On the other hand, the negative effect of full income on on-farm labour supply was further demonstrated by the compensated labour supply responses. The magnitude of on-farm labour supply elasticity was reduced from 0.38 to 0.27 in the marketable surplus case. In the total output case, the sign of price elasticity was changed from positive (0.36) to negative (-0.04) due to full income effects. Thus, there was a tendency for own-consumption to rise but for on-farm labour supply to decline in Chinese grain production after taking account of full income effects.

    * *The effect of own-consumption on marketable surplus (unconditional supply responses)* Taking account of own-consumption, marketable surplus supply response with respect to output price was negative(-0.84). This may be contrasted with the positive (0.33) positive conditional elasticity. Thus, the negative effect of own-consumption on marketable surplus is large and strong. The decline in farm labour supply and the increase in own-consumption due to full income effects will tend to lead to a loss of marketable surplus supply.

* The effect of on-farm return and off-farm wage on labour supply
Both on-farm and off-farm labour supply respond positively to their respective incomes. However, the off-farm wage effect (elasticity 2.79) is much stronger than the effect of on-farm return (elasticity 0.86). These results indicate that Chinese farm households respond much more strongly to the off-farm wage than that to the on-farm return.

* The cross income effect on labour supply Cross income elasticities of labour supply show that the off-farm wage effect on on-farm labour (elasticity -0.87) is rather strong whereas the impact of on-farm return on off-farm labour is negligible (elasticity -0.06). This is consistent with the trend of rural labour flow in recent years. It is also consistent with the estimated labour responses to consumption expenditure, where the off-farm effect (0.52) is much stronger than the on-farm effect (0.10).

* The effect of off-farm labour allocation on marketable surplus supply
Comparing the unconditional marketable surplus supply elasticity (-0.272) with the conditional supply elasticities (0.221), shows the strong negative effect of off-farm work on surplus supply. The results show that the growth of off-farm income opportunities during the reform period has been a key factor influencing marketable surplus supply response, particularly after the liberalisation of factor markets.

9.3   Some implications for policy and future research

Although it is beyond the scope of this book to consider policy issues in detail, it is nevertheless appropriate to outline some of the implications for policy which may arise from this work. This discussion is based on a paper by Zong and Davis (1998). . Government policy towards the grain sector is still very much centred around the long-run aim of national self-sufficiency in grain. This policy has had greater staying power than other slogans from the Maoist era, reinforced by memories of China's vulnerability during the Great Famine of the early 1960s (Wang and Davis 1998). The most recent major initiative in pursuit of this aim was the introduction in late 1994 of the Provincial Governors' Grain Responsibility policy. Amongst other things Provincial Governors now have a responsibility to increase the level of grain marketable surplus at the provincial level, even though this can be greatly at odds with the objective of efficiency in overall resource allocation (Lu 1996). However, as the Chinese rural economy continues to diversify and becomes more integrated into the wider economy, the tendency to allocate more farm household labour towards the off-farm sector will continue: as the analysis in this book has shown, this will tend to have negative consequences for gain marketable surplus supply. Price incentives for grain production in themselves may not be adequate to counter this trend and ensure sustainable growth in marketable surplus supply: in any case we have shown that the pure price effect on marketable surplus is at best very weak. Thus it is likely that more capital intensive methods will be required and incentives to promote technical progress and capital investment will be needed alongside grain price incentives. Li et al. (1998) argue that the Chinese government must take greater responsibility for promoting these measures and that it should also increase its direct investment in agricultural infrastructure and research and development: they argue that this would be no more than a 'refunding' of past exploitation of agriculture. Alongside the need for such investment is the necessity for deeper reforms to the land tenure system, in order to overcome the weaknesses associated with the Household Responsibility System. At the moment the country is experimenting with four main types of land reform system. Ultimately it must decide whether and how one or more of these models might be more widely adopted. For a detailed discussion of these issues see Fu et al. (1997). Clearly, there is very considerable further work needed to translate these broad policy prescriptions into policy programmes and measures which can take account of the very different conditions and levels of development of the grain economy in the various regions of China. Nevertheless, such work is essential if China is to sustain the development of its grain sector in the context of a national autarky objective.

It seems clear to us that unless policy makers seek to understand better the unique features of the Chinese grain economy highlighted in this book, and adopt an appropriate mix of measures, it will be quite unlikely that the full potential in grain production and output can be realised.

It is arguable that theoretical and empirical work on grain price policy and farm households' supply behaviour is only just beginning. Accordingly, we see four further avenues of research that could be fruitful.

Firstly, this study has shed some light on how the effect of price adjustment was weakened by the state intervention, including use of the two-tier price system. The state purchase price and free market prices co-existed and interplayed with each other. Although a number of researchers have already studied this area, research on this topic is incomplete, both theoretically and empirically. Theoretical and empirical modelling of this feature is difficult but important. It can be expected that, with the publication of more detailed price and procurement data, further research might seek to disentangle the impacts of these two distinct prices on marketable surplus supply.

Secondly, although price distortions and institutional constraints have been discussed in this study, the quantitative analysis of such effects on marketable surplus is rather difficult. The price distortions caused by government intervention in the output and input markets are visible. For example, in the output markets, state contract and negotiated purchase accounted for over 80 percent of total grain sales in the 1980s and early 1990s; in the input markets, in the 1990s major input subsidies were linked to contract procurement, eg. providing fertiliser, pesticides, fuel and plastic sheeting at subsidised prices to farmers who fulfilled the state procurement contract. These factors undoubtedly influenced farm households' supply behaviour. However, they are difficult to incorporate into an empirical model. Use of a shadow-price profit frontier to model price and market distortions in China was proposed by Wang et al. (1996). Further developing their approach into an integrated framework to measure such effects on marketable surplus supply may be worthwhile.

Thirdly, although the economic integration between the farm and non-farm sectors was a focus for this study, the impact of greater economic integration within agricultural production was not investigated. The opportunity cost of grain production is an important consideration in supply response. Changes in the prices of cash crops and animal products will affect the supply and demand of grain through cross price supply elasticities and through demand for animal feed. Further research in this area within an integrated framework may be appropriate.

Finally, the whole area of investment behaviour by farm households with regard to eg. livestock, buildings, machinery, irrigation etc. may need to be researched particularly as it might be expected to affect grain supply in the long-run.

- / -

Bibliography

Abbott, M. and Ashenfelter, O. (1976), *Labour Supply, Commodity Demand and the Allocation of Time*, Review of Economic Studies, (43): pp. 389-411.

Adelman, I. and Taylor, J. E., (1991), *The Use of Farm Level Data for Policy Analysis*, Working Paper, Department of Agricultural and Resource Economics, University of California at Berkeley, No: 597.

Ahluwalia, I. (1979), *An Analysis of Price and Output Behaviour in the Indian Economy: 1951-1973*, Journal of Development Economics, (6), pp. 363-390.

Alderman, H. and Sahn, D. E. (1993), *Substitution between Goods and Leisure in a Developing Country*, American Journal of Agricultural Economics, (75), pp. 875-883.

Almon, S. (1965), *The Distributed Lag between Capital Appropriations and Expenditures*, Econometrics: 33.

An, X. J. (1992), *Prices, Costs and Farm Income in Mainland China, Rules of Farmer Behaviour in a Uniquely Mixed Economy*, in Cakins, P., Chen, W.S. and Tuan, F.C., (eds), Rural Development in Taiwan and Mainland China.

--------(1989) *The Development and Improvement of Agricultural Marketing in China, China's Rural Development Miracle: with International Comparisons*, J. Longworth., ed., University of Queensland Press, Australia.

Anderson, K. and Tyers, R. (1987), *Economic Growth and Market Liberalisation in China: Implications for Agricultural Trade*, The Developing Economies, XXV-2, pp. 124-151.

190

Ash, R. F. (1993), *Agricultural Policy Under the Impact of Reform*, in Kueh, Y.Y. and Ash, R. (eds) Economic Trends in Chinese Agriculture, Clarendon Press.

Askari, H. (1965), *The Marketable Function for a Subsistence Crop: An Analysis with Indian Data*, The Economic Weekly, Vol. 17, February, pp. 309-320.

Askari, H. and Cummings, J. T. (1976), *Agricultural Supply Response: A Survey of the Economic Evidence*, Praeger Publishers: New York.

Bai, M. Q. (1993), China Consumer Post, 31 May, 1993, p 2.

Banister, J. and Harbaugh, C. W. (1992), *Rural Labour Force Trends in China*, China Agriculture and Trade Report Situation and Outlook Series, USDA, Economic Research Service, (3): pp. 59-68.

Barber, W. J. (1960). *Economic Rationality and Behaviour Patterns in an Underdeveloped Area: A case Study of African Economic Behaviour in the Rhodesias*, Economic Development and Cultural Change (8), pp. 237-251;

Bardhan, K. (1970), *Price and Output Response of Marketed Surplus of Food Grains: A Cross-Sectional Study of Some North Indian Villages*, American Journal of Agricultural Economics, February, (52), pp. 51-61.

Bardhan, P. and Bardhan, K. (1971), *Price Response of Marketed Surplus of Food Grains An Analysis of Indian Time-Series Data*, Oxford Economic Papers, (23), pp. 255-267.

Barnum, H.N. and Squire, L. (1979a), *An Economic Application of the Theory of the Farm-Household*. Journal of Development Economics, (6), pp. 79-102.

--------(1979b). *A Model of An Agricultural Household*, World Bank Occasional Paper, Washington. D.C.

Bateman, M. J. (1965), *Aggregate and Regional Supply Functions for Ghanaian Cocoa, 1946-1962*, Journal of Farm Economics, (47), pp. 384-401.

Bauer, P.T. and Yamey, B. S. (1959), *A Case Study of Response to Price in an Underdeveloped Country*, Economic Journal, (69), pp. 800-805.

Baxter, N.D. and Cragg, J.L. (1970), *Corporate Choice among Long-term Financing Instruments*, Review Economic Statistics, (52), pp. 225-235.

Becker, G.S. (1976), *The Economic Approach to Human Behaviour*, The University of Chicago Press.

Becker, G.S. (1965), *A Theory of the Allocation of Time,* The Economic Journal, Vol. LXXV, pp. 493-517.

Becker, H. (1990), *Labour Input Decisions of Subsistence Farm Households in Southern Malawi*, Journal of Agricultural Economics,

(41), pp. 162-171.

Behrman, J. (1989), *Agricultural Supply*, in Eatwell, J., Milgate, M. and Newman, P. (eds), The New Palgrave: Economic Development, Macmillan, pp. 35-42.

--------(1968), *Supply Response in Underdeveloped Agriculture: A case Study of Farm Major Annual Crops in Thailand: 1937-1963*, North-Holland: Amsterdam.

--------(1966), *Price Elasticity of the Marketed Surplus of a Subsistence Crop*, Journal of Farm Economics, Nov. Vol. 48, (4), pp. 875-893.

Beijing Review, (1986), *Rural Industries Take on Technology*, 10 February 1986.

Benjamin, C. and Guyomard, H. (1994), *Off-Farm Work Decisions of French Agricultural Households*, in Caillavey, F. et al (eds), *Agricultural Household Modelling and Family Economics*, Elsevier.

Blackorby, C., Boyce, R. and Russell, R. (1978), *Estimation of Demand Systems Generated by the Gorman Polar Form: A Generalization of the S-Branch Utility Tree*, Econometrica, (46), pp. 345-363.

Boussard, J-M., (1985), *Is Agricultural Production Responsive to Prices?* European Review of Agricultural Economics, Vol. 12-1/2, pp. 31-44.

Brown, L.R, Webb, P. and Haddad, L. (1994), *The Role of Labour in Household Food Security: Implications of AID in Africa.* Food Policy, (6), pp. 568-573.

Brown, M. and Heien, D. (1972), *The S-Branch Utility Tree: A Generalization of the Linear Expenditure System*, Econometrica, (40), pp. 737-747

Buck, J.L. (1937), *Land Utilization in China*, Nanking, University of Nanking.

Butterfield, F. (1979), *China's Modernisation Said to Cause 1979 Deficit*, New York Times, 5 June 1979.

Caillavet, F., Guyomard, H. and Lifran, R., (eds), (1994), *Agricultural Household Modelling and Family Economics*, Elsevier Science B.V.

Carter, C.A. and Zhong, F.N., (1991), *China's Past and Future Role in the Grain Trade*, Economic Development and Cultural Change, Vol. 39 (4), pp. 791-814.

--------(1988), *China's Grain Production and Trade An Economic Analysis*, Boulder and London Westview Press.

Catherine, H. and Conrado, G., (1990), *A Policy Analysis of China's Wheat Economy*, American Journal of Agricultural Economics, (73), pp. 268-278.

Chamberlain, G. (1984), *Panel Data*, Chapter 22 in the Griliches and Intriligator (eds), *Handbook of Econometrics*, Elsevier Science

Publishers: The Netherlands.

Chambers, R.G., (1988), *Applied Production Analysis: A Dual Approach*, Cambridge University Press.

Chayanov, A.A. (1966), *The Theory of Peasant Economy*, in Thorner, D., Kerblay, B. and Smith, R.E.F. (eds), Irwin, Homewood, Illinois.

Chen, L.Y. and Buckwell, A., (1991), *Chinese Grain Economy and Policy*, UK. C.A.B. International.

Chen, N.R. and Galeson, W. (1969), *The Chinese Economy Under Communism*, Edinburgh University Press: Edinburgh.

Cheng, C.Y. (1982), *China's Economic Development and Structural Change*, Westview Press: Boulder Colorado.

Cheng, H. (1986), *Analysis of Panel Data*, Cambridge University.

Cheng, L. S., Zheng, S. J. & Cheng, W. H. (1993), *Agricultural Production Response to the Price Under a Dual Pricing System in China*, Economic Research (Chinese), January.

Cheng, Y.S. and Tsang, S. (1994), *The Changing Grain Marketing System in China*, China Quarterly, Vol. 140, (4), pp. 1080-1104.

Cheng, Y.S., Tsang, S. K and Chen, W. H (1993), *Price Response of Chinese Production under the Double-Track Price System*, Economic Research (Chinese), (2), pp. 16-25.

Chinn, D.L (1976), *The Marketed Surplus of a Subsistence Crop: Paddy Rice in Taiwan*, American Journal of Agricultural Economics, (58), pp. 583-587.

Chou, Z. Z. (1984), *Chinese Economy*, Chinese Economic Publishing House.

Christiansen, F. (1991), *Chinese Rural Policy Issues 1987-90*, paper presented at The Second European Conference on Agricultural and Rural Development in China, University of Leiden, 14-18 January, 1991.

Claude, A. 1990, *The Agricultural Crisis in China at the end of the 1980s*, in Delma, J. (ed) Remaking Peasant China.

Colby, W. H., Crook, F. W. and Webb, S-E. H. (1992), *Agricultural Statistics of The People's Republic of China, 1949-90*, USDA Washington DC.

Colman, D. (1983), *A Review of the Arts of Supply Rsponse Analysis*, Review of Marketing and Agricultural Economics, Vol. 53, No.3,pp 201-230.

--------(1972), *The United Kingdom Cereal Market: An Econometric Investigation into the Effects of Price Policies*, Manchester University Press: Manchester.

Cormick, B. J. (1994), *Macroeconomics and the Development of Political Economic Theory*, The Pentland Press.

Crook, F. (1994), *Grain Production for 1994 Projected at 450 Million*

Tonnes, International Agriculture and Trade Reports, pp. 13-17.

Dantwala, M. L. (ed) (1970), *Symposium on Farmer Response to Prices*, Journal of Indian Social of Agricultural Statistics, Vol. 22, June.

Davis, J. and Zong, P. (1995), *Rural Reforms and Economic Behaviour of Farmers in China, 1978-93*, in Copus, A.K. and Marr, P. J (eds) Rural Realities, Trends and Choices, Proceedings of the 35th EAAE Seminar Aberdeen Scotland.

Dean, E. (1966), *The Supply Response of African Farmers: Theory and Measurement,* in Malawi, North-Holland: Amsterdam.

Deaton, A.S. and Muellauer, J. (1980a), *An Almost Ideal Demand System*, American Economic Review, (70), pp. 321-326.

Deaton, A. and Bauer, J. M. (1989), *Economics and Consumer Behaviour*, Cambridge University Press.

Delforce, J. C. (1994), *Reparability in Farm-Household Economics: An Experiment with Linear Programming*, Agricultural Economics, (10), pp. 165-177.

Deng, Y. M. (1989), *On the Transfer of the Rural Labour Force in Underdeveloped Areas in China*, Journal of Population Science (Chinese) Vol. 1, (3), pp. 262-273.

Diewert, W. E. (1971), *An Application of The Shephard Duality Theorem: A Generalized Leontief Production Function*, Journal of Political Economics, (79), pp. 481-507.

Dong, F. (1982), *Relationship Between Accumulation and Consumption*, in Xu, D. X. et al, *China's Search for Economic Growth*, Beijing Review, New World Press.

Donnithorne, A. (1967), *China's Economic System*, George Allen & Unwin Ltd: London.

Du, W. C., (1995), *Agricultural Marketed Surplus Response in China*, Avebury.

Ellis, F. (1988), *Peasant Economics: Farm Household and Agrarian Development*, Cambridge University Press.

Epstein, L. (1981a), *Generalized Duality and Integrability*. Econometrica, (49), pp. 655-678.

--------(1981b), *Duality Theory and Functional Forms for Dynamic Factor Demands,* Review of Economic Studies, (48),pp. 81-95.

--------(1975), *A Desegregate Analysis of Consumer Choice under Uncertainty*, Econometrica, (43), pp. 871-892.

Evenson, R. E. (1978), *Time Allocation in Rural Philippine Households*, American Journal of Agricultural Economics, (60), pp. 322-330.

Fan, S. G. Wailes, E. J. and Cramer, G. L., (1995), *Household Demand in Rural China: A Two Stage LES-AIDS Model*, American Journal of Agricultural Economics, (77), pp. 54-62.

194

Falcon, W. P. (1964), *Farmers' Response to Price in a Subsistence Economy: The Case of West Pakistan*, American Economics Review, Papers and Proceedings, May.

Ferber, R. (1962), *Research on Household Behaviour*, American Economic Review, 52, pp. 19-63.

Fisher, F. (1963), *A Theoretical Analysis of the Impact of Food Surplus Disposal on Agricultural Production in Recipient Countries*, Journal of Farm Economics, (45), pp. 863-875.

Fu, C., Davis, J. and Wang, L. (1997), *Current Issues in China's Land Reforms.* Working Paper 1/97, Centre for Rural Studies, The Queen's University of Belfast.

Gao, X.M. (1989a), *Present Situation and Reform of Grain Purchase and Marketing System in China*, Developing Communication (internal, Chinese), No. 12.

--------(1989b), *The Formation of Surplus Adjustment Mechanism in the Supply of Agricultural Products and Characteristics of its Market Equilibrium*, Economic Research (Chinese), (8), pp. 12-19.

Ghatak, S. and Ingersent, K. (1984), *Agriculture and Economic Development*, WheatSheaf Books Ltd.

Gilbert, R. G. and Becker, G. S. (1975), *The Allocation of Time and Goods Over The Life Cycle,* Columbia University Press.

Gorman, W. M., (1953), *Community Preference Field*, Econometrica, (21), pp. 63-80.

Gould, J. P. and Ferguson, C. E. (1980), *Microeconomic Theory*, Richard D. Irwin, Inc.

Gravelle, H. and Rees, R. (1981), *Microeconomics*, Longman.

Gravelle, H and Rees, R. (1992), *Microeconomics*, Longman.

Greenaway, D. (ed), (1989), *Current Issues in Macroeconomics*, Macmillan.

Greene, W. H. (1993), *Econometric Analysis*, (Second edition), Macmillan Publishing Company.

Griffiths, W. E., Hill, R. C. and Judge, G.G. (1993), *Learning and Practicing Econometrics*, John Wiley & Sons Inc.

Gronau, R. (1980), *Leisure, Home Production and Work*, The Theory of the Allocation of Time Revisited, in: Rural Household Studies in Asia, Binswanger, H.P. et al. (eds).

Gularati, D. N. (1988), *Basic Econometrics*, McGraw-Hill International Editions, McGraw-Hill Book Company.

Guo, S. T. (1988), *Shortage and Policy Decision in Chinese Food Problems*, The Chinese People's University Press.

Haessel, W. (1975), *The Price and Income Elasticities of Home Consumption and Marketed Surplus of Food Grain*, American

Journal of Agricultural Economics, (57), pp. 111-115.

Halbrendt, C., Tuan, F., Gempesaw, C. and Dolk-Etz, D. (1994), *Rural Chinese Food Consumption: The Case of Guangdong*, American Journal of Agricultural Economics, (76), pp. 794-799.

Han, J. (1993), *Solving Rural Problems by Deepening Reform: an Interview with Mr Liu Jiang*, the Minister of Agriculture, China Rural Economy, (107), pp. 1-9.

Harvey, D. R. (ed), (1987). *The Future of the Agricultural and Food System and the Implications for Agricultural and Food R &D*, Working Paper No. 1, Department of Agricultural Economics and Management, Reading University.

Hayami, Y. and Ruttan, V. W. (1971), *Agricultural Development: An International Perspective*, The Johns Hopkins Press.

Henderson, J. M. and Quandt, R. E. (1980), *Microeconomic Theory, A Mathematical Approach*, McGraw-Hill Book Company: New York.

Henneberry, S. R. and Tweeten, L. G. (1991), *A Review of International Agricultural Supply Response*, Journal of International Food and Agribusiness Marketing, 2 (3/4), pp. 49-95.

Hinton, W. (1991), *The Privatisation of China*, London: Earthscan Press.

Holden, S. (1993), *Peasant Household Modelling: Farming Systems Evolution and Sustainability in Northern Zambia*, Agricultural Economics (9), pp. 241-267.

Hotelling, H. (1932), *Edgeworth's Taxation Paradox and the Nature of Demand and Supply Functions*, Journal of Political Economy, (5), pp. 577-616.

Howe, H., Pollak, R. A. and Wales, T. T. (1979), *Theory and Time Series Estimation of the Quadratic Expenditure System*, Econometrica, Vol. 47 (5), pp. 1231-1247.

Hsiao, C. (1986), *Analysis of Panel Data*, Cambridge University Press, London.

Hu, B. D. (1989), *Contemporary China's Price*, China Social Science Publishing House.

Hu, Y. K. (1985), *The Reform of Household Regulations and the Needs of Economic Development*, Social Science, (Chinese), (6), pp. 37.

Huang, J. K and Rozelle, S., (1995), *Environmental Stress and Grain Yields in China*, American Journal of Agricultural Economics, (77), pp. 853-864.

Huffman, W. E. and Lange, M. (1989), *Off-Farm Work Decisions of Husbands and Wives: Joint Decision Making*, Review of Economics and Statistics, (71), pp. 471-480.

Ishikawa, S. (1960), *Capital Formation in China*, Tokyo: Tokyo Book Store, pp. 139-85.

Jacoby, H. (1993), *Shadow Wages and Peasant Family Labour Supply: An Econometric Application to the Peruvian Sierra,* Review of Economic Studies, 60.4, pp. 903-921.

Jiang, J. and Luo, X. (1989), *Changes in Income of Chinese Peasants since 1978,* in Longworth, J. (ed), China's Rural Development Miracle: with International Comparisons, University of Queensland Press.

Jin, H. H. (1990), *Plan Market and Supply Behaviour of Food Grain of Chinese Peasants,* Economic Research, (9), pp. 62-68.

Katz, E and Stark, O. (1986), *Labour Migration and Risk Aversion in Less Developed Countries,* Journal of Labour Economics, (4), pp. 134-149.

Ke, B. S. (1991), *The Problems of Price Signals in China's Grain Market,* New China Digest, Vol. 152, (8), pp. 62-64.

Kojima, R. (1989), *Macroeconomic Development of China: "Overheating" in 1984-87 and Problems of Reform,* Journal of Japanese and International Economies, (3) pp. 64-121.

--------(1988), *Agricultural Organization: New Forms, New Contradictions,* China Quarterly, (116), pp. 706-735.

Koyck, L.M. (1964), *Distributed Lags and Investment Analysis,* North-Holland: Amsterdam.

Krishna, R. (1965), *The Marketable Function for a Subsistence Crop: An Analysis with Indian Data,* The Economic Weekly, (17) pp. 309-320.

--------(1963), *Farm Supply Response in Indian-Pakistan: A Case Study of the Punjab Region,* Economic Journal, (73), pp. 477-87;

--------(1962), *A Note on the Elasticity of the Marketable Surplus of a Subsistence Crop,* Indian Journal of Agricultural Economics, July-September, (17), pp. 79-84.

Krishnan, N. T. (1965), *The Marketed Surplus of Food Grain: Is It Inversely Related to Price,* The Economic Weekly, (17), pp. 325-328.

Kueh, Y. Y. and Ash, R. P. (eds), (1993), *Economic Trends in Chinese Agriculture,* Clarendon Press: Oxford.

Kueh, Y.Y. (1993), *Food Consumption and Peasant Incomes,* in Kueh, Y.Y. and Ash, R.F. (eds). Economic Trends in Chinese Agriculture, Clarendon Press: Oxford.

--------(1988), *Food Consumption and Peasant Incomes in the Post-Mao Era,* The China Quarterly, (116), pp. 634-670.

--------(1985), *The Economics of the `Second Land Reform' in China,* China Quarterly, (101), pp. 122-131.

Lancaster, K. J. (1966), *A New Approach to Consumer Theory,* The Journal of Political Economy, (74), pp. 132-157.

--------(1966), *Change and Innovation in the Technology of Consumption,*

American Economic Review, (56), pp. 14-23.

Lardaro, L. (1993), *Applied Econometrics*, Harper Collins College Publishers.

Lardy, N. R. (1992a), *Chinese Foreign Trade*, The China Quarterly, (131), pp. 691-720.

--------(1983a), *Agricultural Price In China*, World Bank Staff Working Papers, No. 606, Washington.

--------(1983b), *Agriculture in China's Modern Economic Development*, Cambridge, University Press, London and New York.

Lau, L. J. and Yotopoulos, P. A. (1972), *Profit Supply and Factor Demand Functions*, American Journal of Agricultural Economics. (54), pp. 11-18.

--------(1971), *A Test of Relative Efficiency: an Application to Indian Agriculture*, American Economic Review, (61), pp. 94-109.

Lau, L. (1978), *Application of Profit Functions, in: Production Economics: A Dual Application to Theory and Applications*, Fuss, M. and McFadden, D. (eds), Northern Holland: Amsterdam.

Lau, L. J., Lin, W. L. and Yotopoulos, P. A. (1978), *The Linear Logarithmic Expenditure System: An Application to Consumption-Leisure Choice*, Econometrica, (46), pp. 843-868.

Lewis, P. and Andrews, N. (1989), *Household Demand in China*, Applied Economics, (21), pp. 793-807.

Li, D., Davis, J. and Wang. L. (1998), *The Impact of Industrialisation on the Sustainability of China's Agriculture.* Working Paper 1/98, Centre for Rural Studies, The Queen's University of Belfast.

Liang, W. S. (1982). *Balance Development of Industry and Agriculture*, in Xu, D.X (et al.), China's Search for Economic Growth, New World Press: Beijing.

Lin, J.Y. (1992), *Rural Reform and Agricultural Growth in China*, The American Economic Review, Vol. 82, (1), pp. 34-51.

--------(1991a), *Reforming the Agricultural Sector in China*, China Working Paper, No 91/1, National Centre for Development Studies, The Australian National University. Lin, J. Y. F.

--------(1991b), *Reforming the Agricultural Sector in China*, China Working Paper No. 91/1, National Centre for Development Studies, The Australian National University.

--------(1989), *The Household Responsibility System in China's Agricultural Reform: a Theoretical and Empirical Study*, Economic Development and Cultural Change, (36), pp. 199-224.

Ling, B. K. (1981), *Price Scissors of Rural Products*, Rural Publishing House, (Chinese), pp. 35-43.

Lipton, M. (1968), *The Theory of the Optimising Peasant*, Journal of

Development Studies, (4), pp. 427-351.

Liu, G. G. (ed), (1984), *The Studies of Strategic Problems of China's Economic Development,* Shanghai People's Publishing House (Chinese).

Liu, M. Q. (1993), *Commune, Responsibility System and China's Agriculture*, in Fan, Q.M. and Nolan, P. (1994) (eds), China's Economic Reform, St Martin's Press.

Liu, Z. F. (1982), *Price Handbook*, China Finance and Economics Publishing House (Chinese).

Livingstone, I., (1977), *Supply Responses of Peasant Producers: The Effect of Our Own-Account Consumption on the Supply of Marketed Output*, Journal of Agricultural Economics, 28(2), pp. 153-8.

Lopez, R. (1986), Structural Models of the Farm Household that Allow for Interdependent Utility and Profit Maximisation Decision, in *Agricultural Household Models*, edited by Singh, I., Squire, L, and Strauss, J., Johns Hopkins University Press, Baltimore, MD.

--------(1984), *Estimating Labour Supply and Production Decisions of Self-Employed Farm Producers*, European Economic Review, (24), pp. 61-82.

--------(1982), *Application of Duality Theory to Agriculture*, Western Journal of Agricultural Economics, (7), pp. 353-65.

Low, A. (1986), *Agricultural Development in Southern Africa*, James Currey: London.

Lu, F. (1996), *Why Does China's Policy Tend to Compromise the Efficiency Objective - A Neglected Issue for China's Grain Policy Research.* Working Paper 1996002., China Centre for Economic Research, Beijing University.

Lu, M. and Dai, X. J. (1987), *Analysis of Peasant's Economic Behaviour at the Present State*, Economic Research, (Chinese), No.7.

Lutz, E. and Scandizzo, P. (1980), *Price Distortions in Developing Countries: A Bias Against Agriculture*, European Review of Agricultural Economics, (7), pp. 5-27.

Maloney, J. (ed) (1992), *What's New in Economics*, Manchester University Press.

Mangahas, M. et al. (1966), *Price and Market Relationships for the Rice and Corn in the Philippines*, Journal of Farm Economics, (48), pp. 685-703.

Mathur, P.N. and Ezekiel, H. (1961), *Marketable Surplus of Food and Price Fluctuations in a Developing Country*, Kyklos Vol. 14, No.3.

Ministry of Agriculture of China (MOA), (1989), *Rural Economic Statistics of China, 1949-86*, Agricultural Press, Beijing.

--------(1983). *Statistics of Agricultural Economy 1949-83*, China Statistics

Bureau, Department of Planning, Internal Publication.

Mubyardto, S. (1965), *The Elasticity of Marketable Surplus of Rice in Indonesia: a Study of Java-Madura*, PhD thesis: Iowa.

McFadden, D. (1962), *Factor Substitutability in the Economic Analysis of Production*, unpublished PhD thesis, Minneapolis, MN: University of Minnesota.

McMillian, J., Whalley, J. and Zhu, L. J. (1989), *The Impact of China's Economic Reforms on Agricultural Productivity Growth*, Journal of Political Economy, Vol. 97, (4), pp. 781-807.

Nakajima, C. (1986), *Subjective Equilibrium Theory of the Farm Household*, Elsevier, Amsterdam.

--------(1970),*Subsistence and Commercial Family Farms: Some Theoretical Models of Subjective Equilibrium*, in Wharton, C.R., (ed), Subsistence Agriculture and Economic Development, London.

Nerlove, M. (1979), *The Dynamics of Supply Response: Retrospect and Prospect*, American Journal of Agricultural Economics, (61), pp. 874-888.

Nerlove, M. (1958), *The Dynamics of Supply Estimation of Farmers' Response to Price*, Johns Hopkins University Press, Baltimore.

--------(1956), *Estimates of the Elasticities of Supply of Selected Agricultural Commodities*, Journal of Farm Economics, 38 (2), pp. 496-509.

Nerlove, M. and Bachman, K.L. (1960), *The Analysis of Changes in Agricultural Supply Problems and Approaches*, Journal of Farm Economics, (42), pp. 531-554.

Newman, J. and Gertler, P. (1994), *Family Productivity, Labour Supply and Welfare in a Low Income Country*, Journal of Human Resources 29., pp. 989-1026.

Niu, R and Calkins, P. H. (1986), *Towards an Agricultural Economy for China in a New Age: Progress, Problems, Response, and Prospects*, American Journal of Agricultural Economics, (68), pp. 445-450.

Noh, H. M. (1983), *Prospects of Grain Production, Consumption and Trade in China*, PhD Thesis, Kansas University.

Nowshirvani, V. (1967), *Agricultural Supply in India, Some Theoretical and Empirical Studies*, PhD thesis, MIT.

--------(1968), *.A Note on the Elasticity of the Marketable Surplus of a Subsistence Crop- a Comment*, Indian Journal of Agricultural Economics, (22), pp. 110-114.

Oi, J. C. (1989), *State and Peasant in Contemporary China*, University of California Press.

Olson, R. O. (1960), *Impact and Implications of Foreign Surplus Disposal on Underdeveloped Countries*, Journal of Farm Economics, (42), pp.

1042-51.

Oskam, A. J. and Osinga, E. (1982), *Analysis of Demand and Supply in the Daily Sector of the Netherlands*, European Review of Agricultural Economics (9), pp. 365-413.

Paarlberg, D. (1988), *The Backward-Bending Supply Curve: A Myth that Persists*, Choices, First Quarter, pp. 29-30.

Paris, Q. (1970), *The Farmer and the Norms of the Market Economy in Developing Countries: An Analysis of Case Studies*, The Farm Economist, Vol. 11, No. 11, pp. 12.

Perkins, D. H. (1966), *Market Control and Planning in Communist China*, Harvard University Press: Cambridge, Massachusetts.

Peters, G.H. and Hedley, D.D. (eds), (1995), *Agricultural Competitiveness: Market Forces and Policy Choice*, Proceedings of the Twenty-Second International Conference of Agricultural Economists, held at Harare Zimbabwe 22-29 August 1994, Dartmouth.

Phlips, L. (1974), *Applied Consumption Analysis*, North-Holland Publishing Company.

Pollack, R. A. and Watcher, M. L. (1975), *The Relevance of the Household Production Function and Its Implications for the Allocation of Time*, Journal of Political Economy, April.

Rao, J.M. (1989), *Agricultural Supply Response: A Survey*, Agricultural Economics, (3), pp. 1-22.

Raymond, W.F. (1985), *Options for Reducing Inputs to Agriculture: A Non-Economist's View*, Journal of Agricultural Economics, Vol. 36, (3), pp. 345-54.

Robert, E. E. (1978), *Time Allocation in Rural Philippine Households*, American Journal of Agricultural Economics, (60), pp. 322-330.

Rock, C. R. (1985), *Post-reform China*, A Written Summary of Statistics and Analysis from the Rock Creek Research, Fall 1985 China Projection Report, Washington D.C.

Rosenzweig, M. R. (1980), *Neoclassical Theory and the Optimizing Peasant: An Econometric Analysis of Market Family Labour Supply in a Developing Country*, Quarterly Journal of Economics (94), pp. 31-55.

Rozelle, S. (1994), *Trip Report, Liaoning and Hebei Provinces*, Stanford University: Palo Alto, California.

Saha, A. (1994), *Compensated Optimal Response under Uncertainty in Agricultural Household Models*, Agricultural Economics, (11), pp. 111-123.

Sanders, J. and Ruttan, V. (1978), *Biased Choice of Technology in Brazilian Agriculture*, in Binswanger, H. and Ruttan, V. (eds), *Induced Innovation*, Johns Hopkins University Press, Baltimore, MD.

Schiff, M. and Valdes, A. (1992), *A World Bank Comparative Study*, The Political Economy of Agricultural Pricing Policy Vol. (4).

Schnepf, R and Senauer, B. (1989), *Estimation of An Agricultural Household Model for Southern Minnesota Farms,* Staff Papers, Department of Agricultural and Applied Economics, University of Minnesota.

Schultz, T. (1960), *Value of U.S. Farm Surpluses to Underdeveloped Countries*, Journal of Farm Economics, (42), pp. 1019-30.

Schultz, T. (1964), *Transforming Traditional Agriculture*, University of Chicago Press.

Shephard, R.W. (1953), *Cost and Production Functions*, Princeton University Press: Princeton, NJ.

Shi, X. H. (1991), *Micro-Analysis of China's Macro-Control Policy in Agriculture*, Finance and Trade Economy, (Caimao Jing Ji, Chinese), December No. 12.

Sicular, T. (1993a), *The Quest for Sustained Growth in Chinese Agriculture,* in Rayner, A. J. and Colman, D. (eds), Current Issues in Agricultural Economics, Macmillan Press Ltd.

--------(1990), Ten Years of Reform: Progress and Setbacks in Agricultural Planning and Pricing, Harvard Institute of Economic Research Discussion Paper, No. 1474.

--------(1989a), *China's Agricultural Policy During the Reform Period*, Harvard Institute of Economic Research Discussion Paper, No. 1552.

--------(1989b), *China: Food Pricing under Socialism*, in Sicular, T. (ed), Food Price in Asia: A Comparative Study, Cornell University Press,: New York.

--------(1988a), *Grain pricing A key link in Chinese Economic Policy*, Modern China Vol. 14, (4), pp. 451-486.

--------(1988b), *Plan and Market in China's Agricultural Commerce*, Journal of Political Economy, Vol. 96. (2), pp. 283-307.

--------(1988c), *Agricultural Planning and Pricing Policy in the Post-Mao Period,* China's Quarterly, (116), pp. 693-702.

Singh, I., Squire, L. and Strauss, J. (eds), (1986), *Agricultural Household Models: Extensions, Applications and Policy*, Johns Hopkins University Press: Baltimore, MD.

Skoufias, E. (1994), *Using Shadow Wages to Estimate Labour Supply of Agricultural Households*, American Journal Of Agricultural Economics, (76), pp. 215-227.

Song, G. Q. (1987), *From Mandatory Purchase and Sale to Land Tax,* in Gao, X.M. and Song G.Q., (eds), Studies on China's Food-Grain Problems, Beijing: Economic Management Press.

SSB. *Statistical Yearbook of China*, (1987, 1990, 1991, 1993, 1995). Chinese Statistical Publishing House.

--------*Rural Statistical Yearbook of China*, (1989, 1991, 1992, 1993, 1994), Chinese Statistical Publishing House.

--------*China Commerce Yearbook*, 1989-91, Chinese Statistical Publishing House, (1992).

--------*Economic Yearbook of China*, (1989) Chinese Statistical Publishing House, (1990);

---------Statistical Yearbook of Prices, (1994, 1995). Chinese Statistical Publishing House;

--------*Chinese Statistical Abstract*, 1993, Chinese Statistical Publishing House, (1993).

--------*Compilation of Historical Provincial Statistics in China 1949-89*, Chinese Statistical Publishing House, (1990).

--------*Rural Households' Survey Yearbook of China*, 1992, Chinese Statistical Publishing House, (1993).

State Council. (1994), *China's Agricultural Development Programme for the 1990s*, in Renmin Rebao (People's Daily), 19 January 1994.

State Planning Commission, (1993-1994), China Prices 1993-1994, State Planning Commission, Price Institute, Monthly Issues.

Stern, R. M. (1962), *The Price Responsiveness of Primary Producers*, Review of Economics and Statistics, (44), pp. 202-207.

Stone, B. (1988), *Relative Prices in the People's Republic of China: Rural Taxation through Public Monopsony*, in Mellor, J. and Ahmed, R. (ed) Agricultural Price Policy for Developing Countries, Johns Hopkins University Press.

Strauss, J. (1984a), *Marketed Surplus of Agricultural Households in Sierra Leone*, American Journal of Agricultural Economics (66), pp. 321-331.

--------(1984b), *Joint Determination of Food Consumption and Production in Rural Sierra Leone*, Journal of Development Economics, (14), pp. 77-103.

--------(1982), *Determinants of Food Consumption in Rural Sierra Leone, Application of the Quadratic Expenditure System to the Consumption-Leisure Component of a Household-Firm Model*, Journal of Development Economics, (11), pp. 327-353.

Su, X. (1979), *Price Scissors Issues*, Social Science, (Chinese), (2), pp. 104-108.

Sumner, D. A. (1982), *The Off-Farm Labour Supply of Farmers*, American Journal of Agricultural Economics, (64), pp. 499-509.

Taluntais, A. F. (1976), *Agricultural Development: Prospects and Possibilities*, Economics and Rural Welfare Research Centre,

Dublin.

Tang, A. M. and Stone, B. (1980), *Food Production in the People's Republic of China*, Research Report 15, International Food Policy Research Institute.

Taylor, J. R. (1993), *Rural Employment Trends and Legacy of Surplus Labour, 1978-89*, in Kueh, Y.Y. and Ash, R.F. (eds), Economic Trends in Chinese Agriculture, Clarendon Press, Oxford.

Theil, H. (1971), *Principles of Econometrics*, A Wiley Hamilton Publication, John Wiley & Sons Inc.

Thijssen, G. (1988), *Estimating a Labour Supply Function of Farm Households*, European Review of Agricultural Economics, (15), pp. 67-78.

Thorner, D. (1965), *A Post-Marxian Theory of Peasant Economy*, The School of A.V. Chayanov, Economic Weekly, February, pp. 227-236.

Timmer, P. (1988), *The Agricultural Transformation*, in Chenery, H. and Srinivasan, T.N. (eds), Handbook of Development Economics, Vol. I, Elsevier Science.

Toquero, Z. et al. (1975), *Marketable Surplus Function for a Subsistence Crop: Rice in the Philippines*, American Journal of Agricultural Economics, (57), pp. 705-709.

USDA, (1993), Agricultural Statistics of the People's Republic of China, 1949-1990, United States Department of Agriculture, Washington DC.

Uzawa, H. (1964), *Duality Principles in the Theory of Cost and Production*, International Economic Review, Vol. 5, (2), pp. 216-220.

Wang, D. H. (1985), *A Course of Lectures on Agricultural Price: Grain and Oil-seeds Prices*, Price Theory and Practice (Chinese) No. 2 and 3.

Wang, L.M. (1995), *An Economic Analysis of Supply and Demand in China's Grain Sector*, unpublished PhD thesis, The Queen's University of Belfast.

Wang, L.M. and Davis, J. (1998) *Can China Feed Its People Into the Next Millennium? Projections for Grain Supply and Demand to 2010.* International Review of Applied Economics, 12: pp 53-67.

--------(1992),*The Development of Reform and the Rural Marketing System in China*, in Vermeer, E. B. (ed) From Peasant to Entrepreneur: Growth and Change in Rural China, Pudoc: Wageningen, Netherlands, pp. 69-82

--------(1991), *Supply Response of China's Grain Sector*, Conference paper, The Third Annual Conference of Chinese Economic Association (UK), London.

Wang, J. R., Wailes, E. J. and Cramer, G. L. (1996), *A Shadow-Price*

Frontier Measurement of Profit Efficiency in Chinese Agriculture, American Journal of Agricultural Economics, (78), pp. 146-156.

Watson, A. (1988), *The Reform of Agricultural Marketing in China Since 1978*, The China Quarterly, (113), pp. 1-28.

Wen, J. G. (1989), *The Current Land Tenure System and Its Impacts on Long Term Performance of the Farming Sector: The Case of Modern China*, PhD thesis, University of Chicago.

Wiens, T. B. (1987), *Issues in the Structural Reform of Chinese Agriculture*, Journal of Comparative Economics, (11), pp. 372-384.

William, E. G., Hill, R. C. and Judge, G. G. (1993), *Learning and Practicing Econometrics*, John Wiley & Sons Inc.

World Bank, (1986), *China: Agriculture to the Year 2000, Annex 2 to China Long-Term Development Issues and Options*, A World Country Economic Report, Johns Hopkins University Press, Baltimore and London.

--------(1991), *China: Options for Reform in the Grain Sector*, World Bank Country Study, World Bank, Washington, D.C.

--------(1993), *The Achievement and Challenge of Price Reform*, International Bank for Reconstruction and Development, Washington DC.

Wu, P. Z (1995), *An Economic Analysis of Supply Response for the Main Grain Crops In China, with Particular Emphasis on the Impact of Reforms since 1979*, PhD Thesis, the Queen's University of Belfast.

Wu, Z . and Kirke, A.W. (1994), *An Assessment of Some Key Chinese Agricultural Statistics.* China Information, Vol. IX, No. 1, Summer 1994.

Xue, M. Q. (1983), *Problems of Stabilising and Adjusting Price Since 1979*, Economic Research (Chinese) No. 6.

Yang, Q. R. and Ming, Y. L. (1991), *Chinese Grain Policy Study*, in China's Grain Policy Research Reports by the Chinese Agricultural Department, Unpublished Research Reports.

Yao, X. G. (1981), *Cost Price and Value of Farm Products: Report of an Investigation and Calculation of Farm Costs for Jiading County*, Fudan University Bulletin, (1), pp. 109-110.

Yotopoulos, P.A., Lau, L. J. and Lin, W. L. (1976), *Microeconomic Output Supply and Factor Demand Functions in the Agriculture of the Province of Taiwan*, American Journal of Agricultural Economics (58), pp. 333-340.

You, L. J. (1985), *On the Road to Price Reform With the Chinese Characteristics*, Economic Research. (Chinese), No. 2.

Yu, C. J. (1991), *Chinese Grain Economy and Policy*, Redwood Press.

Zhang, C. Y. (1991), *Correlation between Rural Population Probability*

205

and Their Income Increase, Population Science of China, (5), pp. 13-19.

Zhu, L. (1991), *Rural Reform and Peasant Income in China*, London, Macmillan Press.

Zong, P. (1994), *From State Control to a Managed or Liberalised Market: Dilemmas in the Reform of the Grain Price System in China*, in Lowe, P. et al. (eds). Regulating Agriculture, David Fulton Publishers Ltd: London.

--------(1992),. *The Government Adjustment and Market Regulation in the Dual Price System in China*, presented at the Queen's University of Belfast one day ESRC Conference, 24 March 1993.

Zong, P. and Davis, J. (1998), *Off-farm Employment and Grain Marketable Surplus in China*. Journal of Agricultural Economics, September 1998.